C000229807

THE BEERS OF WALLONIA

BELGIUM'S BEST KEPT SECRET

By

JOHN WOODS
and
KEITH RIGLEY

Dedications

To Rachel – for her continued good humour and support throughout a project that inevitably took much more time and effort than originally envisaged.

John Woods

To Janet – for the support and her belief that this was one project which might just reach fruition.

Also to Lawrence, Robert and Arthur – who have had to endure over two years of obsessive behaviour around the home and the occasional detour on holidays for "research".

Keith Rigley

Acknowledgements

The authors would like to thank the following for permission to use the photographs listed below:

Abbaye Notre Dame D'Orval – pp. 25, 26
Abbaye Notre Dame de St. Remy – pp. 28, 29
Abbaye Notre Dame de Scourmont – pp. 32, 33, 34.
Brasserie Dubuisson – p. 74 (bottom).
Brasserie Friart – p. 94 (bottom).
Brasserie Piron – p. 124.
Brasserie l'Union – p. 147.
Neil Pakenham-Walsh – pp. 4, 13, 45 (bottom).

The authors also gratefully acknowledge the translation services of Valou Zitoun of VZ Translations, Charlbury, Oxon., and the proof reading services of Richard Palmer of Straitext, Charlbury, Oxon.

ISBN 0 9529238 0 7

© 1996 The Artisan Press

All rights reserved. No part of this publication may be reproduced, stored in a retrieval system, or transmitted in any form or by any means, electronic, mechanical or otherwise, without the prior written permission of the copyright holders.

A CIP catalogue record for this book is available from the British Library.

All research, photography (except as stated), editorial, design and typesetting by the authors.
Printed and bound by Information Press, Eynsham, Oxford

The Artisan Press
PO Box 1098, Winscombe, Bristol BS25 1DT

Contents

INTRODUCTION

This book gives a comprehensive insight into the beers and breweries of Wallonia – a region relatively unknown to beer drinkers around the world, despite making up almost half the land area of the great beer-producing country of Belgium. Flanders, the Flemish-speaking north has always had the lion's share of the limelight, yet the beers of Wallonia, the French-speaking south, are just as high in quality and most exude a wonderful rural, artisanal character, sadly lacking in the vast majority of beers today.

Each brewery has been personally visited and every beer sampled by both authors on more than one occasion. This gives the book a consistent approach to describing beers and by having two independent sets of notes we hope to give readers a good appreciation of what they may expect to find in what is, after all, such an individual experience. Everybody has slightly different responses to taste which can vary depending on how they feel or what they have eaten. For this reason we have opted to show the differences we noted rather than try to agree on some common ground. Maybe you will find that your taste approximates more to John's than Keith's, so in theory you should be able to follow one or the other's notes and know what you are getting in advance.

We both did our "apprenticeships" on the British real ale scene in the 1970s and 1980s but became increasingly impressed with some of Europe's more unusual offerings – especially from Belgium and Germany – on our individual travels. This burgeoning interest was due in part to the desire for something different to (and perhaps more interesting than) the British milds, bitters and strong ales.

Although we met in 1987 (in Belgium, appropriately) it was not until 1990 that we really started searching out Belgium's special beers together in earnest. Inspired by Michael Jackson's *Beer Hunter* series on TV we hit the Senne Valley in a big way, starting at the elusive Congo Bar featured in the first programme. We ended the day at the Drie Fonteinen in Beersel having just about had enough of real Lambic – there is a limit to how much acidic beer one's body can take in one session and we were perilously close to it. After the likes of Belle-Vue, previously considered quite drinkable, the real stuff was a definite eye-opener – and commercial lambic was never entertained again.

We had an excellent excuse for visiting Belgium as we were both members of a federation of motorcycle clubs, the Belgian one of which organised a four-day rally every Easter. By 1991 we were equipped with Michael Jackson's *Pocket Guide to World Beers* and worked our way through the recommended bars in Antwerp, Brussels and Gent. It was around this time that we came across De Dolle's Bos Keun which impressed us so much we just had to visit the brewery. So started some serious searching out of bars, beers and breweries. Initially this was always in Flanders because the rallies were always held there and it was easy to find information relevant to the area, but eventually we came across some Wallonian beers in a few bars. We were immediately taken with their taste so started travelling to Wallonia specifically to find them.

This was when the real fun began.

Even in Wallonia they were difficult to locate and, to make matters worse, there were just nine bars and the same number of breweries covered in the *Pocket Guide*. The arrival of CAMRA's *Good Beer Guide to Belgium and Holland* in 1992 did not help much as the vast majority of the book was taken up with the bars and breweries of Flanders. This was when we decided to start researching for this book as we sought out obscure, not so obscure, and non-existent breweries.

There is a tremendous amount of fun to be had in this genuine beer-hunting but we also wasted an awful lot of time (and no doubt a fair bit of money) in the process. The aim of this book is not to take the fun out of it for you but to make sure you are pointed in the right direction. To the best of our knowledge it is accurate as of July 1996.

We hope that reading this book will encourage you to try to find some of these Wallonian beers. Although most breweries have recommended bars and shops where you can find their products, you will probably still have to visit the brewery itself if you want to buy the full range. We found the vast majority of brewers very hospitable and keen to show off their brewery and its beers – probably due to the size, or lack of it. Being small (in many cases a one-man show) there is a great deal of personal satisfaction – and no small amount of passion – in it for the brewer and they are only too happy to share this. However, as very small enterprises which have to keep operating in order to exist they are often busy, so please bear in mind the notice period required for a brewery tour.

For those who are new to Belgian beer there are a few things you need to bear in mind. About 70% of the beer sold in Belgium is of the Pils style, with a fair proportion coming from Jupiler. With the exception of Jupiler very little Pils is produced in Wallonia but it is a ubiquitous product and you will find some variety of Pils in every bar in Belgium. This is the equivalent of an English bitter and just as you will be served a pint of ordinary bitter if you walk into an English pub and ask for a beer, so you will get a glass (usually 25cl) of Pils if you walk into a Walloon bar and ask for "Une bière, s'il vous plaît". The interesting beers are known as special beers and although some bars have them displayed on a wallchart many have a beer list (much like a menu) which lists the full range, sometimes alphabetically, sometimes by style, sometimes in no particular order. If you can't see a beer list, ask the waiter (in Wallonia, it is called a "carte de bières").

So, you have your beer list and you have chosen a beer, possibly prompted by this book. You will notice that you have what looks more like a wine glass than a beer mug. There are a number of reasons for this, for instance: it is aesthetically pleasing; it encourages you to drink the beer more slowly; it can enhance the whole experience (concentrating the aroma or encouraging the longevity of the beer's head for example); it can add a distinctiveness to the brand image. Almost every Belgian special beer has its own glass, some of which are unique designs, others just a utilitarian shape with the brewery logo added. Approach the beer not as a pint of bitter or lager to be knocked back without touching the sides, but rather as a glass of fine wine. Take in the appearance of the beer in its chosen glass, savour the aroma, extract the full flavour from the liquid, wonder when the finish will end, but, above all, take your time. These beers are not designed to be consumed quickly – ignoring all else, think of the alcohol content, it will probably be between 6% and 9% by volume. The whole thing about Belgian special beers is that they are an experience and, as it is always nice to share an experience, the brewers – particularly in

Wallonia – have been very obliging and most produce beers in 75cl corked bottles which are just perfect for sharing. In fact some breweries only sell their beers in 75cl bottles.

As stated earlier we have included a list of bars recommended by each of the breweries (as well as some recommended by ourselves), but it should be pointed out that occasionally even Belgian bar staff will not pour your beer correctly. It is very important that the sediment is left out of many beers, so it is worthwhile watching how the beers are poured in that particular bar. If, for instance, the barman throws the bottles around and slams them on the bar he will probably have just ruined a perfectly good beer which will need to stand for another 24 hours or more before it can be served in the correct condition. An organisation called "l'Office Belge du Service de la Bière" (BSB) has recently introduced courses for barstaff which includes handling and pouring sedimented ales. Special beers are not cheap, so be prepared to ask if you can pour your own rather than risk wasting your money – we have done this on many occasions and rarely received more than a raised eyebrow. If you wish to pour your own beer you should say: "Est-ce que je peux la servir moi-même, s'il vous plaît" to the bar staff.

A sign to watch for outside a bar or cafe.

One of the great appeals of Belgian beers is the sometimes outrageous tastes which unfortunately do not appeal to everybody. There is currently a trend towards making the beers more bland in an effort to make them appeal to a wider audience. We would encourage you to waste no time in making your foray into Belgian beer as during the last year three, previously superb, Wallonian beers – Praile's Cuvée d'Aristée, Silenrieux's Sara and Vapeur's Cochonne – have had a recipe change in an effort to induce wider sales. For the benefit of the brewery we hope this succeeds but it is a shame that it is always to the detriment of the quality and character of the beer.

Hopefully, we have now whetted your appetite for a Belgian beer. To whet your appetite for a little beer-hunting we will cite some of our experiences – a couple of failures and a success. Peter Crombecq's excellent *Bier Jaarboek* for 1993/4 suggested there was a Brasserie d'Avignon at Nismes, in the province of Namur. We drove there to find the row of terraced houses with Rue d'Eglise 15, the supposed address, in the centre. Enquiries in a bar sent us down a road to a derelict factory – obviously not a brewery started in 1992. We eventually knocked on the door of number 15 where we found the pensioner who answered the door had amazingly worked at the brewery that was now the derelict factory (it closed decades earlier) but knew nothing at all about a current brewery. One more off the list.

On another occasion we found an article in a local magazine giving names of breweries we had not previously heard of. Armed with this article we went in search of Brasserie Perez at Gaumain-Ramecroix. We deciding to stay overnight in nearby Tournai, as a bar in the town – Le Damier – was quoted as selling his beers but the article gave no address for the bar or the brewery. We asked the owner of one of our regular haunts, Le Moine Austère, if he knew of the bar. He knew nothing of the brewery but gave directions to Le Damier, outside which was a poster for Cuvée du Marais (the Perez blonde beer) – things were looking up. Inside we found some 75cl and more reasonably-priced 33cl bottles behind the bar which we sampled, but definitely did not enjoy. The owner knew nothing about Brasserie Perez, despite marketing their beer so prominently – then we discovered she had only bought the bar that day. We borrowed her phone book but could find nothing under the name Perez in the locality. Next morning we drove to Gaumain-Ramecroix and, although we managed to get directions to the approximate area, we still could not find a brewery. Nobody – including the four houses up the road from him – knew of a Mr Perez, despite the fact that he is a Basque and supposedly ran a brewery. By using a process of elimination, we eventually knocked on the door of a house where the man himself answered only to tell us he couldn't find enough outlets to make brewing viable so had given it up. A disappointing end, but an adventure in itself.

Brasserie De La Tour was another brewery gleaned from that article, which suggested it was currently operating in Comblain-La-Tour where we went to look for the brewery, Receiving largely blank looks we were eventually given directions up a hill via some country lanes. Needless to say we did not find the brewery, so we resorted to our usual ploy of adjourning to the nearest bar. We asked the owner about the brewery, at which point he disappeared out to the back of the bar. After a couple of minutes Antoine, the de la Tour brewer, walked in the door – quite by chance he had been building a wall for the house next door. He told us he had not yet received his commercial brewing licence, so we arranged to meet him in the bar on our next visit so he could show us the way to the brewery. It transpired that we used the drive of his house for a three-point turn before retiring to the bar.

You can avoid incidents like these in your initial Wallonian beer-hunting as we not only give you an address but also directions to each brewery. New breweries are sprouting up quite regularly these days, so if you hear of one subsequent to this book's publication, we hope you have as much fun seeking them out as we did.

At this point we should mention that not every Wallonian brewery wants publicity. This can be particularly true within the table beer market. For instance, Brasserie Poncelet specifically asked not to be included in the brewery section as they only produce blonde and brune table beers which are locally delivered and not available in bars or shops, and the facilities are not legally capable of supporting visitors.

Although, generally speaking, Wallonian beers are still difficult to find, the situation is getting better – in fact now you don't even need to go to Belgium. Some are stocked by the specialist beer shops in the UK, while the Belgo restaurants in London even have Saison Dupont Biologique as their house beer, labelled as Belgo.

The authors – John Woods (left) and Keith Rigley.

HOW TO BE A BEER SNOB

With wine snobbery currently reaching new heights it is about time the beer world hit back

There is a stigma that society has bestowed upon people who drink beer. It is assumed that anyone expressing a preference for beer over wine may be uneducated in the finer things in life, probably working-class and might even be capable of loutish behaviour.

For years now there has been a trend by the 30-somethings and older to drink more wine and less beer. Usually this is in the mistaken belief that wine has more finesse and a wider range of taste and character than beer, doubtless this opinion being based on the bland offerings from the multi-national breweries. The authors appreciate wine as well as beer, and would argue that both have a place in this world – neither deserving to be regarded as the inferior product.

The esteem (and etiquette) given to wine in countries like France is applied to beer in Belgium, mainly because it cannot grow vines successfully due to its geographical location and until recent decades the average person could not afford decent imported wine. The ingredients, production process and maturation methods give a beer its unique character just as they do a wine. Hops and barleys, like grapes, differ according to varieties used and the soil and climate of the area in which they are grown. The yeast strain has a great effect on the character of a beer, as does the brewing process where variations can include dry hopping, spicing (considered sacrilege in wine) and decoction or stepped infusion mashing. Maturation, storage and ageing apply as much, if not more, to beer as to modern, cheap wines.

Opening a corked 75cl bottle of vintage beer with its attendant ceremony is just as appropriate as the cracking open of a good wine. The aromas and flavours encountered, whilst obviously very different, need be no less complex or satisfying to the discerning nose or palate and the alcohol content may be no more than two or three percent lower. The main difference is that the "good" wine will cost much more than the vintage beer and most people will not even truthfully appreciate the fact that it was much superior to a standard supermarket wine.

Once you are familiar with the special beer world, it is possible to assign various beers (even limiting the choice to Wallonia) to an equivalent wine, spirit or fortified wine in French cuisine. For instance, in place of the pastis an Orval or a Marlagne Blanche would be ideal. A Bush Beer (or perhaps a Fantôme) and a Vapeur en Folie could be used in place of a vermouth and fino sherry respectively as aperitifs. Offer your guests a Moinette Blonde instead of a dry white wine. Where you would serve a Claret, fetch a full and fruity beer such as a Binchoise Brune. Cheese has the perfect accompaniment in Chimay Bleue and desserts go down well with a Blanche de Namur. The after-dinner period is the preserve of Rochefort 8 or 10 and some of the heavier Spéciale Noëls – and you don't have to pass it to the left!

Looking around the beer shelves and racks of a well-stocked cellar when wondering what to pick for that particular occasion, especially with a good selection of vintage ales, you can find a greater variety and choice than a cellar full of wine – and in comparison it won't have broken the bank to stock.

Perhaps it's time for the beer snobs to start looking down *their* noses.

WHERE IS WALLONIA – AND WHAT IS IT?

Essentially Wallonia is the southern half of Belgium and the inhabitants speak French rather than the Flemish spoken in the northern half. However, to be more specific it is an administrative division of Belgium whose southern, eastern and western borders are well defined by the national borders with France, Luxembourg and Germany. The northern border, identified by signs alongside the major roads (much as English Counties are) has moved many times over the years and currently runs east-west in a line just south of Brussels from north of Liège in the east to north of Tournai in the west. Although French is the principal language of Wallonia, not everybody speaks it as there are two areas in the east (the Cantons de l'Est) where 68,000 inhabitants speak German.

Needless to say, that is not the whole story but perhaps it is best to approach the subject of Wallonia and Walloons from the historical viewpoint. The following is a brief summary of the major points of importance in the development of Belgium from Roman times when it was part of Gaul and occupied by the Belgae, an ancient Celtic tribe from whom the name Belgium derives.

C3rd & C4th	The Salic Franks (from Germany), moved in from the north-east, pushing the Romans back to a position roughly in line with the current Flemish/Walloon border, a line of natural coal forests.
C5th	Withdrawal of Roman garrisons. The Franks pushed further south adopting the language of the Romanised Gauls which became French. Those that stayed in the north retained their Germanic language which became Dutch and Flemish.
C14th	Philip of Burgundy gained control of Flanders.
late C15th	The Houses of Burgundy and Habsburg unite through marriage.
1504	The area that is present day Belgium came under rule of Spanish Habsburgs.
1579	Southern Spanish provinces formed the union of Arras pledging allegiance to Spanish king and Roman Catholicism. The Protestant northern provinces formed the United Provinces of the Netherlands.
1713	Following the War of Spanish Succession the Spanish Netherlands, including Belgium, was ceded to the Austrian Habsburgs and became the Austrian Netherlands.
1794-1814	Belgium annexed to France.
1815	Belgium reunited with the Netherlands as one country, the United Kingdom of the Netherlands, ruled by the Protestant House of Orange.
1830	Catholic Belgians revolt against Protestant Dutch rule.

1831	Independent Belgium created with Prince Leopold of Saxe-Coburg elected as King Leopold I.
C19th	A Flemish equality movement attempted to raise the position of the Flemish population. The Flemings outnumbered the Walloons but French was the language of the upper classes therefore Walloon interests were disproportionately represented in the national government. Tensions grew between Dutch and French speakers.
1898	Flemish became the official language.
1930	Belgian parliament turned the country into two linguistic regions with different administrations.
1950-60	Wallonia had rigid industrial structure relying on large state subsidies, whereas Flanders attracted much of its investment from abroad. The Flemings objected to subsidising the Walloons who, in turn, feared the more numerous and prosperous Flemings would dominate the state. Economic and linguistic tensions were now inextricably linked.
1961	Massive strikes in Wallonia brought the tensions to a head.
1962/3	An immovable linguistic border was defined by act of parliament and a new special arrangement allowed for the bilingual area around Brussels.
1968	Tensions led to the division of bilingual University of Leuven into a Dutch speaking campus in Flanders and a French speaking campus in Wallonia. This sparked off a slow process of federalisation.
1971	Parliament accorded cultural autonomy to the Flemish and Walloon regions.
1980	Constitution revised to allow for creation of an independent administration within each region.
1988/9	Another constitutional revision extended cultural autonomy to encompass economy and education. It also gave bilingual Brussels the status of a third independent region with its own administration and explicitly turned Belgium into a federal state.

From the above it can be seen that the roots of the two areas go very deep with more than just language dividing them. This also helps to explain the way Walloons view Flemings and vice versa, something you will notice if you travel around the country and talk to the people. There are obviously still problems and some political and constitutional commentators are predicting the break up of the national state of Belgium into two distinct independent nations before the end of the century. With Brussels being officially bilingual it could well be left as a political island which would be particularly ironic, considering Brussels is the current focal point of European unity.

The population of Belgium in 1994 was 10,680,000 with 10% of those living in Brussels. Those 10% are officially bilingual (French and Flemish) while another 57% speak Flemish, 32% speak French and 1% speak German. Of ethnic groups, the 91% of the people who are officially Belgian is made up of 57% Fleming and 32% Walloon.

The German element is very significant because this adds another complication. Although there is basically a north/south divide with

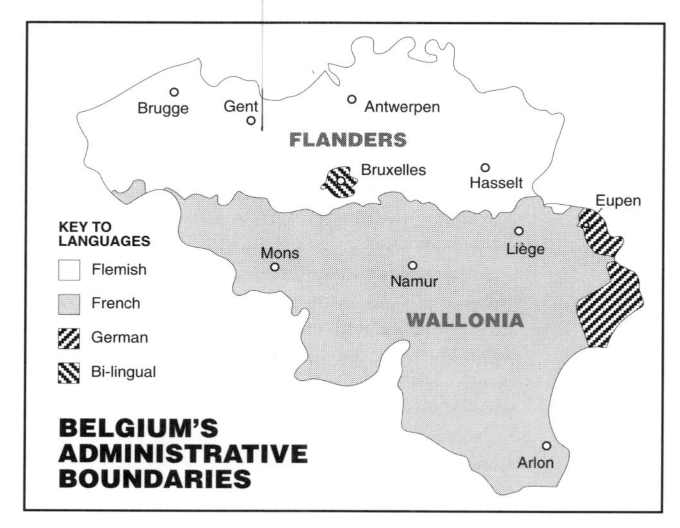

the bilingual pocket of Brussels in Flanders, there is also a German speaking pocket in Wallonia (see map). In fact there are two distinct areas that are not quite joined where they speak German, display German characteristics and brew German style beer. This area has its own local government but answers to the Wallonian administration and at the national level is deemed to be part of Wallonia. For the purposes of this book though we have concentrated on French speaking Wallonia primarily because neither the German nor the French speakers really want these areas to be considered part of Wallonia.

There is only one brewery in the German speaking area, the Eupener Bierbrauerei, Paveestrasse 12-14, 4700 Eupen. It can trace its history back to 1834 and is centrally situated in the town of Eupen, concentrating on producing beers loosely in the German style for mainly local consumption. We sampled a Pils (4.5% alc/vol.), Export (4% alc/vol.), Klosterbier (6.5% alc/vol.) and a Caramel (1.8% alc/vol.), though we believe they also brew a Caramel table beer (1.5% alc/vol.) and an Extra Light (2.5% alc/vol.). We found the Pils to be surprisingly good with plenty of pale malt, hops and dryness, but the Export, Klosterbier and Caramel were all disappointing.

Wallonia is very much a land of contrasts. The north – a band running through Mons, Charleroi, Namur and Liège – has a reasonably high density of population and grew up around the heavy industries that originally came with the coal mining. Industries such as glass manufacture, iron production, zinc metallurgy, chemical and electrical industries. There is a large coalfield in the Sambre-Meuse Valley, centred on the cities of Charleroi and Liège, though production has declined in recent years with uneconomic mines being closed. The south, on the other hand, is very rural with a low level of population – about 50 people per square kilometre on the Ardennes plateau – and contains much agricultural land with large areas still forested. This is the area in which you will find almost all the 3.1% of the national population that do not live in an 'urban' area. The official figure of 96.9% urbanisation makes Belgium the most 'urban' of any reasonable sized independent state. With 323 people per square kilometre, it is also one of Europe's most crowded nations. However, if you were to enter the country from the south and travel up through the Ardennes you would find these statistics very hard to believe.

The Ardennes not only represents a vast rural playground for the northern Belgians but also attracts many other European holiday-makers in search of the great outdoors. It is essentially an area of moorland, peat bogs and woodland with rivers, gorges and big hills – as opposed to mountains (Mount Botrange, south east of Verviers, at 694m being the highest) – which is in stark contrast to the cultivated rolling plains of the north. The area is by no means uninhabited, it is full of small villages, compared to densely-populated Flanders and northern Wallonia which have little distance between much larger towns and cities.

From the beer viewpoint the Flemings can lay claim to white, lambic, old brown and red beer styles whilst Wallonia only really has Saison as a recognised style. However, with the historical prevalence for spicing their beers it could be argued that spiced beer is very much a Walloon beer style, as are the ubiquitous blondes and brunes now produced by many Wallonian breweries.

Saison is a very old beer style and was traditionally made by farmer-brewers during the winter to be laid down until the summer when they were provided as a thirst quencher for landworkers, probably forming part of their payment. To be a thirst quencher they must not be too strong and those that survive are mostly 5-6.5% alc/vol. All are presented, as is traditional, in corked champagne bottles of 75cl. Only a few years ago this style of bottling was almost unique to Wallonia, but now there are probably more beers in Belgium available in 75cl bottles than not.

Another feature of the beer is its artisanal character. Most Wallonian breweries are very small – and not just the very new ones – with a great affinity for their locality and a very small distribution area. This artisanality comes through in the distinctiveness of many of the beers, giving a true "farmhouse" quality, making Wallonia an area worthy of closer consideration by any beer enthusiast. The character of the breweries and their beers can be explained in part by the nature of the area and its people. Being more rural than Flanders it encourages a perhaps less sophisticated approach to production and presentation of their beers. Whilst this can be detected in the taste of its beers (many have an earthy appeal) it in no way detracts from their quality. Many beers produced here are of a very high quality and the brewers are generally very professional in their operation.

It is unfortunately the case that the two major lingual groups in Belgium have a natural affinity towards a beer produced in their half of the country and they probably expect its name or identity to reflect this. Some beers do cross over the language barrier – such as Cuvée des Flandres Triple and Cervoise des Ancêtres – but most appear to come from Flemish breweries which target Wallonia in their marketing strategy (like Van Honsebrouck and Huyghe), while other beers are given two names – e.g. Kasteel Bier (sold in Wallonia as Bière du Château) and Binchoise Blonde (sold in Flanders as Fakir). On the whole, however, anyone drinking in Flanders will usually only see Flemish beer just as Walloons prefer to sell their own products.

Most beer drinkers tend to identify "Belgian" as meaning "Flemish". If you are one of these people, we would like to suggest that perhaps you only know half the story!

Wallonia's emblem – the red cockerel.

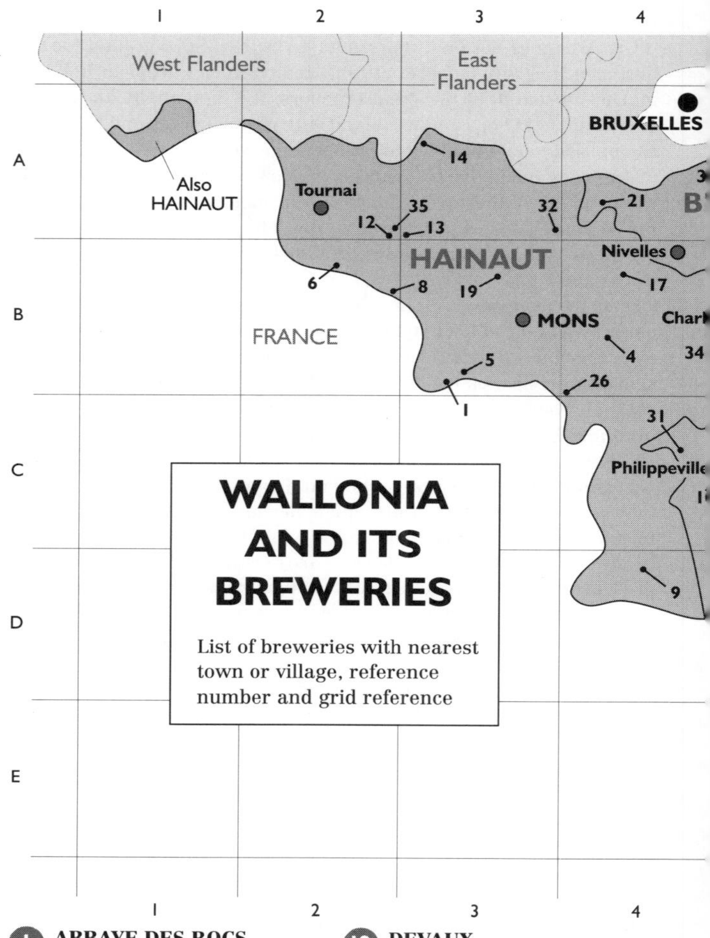

1. **ABBAYE DES ROCS** Montignies-sur-Roc (B3)
2. **ACHOUFFE** Achouffe (C8)
3. **AMBLY** Nassogne (C6)
4. **BINCHOISE** Binche (B4)
5. **BLAUGIES** Blaugies (B3)
6. **BRUNEHAUT** Rongy (B2)
7. **CARACOLE** Falmignoul (C5)
8. **CAULIER** Peruwelz (B2)
9. **CHIMAY** Chimay (D4)
10. **DEVAUX** Philippeville (C5)
11. **DU BOCQ** Purnode (C6)
12. **DUBUISSON** Pipaix (A2)
13. **DUPONT** Tourpes (A3)
14. **ELLEZELLOISE** Ellezelles (A3)
15. **FANTÔME** Soy (C7)
16. **FERME AU CHÊNE** Durbuy (B7)
17. **FRIART** Le Rœulx (B4)
18. **GIGI** Gerouville (E7)

19 **HAMEAU**
Lens (B3)

20 **JUPILER**
Jupille-sur-Meuse (A7)

21 **LEFEBVRE**
Quenast (A4)

22 **MIBRANA**
Namur (B5)

23 **OLEYE**
Waremme (A6)

24 **ORVAL**
Villers-Devant-Orval (E6)

25 **PIRON**
Aubel (A8)

26 **PRAILE**
Peissant (B4)

27 **ROCHEFORT**
Rochefort (C6)

28 **ROCHEFORTOISE**
Rochefort (C6)

29 **RUWET**
Verviers (B8)

30 **ST. GUIBERT**
Mont St. Guibert (A5)

31 **SILENRIEUX**
Silenrieux (C4)

32 **SILLY**
Silly (A3)

33 **TOUR**
Comblain-la-Tour (B7)

34 **UNION**
Jumet, Charleroi (B5)

35 **VAPEUR**
Pipaix (A2)

36 **VERVIFONTAINE**
Jalhay (B8)

Beer Label Interpretation

Some basic translations to help you understand the label

Wallonian beer labels convey a fair bit of information, sometimes in Flemish, sometimes even in English, but always in French. To make deciphering this information a little easier we have included here a list of the more common phrases and symbols used along with an explanation of their meaning.

A consommer de préference avant fin ...	Best before end date.
Aucun (or) Sans additives	Without additives.
Bière artisanale	A handcrafted beer.
Biologique	Organic.
Brassée et embouteillée à ...	Brewed and bottled at ...
Cat. S	Category S (Superior). One of the legal classifications of beer in Belgium.
Consigné (or) Verre Consigné	Returnable bottle. Often used in conjunction with a value e.g. 7 BEF
Embouteillée le ...	Bottled date.
... ans de conservation	Will keep for ... years.
Fermentation haute	Top fermented.
Froment	Wheat.
Glass symbol e.g.	Signifies the type of glass the brewery recommends drinking the beer from.
Goût évolutif (or) Goût en progression	An evolving taste. Beer will change over time.
Mis en bouteille ...	Bottled by ...
Non Filtrée	Unfiltered.
Non Pasteurisée	Unpasteurised.
Orge	Barley.
Pur Malt	Pure malt. Uses no other grain.
Refermentée en bouteille (or) Bière sur lie (or) Bière vivante	Refermented in the bottle. (Literally, beer on yeast) (Literally, live beer)
Servir frais/Servir à ... Servir entre ... à ...	Serve cool / Serve at ... (temperature) Serve between ... and ... (temperature)
	The logo of the OBP (Objectieve Bierproevers), a Flemish-based consumer association rather like CAMRA in the UK, signifying that they have approved the details on the label.
	Recyclable. Most countries now have a legal requirement that packaging should state if it is recyclable.

THE STEAMY SIDE OF WALLONIAN BREWING

Vapeur by name, Vapeur by nature . . .

Many breweries offer the possibility of a visit and a tour, though you often have to use your imagination to visualise the operation in full flow. Jean-Louis Dits at Brasserie à Vapeur actually opens his doors to the public on the one day in the month that he brews. By booking in advance and paying a minimal sum, you can join him as he brings the past to life, using the steam-powered brewery equipment which originated in the last century to produce a beer for today in his own individualistic style. This is an account of our day spent there and should give you an indication of what to expect as well as an insight into the brewing process employed at Vapeur.

The Vapeur brewery has a couple of things that make it stand out from others. One is the fact that it claims to be the last working (i.e. still producing on a commercial basis) steam brewery in the world. The steam provides not only the heat but also the power for the majority of the brewing operation which uses belt-driven equipment powered by the original steam engine from 1896 and centres around the 'antique' mash tun. The other notable attribute is the brewer. Many Wallonian breweries seem to have someone who stands out from the crowd, but Jean-Louis does so more than most. In spite of taking on a brewery that is, in many respects, antiquated, he still manages to hold down a part time job as a history teacher. He cures his own ham, and bakes his own bread. His appearance and beliefs could encourage you to describe him as the epitomy of a 'green'. Most important is probably his sense of tradition, a prime factor in determining the character of his beer range, though the realities of the commercial world are now creeping in as Vapeur Cochonne gets sweeter in order to appeal to the modern palate.

The brewery is situated in the centre of Pipaix near Leuze-en-Hainaut, almost opposite the school. In appearance it is a large brick built, industrial style building and entering through the gate reveals more of the same at the back where you will find the bottling plant,

Bernard keeps an eye on the steam engine.

cellar and beer shop. The business part of the brewery, as well as the living quarters, is that which adjoins the road. Some of the buildings date from the 14th century but the brewery was not founded until 1785 – the year that Saison de Pipaix was developed. It is still brewed to the original recipe though with some necessary changes. The 1785 recipe called for the addition of a lichen but with the less pure air of the 1980s (when Jean-Louis recreated it) it was found to be no longer suitable as a beer ingredient – instead pepper has been substituted. The brewery site extends to buildings and land across the road. Here can be found a nicely laid out and characterful little tasting room as well as, in another building, a kitchen and large room used for entertaining.

Having been started in 1785 by Cosne-Damien Cuvelier and Marie-Alexandrine Moulin the brewery then passed through a further five generations of the family before being sold to Jean-Louis Dits and Anne-Marie Lemaire in 1984. In 1896 the brewery had been modernised with the addition of steam power, and with the exception of the boiler that equipment is still in use today. The brewery fell into disuse when it became too much for the 86-year-old Gaston Bizet to manage. Unable to face the prospect of such a landmark of local heritage departing the scene, Jean-Louis stepped in and became the proud owner. Having taken on such a mammoth project he needed to make it generate a little revenue. The name was changed from Brasserie Bizet-Cuvelier to Brasserie à Vapeur and the first brew was produced in October 1984. The second brew was in 1985, along with another seven. 1986 saw that rise to 12, 1987 to 18 of 50hl and 1988 to 14 of 60hl. By 1994 things had steadied to a brew of 40hl on the last Saturday of each month. Although there has been a healthy level of production, things could not have got off to a worse start in the early days when the ancient steam boiler exploded, tragically killing Anne-Marie. It says a lot for Jean-Louis that he managed to overcome this tragedy and continue running the brewery.

For the observer of the monthly brew the day starts at 9am but for Jean-Louis it starts much earlier. The boiler has to be fired up at 4am as it must heat 4000 litres of water to 85°C before the start of the brewing, and the malt has to be milled into the hopper where it awaits release to the first stage of its transformation into Vapeur Cochonne (in this instance).

The day we joined him we were just two of an audience of about 20 people (apparently anywhere between five and 20 is normal), all of whom were stood around the mash tun awaiting the start at precisely 9am. At one end of the room the steam engine, rapidly approaching its one hundredth birthday, was chugging away merrily. This provided all the power to run the brewing operation via a series of drive belts which were largely unprotected – not a place to let little small children run around unattended. Luckily this party only consisted of big kids who were fascinated by what was about to unfold before them.

When Jean-Louis was ready to begin he gave the signal and Vinciane opened a valve that released a small amount of water into the chamber of the worm screw at the bottom of the grist hopper. Jean-Louis started the worm screw and slowly the grist – mixed with a little water – started to appear and drop into the mash tun. The grist consisted of one-third pale malt (2.5 ebc) and two-thirds amber malt (22 ebc). As this mixture started to pile up on the base of the mash tun the signal was given to Bernard. A pull on the right-hand chain and he shifted the drivebelt from the idler wheel to the drive wheel above our heads and the stirring rakes started to move. They are mounted on two arms extending either side of a central crown wheel, there are four rakes on each arm and they rotate as the arms travel around the vessel.

The hot, steamy grist starts to flow.

With all the grist added and the temperature at about 45°C this was stirred for 15 minutes. Hot water – at 85°C – was added to bring the temperature up to 55°C, where it remained for 20 minutes, being stirred reasonably slowly. All the while, the steam engine continued puffing away behind us providing the power, with the hot water coming directly from the boiler in the next room, as did the steam which was about to be used.

After its 20 minutes at 55°C, things speeded up as the temperature was rapidly raised to 62°C by the addition of more hot water and also the injection of steam from the base of the vessel. The stirrer seemed to be going flat out at this point in an effort to keep the mash turning over to avoid any damage from prolonged contact with the steam. By now the environment was more reminiscent of a sauna than a brewery, visibility was down to a few feet and the temperature and humidity level high enough to remove any need there may have earlier been for a jacket or pullover. The 'Vapeur' in the brewery name is apt indeed! When the temperature of the mash reached 62°C things slowed down a little and it was left here for 30 minutes – long enough for us all to adjourn to the tasting room and sample some amazing vintage Saison de

Controlling the temperature of the mash using hot water and steam is a fine art. In the foreground a sample jug of the mash is tested with a thermometer.

Early on in the brewing process it is possible to see other visitors across the mash tun. Later on it becomes a lot hotter, a lot steamier and a lot more difficult to see.

Pipaix which had an exceptional complexity of taste and in spite of being many years old suggested that it may last a couple more yet.

Back in the brewery the temperature had been raised to 68°C for 15 minutes and then to 74°C for 15 minutes before the wort was run off. Jean-Louis does not normally pause at these temperatures but the Cochonne is sweeter than the other Vapeur beers and needs the non-fermentable sugars to be released to achieve that sweetness.

After this the wort is filtered through the grain bed as many times as is felt necessary before being pumped upstairs, via a small holding tank, to the kettle. Sparging, with water at 80°C takes place soon after the grain bed becomes visible. This brew produced about 38 hl. The kettles are large steel affairs with large diameter copper pipes in the base which, when enough steam is pumped through them to boil the wort, serve as heating elements.

A handful of hops is added at the start of the three hour boil. 200 kg of sugar and a tubfull of coriander seeds, bits of dried roasted chicory and orange peel are added about half an hour before the end of the boil as are 10 kg of Goldings hops in pellet form.

The natural break in proceedings provided by the long boil allowed everybody to adjourn to the 'hall' next to the tasting room for lunch. This only happens when there is a large enough party but if you are lucky you may get the treat, as we did, of being able to partake of some excellent beer cuisine. It was prepared by the chef from a local restuarant and uses Vapeur beers in almost every course. We were treated to such delights as pâté with Saison de Pipaix, mussels in Folie, pork in a Folie sauce and cheese made with Cochonne. Needless to say this was accompanied by large quantities of the beers themselves. All in all a superb experience.

Whilst we were enjoying our meal and the boil was progressing the hard work had started downstairs in the brewery – cleaning out the mash tun. This is done by three people, a brush, a shovel and a wheel-

True to Jean-Louis' green philosophy nothing goes to waste. From the brewery the spent grains go for cattle feed.

barrow. The spent grains are shovelled out of the mash tun into the wheelbarrow which is taken outside by a farmer friend, and up onto the trailer behind his tractor to be given to his cows. Having got the mash tun quite clean, the filter plates are lifted out of the base and washed. Below the filter plates are more plates covering the steam channels, these also have to be removed and washed.

When everyone has left, around 6pm, Jean-Louis moves onto his next task (along with the obligatory glass of Cochonne) – that of bread making. This bread, predictably, uses some of the spent grains from the brew which didn't go off for cattle feed, and is made in a gas fired bread oven in the tasting room (perhaps Jean-Louis has had enough of steam by now). It was amazing – although there was no fermentation the bread definitely tasted alcoholic. So what with bread making and cow feeding, nothing goes to waste.

As a visitor to the brewing day that is all you will see, but there is still a lot to happen in the process. After being cooled the fermentation takes place, usually four to six days at 25°C, and then the bottling. The brewing can be done with two people but the bottling takes a minimum of four (five or six is better). It will take about three hours if all the production goes into 75cl bottles, but if it is split between 75cl and 25cl it will be more like five hours. After bottling the beer is stored in a warm room for five days to encourage a healthy refermentation, then transferred to the cellar – ideally for three months – before being brought up to the shop for sale.

This brewery is a working museum in many ways, a lot of the equipment and some of the techniques would be considered, in this high tech world, to be antiquated. This must, however, have an influence on the nature of what is produced – a product that, if not unique, is certainly highly individual and often of very high quality. The equipment, environment and techniques possibly also exert their influence on the occasional variations in quality and character of the beer, though to our minds that is not necessarily detrimental. It is nice to have a little variety as it heightens the anticipation of not knowing whether you are about to taste a beer that only merits a seven or is truly worthy of a ten.

A treat for the visitors – Jean-Louis pours each a glass of vintage Saison de Pipaix in the less-steamy environment of the tasting room across the road.

Trappist Temptations

A potted history of the monks who (latterly with a little help from less spiritual workers) produce those hallowed ales worshipped by beer-lovers around the world

The word Trappist usually conjures up one of three images. Most people will simply think of a silent order of monks in an abbey. Those with a basic knowledge of beer will associate the word with quality strong ales made in Belgian abbeys. Beer connoisseurs will no doubt appreciate that those quality strong ales are not made in just any Belgian abbey but in one occupied by monks of the strictest Benedictine order – the Trappists. They will also know that they are to be found in the Netherlands as well.

Today the use of the word Trappist to describe a beer is controlled by law. "Trappist" is an appellation of origin, rather than style – a little like Champagne or Wensleydale, except that these latter are geographical appellations. The epithet Trappist, therefore, can only be used when Trappist monks have produced the end product. To us it usually means beer but it also applies to their other produce, notably cheese. There are only six Trappist breweries in the world. The Netherlands has one – Schaapskoi at Koeningshoeven, which produces the La Trappe range of beers – and Belgium has the other five. Westmalle and Sint-Sixtus at Westvleteren (in the provinces of Antwerpen and West Flanders respectively) are in Flanders while the other three are all in Wallonia – Chimay, Orval and Rochefort (or to give them their proper names: Abbaye Notre Dame de Scourmont, Abbaye Notre Dame d'Orval and Abbaye Notre Dame de St. Remy).

The use of the word Trappist is quite rightly being vehemently defended by the abbeys these days as other parties try to acquire some of the kudos imparted on a product simply by mentioning Trappists. Over the years the monasteries have built up a reputation for quality in their products and this is never more true than with the Trappist beers. That reputation is based upon the use of only the best materials, a high degree of skill, traditional methods and great dedication. Unfortunately, many of these elements are missing in the wider world's process of satisfying an ever-growing demand for consumer products for which price is one of the main criteria. In these times of mass-marketing and the advertisement-drunk mind of fickle consumers, some unscrupulous companies have been tempted to try to sell a perceived quality that, in reality, may be lacking in

The logo used to show a genuine Trappist product.

Découvrez la microbrasserie de Namur

Visit Namur's microbrewery

Ontdek de huisbrouwerij van Namen

Besuchen Sie die Gasthausbrauerei von Namur

Du malt à la bière : 20 siècles de tradition brassicole belge à l'honneur dans une des plus petites brasseries du pays. Venez découvrir ses installations et déguster ses bières spéciales. Laissez-vous tenter par son restaurant et sa cuisine traditionnelle à la bière.

From malt to beer : 20 centuries of belgian brewing tradition concentrated in one of the smallest breweries in the country. Discover the tavern, taste the beers and visit the brewing plant. Try the restaurant with its traditional belgian food cooked with beer.

Place de la Station, 2
B-5000 NAMUR

Tél. : (081) 23.16.94
Fax : (081) 22.15.09

Taverne - Restaurant - Microbrasserie

Ouvert tous les jours de 10h00 à 24h00,
le dimanche de 15h00 à 24h00.

Tavern - Restaurant - Pubbrewery

Open every day from 10h00 a.m. until midnight,
from 15h00 until midnight on sunday.

Taverne - Restaurant - Huisbrouwerij

Open elke dag van 10h00 to 24h00,
van 15h00 tot 24h00 op zondag.

Gasthausbrauerei

Täglich geöffnet von 10 Uhr bis 24 Uhr,
Sonntag von 15 Uhr bis 24 Uhr.

Van malt tot beer : 20 eeuwen belgische bierkunst in één van de kleinste brouwerijen van het land. Probeer onze speciale bieren en bezoek onze brouwerij. Proef de belgische keuken met bier fantazieën in het restaurant.

Vom Hopfen und Malz zum frischen Bier : die gesamte belgische Biertradition in einer der kleinsten, aber feinsten Braustätten des Landes. Probieren Sie unsere Spezialbiere und entdecken Sie unsere Erlebnisbrauerei mitsamt zünftiger Gaststätte und seiner originellen, gambrinalen Gastronomie.

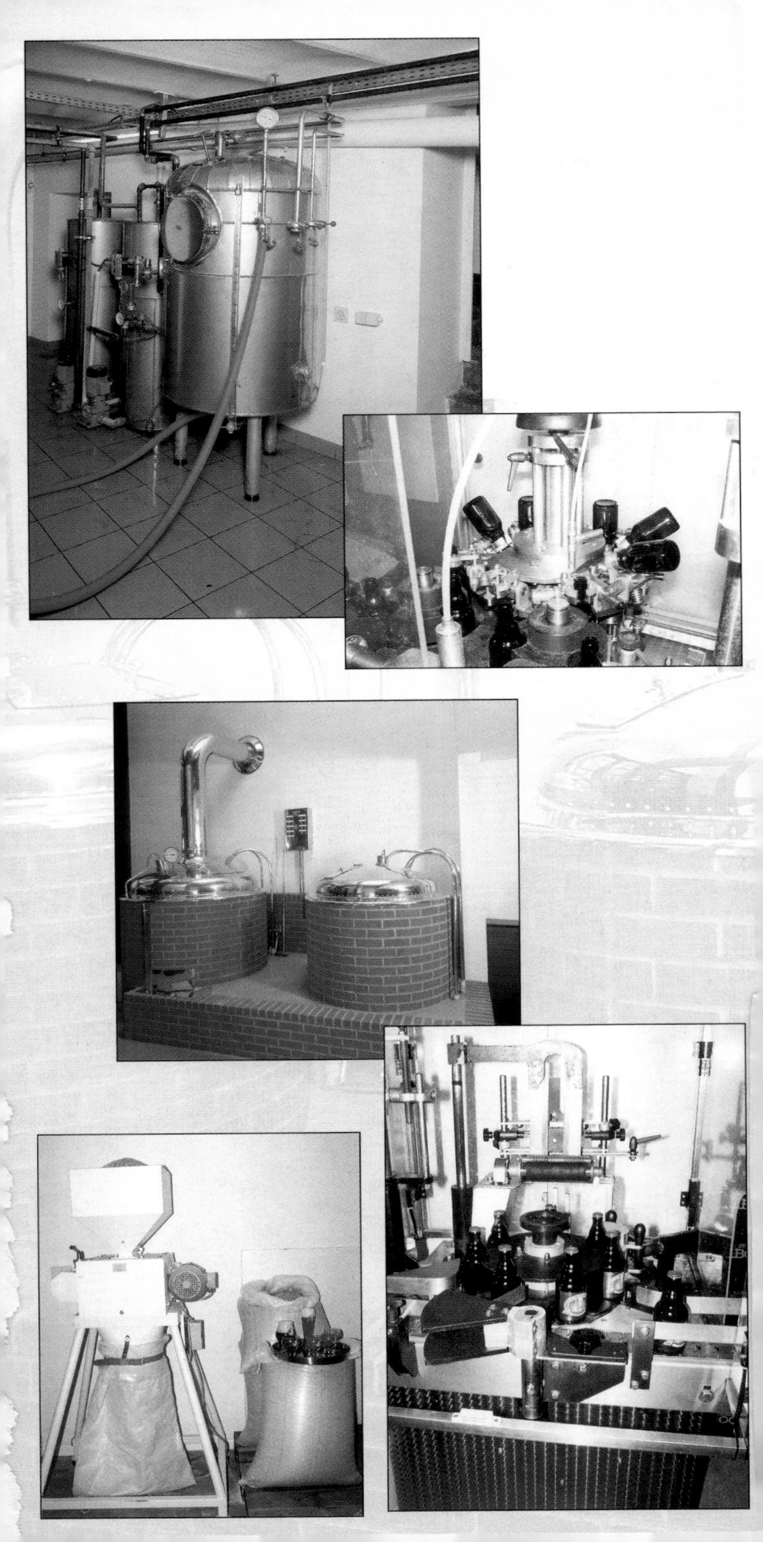

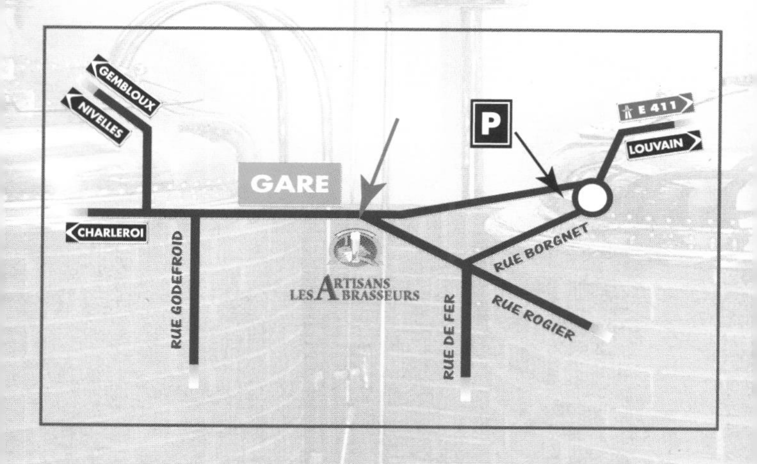
GEMBLOUX
NIVELLES
CHARLEROI
GARE
P
E 411
LOUVAIN
RUE GODEFROID
LES ARTISANS BRASSEURS
RUE DE FER
RUE BORGNET
RUE ROGIER

Trappist monks are easily recognisable with their white robes. Pictured is a service at Abbaye Notre Dame de Scourmont.

substance. Of course this applies to many aspects of consumerism, but here we are only interested in beer.

A habit prevalent throughout Belgium, as in other countries, is to give a beer an air of quality by calling it an abbey beer and giving it a monastic identity with the use of stained glass windows and religious figures on the label. Many of these are good beers in their own right, but equally as many are very pale imitations of beers genuinely produced in monasteries.

Some abbey beers do provide funds for existing abbeys – but none are made in the abbey and the monks are not Trappists. In most cases, however, the abbey is little more than a ruin and the brewery which makes the beer has nothing in common with an abbey and simply sells an historical brand name. It must be clearly understood that abbey beers are generally made by large commercial breweries, well away from any monks, and that Trappist beers are only made at a Trappist monastery with at least a little input to the operation of the brewery by one or more Trappist monks.

Another common misconception regarding Trappist beer – and a feature of virtually all abbey beers – is that their products fall easily into the styles of Double and Triple (Dubbel and Tripel in Flemish).

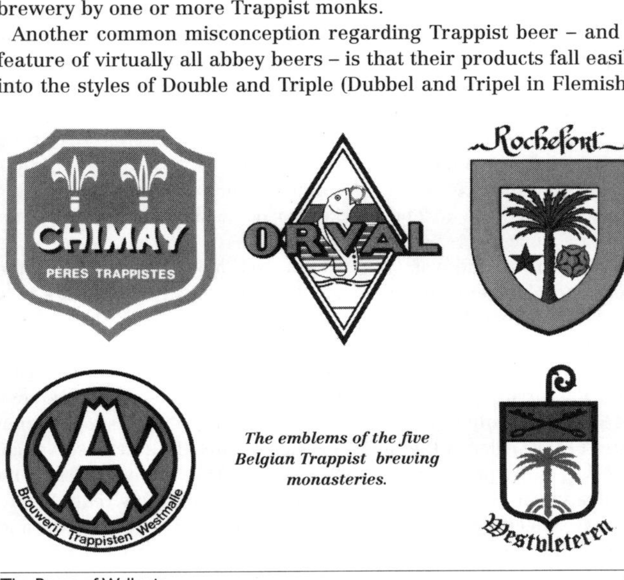

The emblems of the five Belgian Trappist brewing monasteries.

Westmalle presumably started this trend, having two such beers, but the two lowest gravity St. Sixtus beers can only loosely be so described and that doesn't take into account the Westvleteren Abt (its strongest beer). Schaapskoi has taken this a stage further by naming its strongest La Trappe beer as "Quadrupel" in addition to a Dubbel and Tripel. The Wallonian Trappist beers, however, bear little or no resemblance to the archetypal double and triple style. Chimay is the only one to brew a dark brown and a light beer in addition to the famous Chimay Bleue. Rochefort makes three brown ales and Orval produces just one, very original, light ale.

The story of the Trappists starts long ago, in Calabria, Southern Italy – the original home of the Benedictine monks. Moving northwards they established themselves in many other lands. The first Benedictine settlement in present-day Belgium was at Orval in the 11th century (Abbaye d'Orval celebrated its 900th anniversary in 1970). Legend has it that Orval owes its name and its emblem of a fish with a golden ring in its mouth to a certain Countess Matilda, Duchess of Tuscany, when she visited the monks in 1076. Sitting next to a spring (which was later named after her) she accidentally dropped her wedding ring into the water. Beseeching the Virgin Mary for its return she was delighted to see a trout rising out of the water with her ring in its mouth, at which she exclaimed "This is truly a val d'or" (val d'or translates as golden valley, and somewhere in the mists of time the term was bastardised into Orval).

Trappists strictly follow the teachings of St. Bernard (known to the Walloons as St. Benoit).

Although the Benedictine monks lived by a strict code of observance, by the end of the 11th century it was felt by some of them that their life was a little too comfortable. So, in 1098, a group of monks from the abbey of Molesme, led by St. Robert of Molesme, left to found a new order which demanded a solitary life under the strictest interpretation of St. Benedict's teachings. This new order was based at Citeaux, near Dijon in Burgundy and took its name – Cistercians – from Cistercium, the Latin name of the town.

Ironically history was to repeat itself as many abbeys broke their statutes by accumulating wealth and allowing discipline to decline. Then came the Protestant reformation which all but wiped out the monks in northern Europe, leaving those that survived to struggle for their existence.

The monastic life was later resurrected, mostly in France, in the 16th and 17th centuries. The most important instigator must surely be Armand-Jean le Bouthillier de Rance who became abbot of the abbey of La Trappe in Normandy in 1664. He made a great success of restoring the balance of silence, prayer, manual labour and seclusion from the corrupt outside world and the order became popularly known as Trappists rather than the correct but somewhat sesquipedalian term of the Order of the Reformed Cistercians of Strict Observance. Life was not all prayer and silence, however. They were expelled from La Trappe in 1792 and moved to Switzerland for a few years before being expelled again to eke out a nomadic existence in Germany and Russia. It was not until 1814 that they were able to return to La Trappe

– the first religious order to be revived after the disolution of many abbeys following the French revolution.

Life for a Trappist monk is not as hard these days. Until the late 1960s they still slept, ate and worked together in silence and observed strenuous fasts. Latterly, the reforms of the second Vatican Council and the modernisation of the Catholic Church have led to more diversity among the Trappist monasteries and although there is still an emphasis on silence and austerity they no longer enforce the rigid regulations of the early Trappists.

In the late 18th century some Trappists were forced out of their abbeys in France, necessitating a move to Belgium and the Netherlands with the aim of restoring old abbeys or founding new ones. Today there are 12 Trappist monasteries in Belgium (seven of which are in Wallonia) so the colonisation must be considered a success.

A closer look at the history of the three brewing abbeys in Wallonia reflects the scene over the whole of Belgium. The oldest existing site, Orval, though being occupied by monks from as early as the 11th century had the abbey built on its current site in 1132 by Cistercian monks from Trois-Fontaines. It was sacked and plundered in the 17th century, rebuilt, and then destroyed by General Loison in the French Revolution at the end of the 18th century. A long period of absence ended when, in 1926, a new abbey was built on an adjacent site. Rochefort was founded in 1230 and initially used by nuns before being replaced by monks in 1464 who stayed until 1794. The abbey had a new lease of life when it was reoccupied in 1887. Chimay does not have the long, turbulent history of its neighbours as it was founded as recently as 1850 by brothers from the abbey at Westvleteren, which itself had been founded only 19 years earlier.

Despite the strict edicts of the Trappist order and their avoidance of contact with the outside world, things have now relaxed to the point that it is now possible to visit the monasteries (although some are more accessible than others) and the monks even employ secular workers, particularly in the brewing operation. In all cases, however, the brewery is owned by the abbey and a monk is in overall charge. The employment of secular workers must have its advantages as the brothers obey several calls to prayer during the day and these could easily come at an inopportune moment in the brewing process.

Trappist beers tend to be rather on the strong side which could be considered incongruous in a society eschewing the material things in

Thankfully, Trappists take the trouble to ensure the customer will get the appropriate glass in which to enjoy their ale by printing pictograms like those above on their labels.

life (like hangovers!). Perhaps it is because of this that most of the abbeys brew a house beer for the brothers to drink with their meals. These are weaker than the commercially available beers and, unfortunately, and tend not to be available to the public.

All the Trappist beers have a heavy sediment which means, more than most beers, that it is very important to know about the effects of sediment on the taste. In almost all cases we would advise that you do as the Trappist breweries recommend – pour the beer carefully into the glass (making sure it is at least a Trappist glass shape if not the real one for the appropriate brewery) leaving the sediment behind. They then advise you to pour the dregs into a small glass which can be drunk at the end to get the benefit of the vitamins and proteins from the yeast while keeping the beer as it should be sampled. Of course, this is all a matter of taste.

A 15th century wood carving at St. Remy, Rochefort.

We would go further and recommend that with the 8° and 10° Rocheforts and Chimay Bleue, you pour the beer into the glass at least 10 or 15 minutes before drinking. This will avoid the tendency for excessive fizz, leaving you a wonderfully smooth, excellently rich and complex beer which is worthy of the tag "Trappist".

For those who want to try the whole Trappist experience it is possible to buy Chimay à la Bière cheese and Chimay à la Bière sausage to accompany your bottle of Grande Réserve (Chimay products are widely available in good delicatessens throughout Wallonia). For your health you can take Trappist Tablets made from beer yeast. Non-beer products sold by various Trappist and Trappistine sites are: bread, fruit, vegetables, poultry, pâté, cured meats, butter, children's clothing and even the "Trapp" brand of cleaning and hygiene products.

Details of the brewing operations at each of the Wallonian abbeys appear at the start of the brewery section.

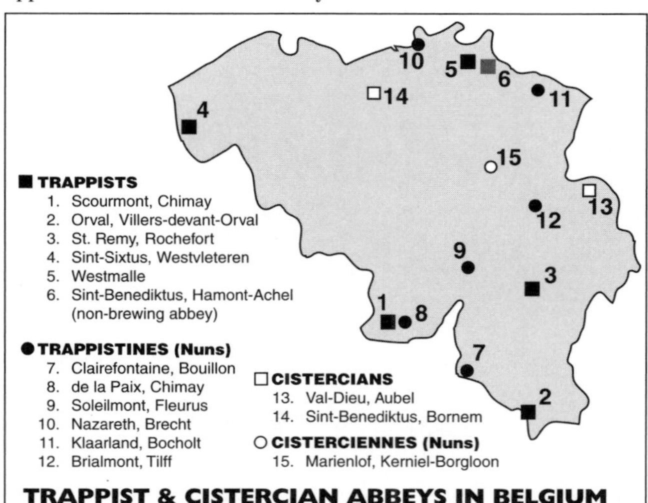

The BREWERIES *and their* BEERS

See overleaf for How To Use This Guide

How To Use This Guide

BREWERY INFORMATION

The amount of information forthcoming from the breweries varied, but we have reproduced the relevant information, such as ingredients and annual production, about the beers where it was available. Understandably the brewers were often guarded when it came to giving full details of ingredients, particularly with regard to the spices used. We have listed everything they told us.

General information about the breweries is contained in the start of each section and is identified by the following symbols:

- ✉ Address.
- ☎ Telephone number (plus fax if appropriate).
- 🕒 Brewery opening times.
- Tour availability, notice required, languages spoken on the tour, charge (if any).
- SHOP What can be bought – cases, individual bottles, glasses.
- Annual production in hectolitres (hl). 1hl = 100 litres.
- ➔ Directions to the brewery.

Information common to the range of beers is recorded in the brewery text.

THE BEERS

Regular beers, seasonal or otherwise, are listed with full details after the brewery text. Under "Other Beers" we list and briefly describe those beers brewed under contract for towns, distributors, fêtes, etc., which are not considered to be part of the brewery's portfolio. The names of relabelled beers (including those marketed under a different name for export) and one-off, special occasion beers appear in bold type in the text.

BEER TASTING NOTES

All beers have been tasted independently on more than one occasion by both authors, generally in a controlled atmosphere at home. The tasting notes reflect a joint opinion, though where they differ greatly this is recorded by using the initials of the relevant author.

HOW THE BEERS WERE MARKED

The marks are out of 10. There are two marks by each author for each beer. The first number represents the appeal the author believes that beer would have to someone looking for that style or type of beer. The second mark is the appeal that beer has for the author (as an indication, a mark of 6 or over suggests that the author would happily buy the beer again).

RECOMMENDED BARS/CAFES AND BEER SHOPS

Whilst researching this book we frequently had problems finding many of the beers without going to the brewery. To ease this situation we asked the breweries to recommend bars and cafes which store and serve their beers in the correct way, along with shops where their beers can be bought should the brewery be closed (most close over the weekend). These recommendations (where given) appear at the end of the appropriate brewery section, and the full collated list (sorted by town and province) can be found in the Recommended Outlets section, along with recommendations from the authors.

Abbaye Notre Dame d'Orval

✉ Orval 2, 6823 Villers-Devant-Orval, Luxembourg.

☎ 061 31 12 61 Fax: 061 31 29 27.

🕓 Mon-Thur 0800-1700, Fri 0800-1200.

Pre-arranged only. Unlikely, but may be possible.

SHOP Cases only and glasses.

37,000hl (in 1995).

➔ N88 south from Florenville to Virton, Abbaye d'Orval is signposted around the local area.

The abbey of Orval is probably the most attractive of the Trappist abbeys, being constructed of a light yellowish stone and enhanced by its idyllic setting on a bend in the old Roman road which linked Trier to Rheims, at the end of a little valley dominated by a lake. It was not always thus, and the ruins of the original abbey bear testiment to the turmoil of the centuries.

Founded by Cistercians in 1132 Orval was gutted by fire just one year later. Undaunted, the monks rebuilt the abbey soon after but it was sacked and plundered in the 17th Century. Following another

All Orval's brewery staff apart from the managing director are secular workers.

rebuilding programme along with extension and improvement it was destroyed once again during the French Revolution.

Although it is difficult to obtain permission to visit the new abbey, the part of the grounds containing the ruins are open to the public at certain times. The ruins also give access to the Matilda Spring, named after the Countess Matilda, Duchess of Tuscany, who visited the monks in 1076 (Matilda's visit also gave rise to the name and emblem of the abbey – see Trappist Temptations, p.20). That we are now able to enjoy the sight of the new abbey owes a lot to the brewery.

Construction of the present abbey started in 1925, but by 1931 funds were running out and the large buildings on the site had still not been finished. A group of people known as the Friends of the Orval Abbey set up the brewery as a public limited company, purely as a means of providing funds to enable the building work to be completed and then help maintain the site once it had reopened. The Friends eventually transferred their shares in the company to the monks. Income from the brewery is now used by the monks for charitable donations.

The brewery building was designed by the architect Henry Vaes and is based on the ruins of the abbey in Villers-la-Ville (south of Brussels). In 1932 he also designed the distinctive and impressive Orval beer glass which is still produced to this day.

There are currently 30 monks living in the abbey but only one works in the brewery. Dom Eric Dion has the role of managing director but the other 30 staff are all secular workers and range from the general manager to the lorry drivers. Only one beer is produced, but enough of it to make Orval brewery the third largest of the five Belgian Trappist breweries. Sales of the beer are pretty evenly spread throughout Belgium though, not surprisingly, the province of Luxembourg has the largest proportion. About ten per cent of production is exported to many countries around the world.

The beer itself is very complex which is probably down to the brewing process employed. In addition

Even at ground level the view of Abbaye d'Orval is impressive. The brewery is housed in the building on the right hand side.

to the water from the Matilda Spring, two types of hops, six malts, and no less than five yeast strains are used. There is a primary fermentation with one yeast and a secondary with five, taking six days to complete. This is followed by three weeks lagering (storage) complete with dry hopping, which helps account for the powerful aroma of Orval beer. Refermentation is started by six weeks in temperature controlled (15°C) warm rooms. Then, ten weeks after starting the brewing process, the beer is ready for sale.

ORVAL

6.2% alc/vol. 33cl crown corked bottles.

Known Ingredients: Triumph, Unterfranken, Prisma, Alexis, Caravienne malts. Styrian Goldings and Hallertau hops. Candy sugar.

Appearance: Golden amber orange with a lovely, creamy head.

Nose: Very complex with an interesting blend of hop aromas and an inviting fruitiness. Bitter orange hints and a distant herbiness. JDW: Apricot notes. KBR: Ground white pepper notes.

Palate: A complexity of multi-faceted hop tastes with their attendant levels of bitterness, citric notes and spiciness. There is a light fruitiness accompanying the bitterness. KBR: A peppery dryness with a distinct bitter orange note. JDW: Dry with a slight tartness.

Finish: Masses of dry hop bitterness with a little tannin and some lingering hints of fruit.

Overall: An amazingly complex, well balanced beer with a strong hop character and a lovely smooth, creamy texture. Gets noticeably drier as it ages. An excellent example of the philosophy of keeping the range small and concentrating on quality.

General: The brewery suggests it reaches maturity at nine months but will keep for five years if stored in the dark at 12-14°C (this is also the recommended serving temperature). It suggests pouring a clear glass of beer and drinking the dregs separately (the oval shaped bottle is designed to facilitate this). When it is offered for sale it has an alcohol content of about 6% but by the time the bottle refermentation has finished approximately 8 or 9 months later, it will have reached 7.1%. First brewed in 1931.

JDW: 10 / 8 KBR: 9 / 10

BARS & CAFES RECOMMENDED BY THE BREWERY

Each of the following should be able to supply at least two vintages:

L'ANGE GARDIEN, Villers-devant-Orval.

AUBERGE DU DAUPHIN, Chaussée de Nivelles 13, Arquennes.

LA VIEILLE POMPE, Membre sur Semois, Vresse sur Semois.

CAFÉ LE COMBATTANT, Grand Place, Morlanwelz.

Abbaye Notre Dame de Saint Remy

✉ Rue de l'Abbaye 8, 5580 Rochefort, Namur.

☎ 084 21 31 81.

🕓 Mon-Fri 0800-1600.

Pre-arranged only, but rare. Charge not known.

SHOP Cases only.

15,000hl (in 1995).

➔ See article.

Abbaye Notre Dame de Saint Remy, better known to most as Rochefort, can trace its origins back to 1230 when the abbey was first inhabited by nuns. Monks took up residence in 1464 and remained there until it closed in the cataclysmic days of the French Revolution in 1794. There then followed a long period of disuse before it was reinhabited again in 1887.

Monastery records show that the first brewery at the abbey dates from 1595 and that it used hops and barley grown in its grounds. Some of the brewery buildings we see today date from 1899 when it was still very much a cottage industry operation providing the monks, travellers and perhaps some of the local people with their wares. The brewery was extended and modernised in the 1950s, but it was not until the new brewhouse was built in 1960 that production reached its current levels. A new bottling plant was added in 1974.

As Trappist monasteries go this is probably the most secretive of them all. In Scourmont and Orval you can at least visit the grounds to sample the ambience – but at Saint Remy John was discour-

Give us this day our daily bread . . . the tables are laid ready for the brothers' meal times.

aged from just peeping through the gate as it was opened for some privileged soul to enter. Nothing was spoken but the face of the monk on the other side of the window said it all to someone stood on the "real world" side of the gate. The offer was made, however, for him to visit the brewery office – if only it was open! The office sells beers by the case

The abbey complex, like the others, is hidden away amongst wooded countryside some distance from the main town, and is approached through rolling farmland to a concealed car park from which you will see the entrance to the abbey.

Finding it is relatively simple – get to Rochefort, head out to the north of the town and follow the signs to Abbaye de St. Remy where it is found just off the N959.

In early 1996 there were 21 monks at St. Remy, five of whom have the enviable task of making Rochefort beer alongside some secular workers.

The brewing monks' day starts very early (at 3.30 am) for the start of the mash and goes through until 5.00 pm by which point the yeast has been pitched and the fermentation has started. Usually the Monday, Tuesday and Wednesday brews will have fermented enough to be transferred to the maturation tanks by the following Saturday morning.

At the bottling stage the beer is at 28°C to ensure the beer reacts quickly when the extra yeast and sugar is added. Eight days later the process is complete and the bottles are ready to be sold.

The beers, called simply 6, 8 and 10, refer to the Belgian degrees scale and are in fact considerably stronger when measured in alc/vol. Essentially they are all the same beer which is fermented out to dif-

Inside the abbey grounds.

The front gate of the abbey – not many people see the other side.

ferent strengths. Despite this, all three have subtle characteristics distinguishing each from the others.

It is only very recently that labels have been used – previously they had the words "Trappistes Rochefort" screen-printed onto the bottles with different crowns to identify each different brew.

ROCHEFORT 6

7.5% alc./vol. 33cl crown corked bottles.

Known Ingredients: Prisma and Alexis malts. Hallertau and Styrian Goldings hops.

Appearance: Rich dark amber colour with a good, compact and persistent head.

Nose: Distinctive fruity malt and pear drops. KBR: Some caramel.

Palate: A little sweet with a distinct malt taste and pear drop notes. JDW: A touch of fruit and hints of cocoa. KBR: Dry pepperiness with a very slight tartness.

Finish: Malty tending towards caramel. JDW: A little dry and cloying, alleviated by those pear drop notes again. KBR: Dry and bitter with darkly spiced fruit.

Overall: Quite full and complex, yet very easy to drink. Tastes considerably weaker than it actually is.

General: First brewed in 1900. A difficult beer to find – it is apparently only brewed intermittently and is intended for distribution only in the local area. Has a red crown.

JDW: 8 / 9 KBR: 9 / 9

ROCHEFORT 8

9.2% alc/vol. 33cl crown corked bottles.

Known Ingredients: Prisma and Alexis malts. Hallertau and Styrian Goldings hops.

Appearance: Very dark chestnut with burgundy highlights and a lasting head of very tight, creamy texture.

Nose: A good strong, deep and complex aroma with masses of fruity malt and pear drops to the fore. A lightly roasted malt base.

PALATE: Starts a little sweet with lashings of dark fruit before strong alcohol and pear drop tastes work their way through. A slight honeyed, peppery dryness adds to the complexity. Hops are present but are well in the background though the bitterness they impart is very noticeable. JDW: The alcohol element gives it a sharper taste than one might expect.
FINISH: Pear drops and a bittersweet alcohol tang which attacks the roof of the mouth (and back of the throat – JDW). Dry and lightly roasted element. Also a mixture of herbal tastes and some spicy hints.
OVERALL: A beautifully balanced, complex beer with great depth and many layers of taste. Has a wonderful texture if served at the correct temperature and left for 10-15 minutes before drinking to allow the initial excessive fizziness to subside. Very rewarding to drink.
GENERAL: First brewed in 1954 and now easily obtainable throughout Belgium. Three times as much 8 is produced as the 10. Has a green crown.

JDW: 10 / 10 KBR: 10 / 10

ROCHEFORT 10

11.3% alc/vol. 33cl crown corked bottles.
KNOWN INGREDIENTS: Prisma and Alexis malts. Hallertau and Styrian Goldings hops.
APPEARANCE: Very, very dark burgundy which appears black unless held against a light. Creamy, lasting head which leaves a beautiful lacework on the glass.
NOSE: Pear drops over a rich roast malt with occasional hints of coffee. Intensely strong in alcohol. KBR: Liquorice and pepper. JDW: Deep and fruity.
PALATE: Very rich, with a full fruity malt taste, some bitter chocolate and liquorice, masses of alcohol. A roast element and a dryness that starts building for the finish. JDW: Reasonably bitter.
FINISH: Long, lingering, dry bitterness with chocolate malt and a warming alcohol. KBR: Has a liqueur chocolate character.
OVERALL: Very uncompromising, complex ale which is full in taste, full in body and extremely heavy on the alcohol. Once accustomed to its excesses you can appreciate its quality and depth. A beer which has to be drunk last of all in an evening as no beer can compete with its formidably strong tastes. Lacks the flexibility (and compromise) of the Rochefort 8 but is the ultimate way to round off an evening when no other beer can fit the bill.
GENERAL: The brewery is unsure when it was first brewed. Like the Rochefort 8 it benefits from "venting" by pouring some 10-15 minutes before drinking to enhance its wonderful creamy texture. Has a blue crown.

JDW: 10 / 10 KBR: 10 / 9

BARS, CAFES & SHOPS RECOMMENDED BY THE BREWERY

So widely available the brewery does not wish to recommend any specific outlet.

Abbaye Notre Dame de Scourmont

✉ Route du Rond-point 294, 6464 Forges-Chimay, Hainaut.
☎ 060 21 30 63 Fax: 060 21 40 19.
🕓 Not applicable.
👥 See article. Phone for times and availability.
SHOP No.
🍾 103,000hl (in 1995).
➔ See article.

Most enthusiasts will have heard of – and doubtless sampled – Chimay beers due to their wide availability in bars, supermarkets and off-licences in many countries. Yet, despite the high profile of its products, the Abbaye Notre Dame de Scourmont (almost always referred to by its famous brand name) has retained the same traditions of inaccessibility and secrecy as the other Trappist abbeys.

The abbey itself is located in the Bois de Chimay, the large area of woodland south of the town of Chimay, very close to the French border. It is constructed of grey stone and is large enough to dominate the landscape if not for the fact that is hidden away behind its "front garden" of large shrubs and trees. To find the abbey, simply follow the "La Trappe" signs for 8km from Chimay where it lies just off the road through Bourlers to Riezes.

Founded in 1850, the abbey built its brewery some 12 years later in 1862, the year that its oldest product – Chimay Rouge – was first produced.

The ravages of the Second World War left their mark so, in 1944, work started on rebuilding the brewery using the most advanced scientific methods available at the time, with the assistance of Professor Jean de Clerck and his associates at the University of Louvain. It was Professor de Clerck who developed the strain of yeast which helps give Chimay beers their distinctive character. Perhaps the other principal ingredient to have a great effect on their character is the water which is drawn from wells beneath the abbey. Professor de Clerck declared it to be perfect for brewing, having very few mineral salts and a low alkalinity. No adjustment is necessary. In 1948 a new beer was added to the range – Chimay Spéciale Noël – which, ten years later, joined the regular beer portfolio as the famous Chimay Bleue.

The Abbaye Notre Dame de Scourmont lies in rolling countryside west of the Meuse valley.

A modernisation programme recently saw the abbey upgrade its plant again, sadly removing its famous gleaming copper kettles. Perhaps the most surprising element of the new operation at the abbey is that the beer leaves the site once the fermentation ceases. At that point it is pumped into tankers and driven 8km to a new installation on an industrial estate on the main road between Chimay and Couvin which was built in the early 1980s to handle the bottling, refermentation, storage, distribution and marketing. After the solemn, spiritual tranquility of the abbey, visiting this site brings you straight back into the real world.

The bottling plant is open to visitors, but only on organised tours which must be pre-booked. During the winter months they require only a couple of days' notice, but in the height of the summer tourist season this can increase to a couple of months (tel: 060 21 03 11).

The brewery itself is, in true Trappist tradition, strictly off limits. The abbey gardens are open to the public and you can wander around the courtyard garden, contemplating the peace and quiet, and stare at the brewery wall. If you look carefully you may even see some of the brewery equipment through a high window; but as Paul Arnott, the brewery's quality control manager, said: "If the wind is blowing in the right direction you can at least smell the production".

Like other Trappist breweries, the staff are almost entirely secular workers. Of the 20 monks at the abbey only two are involved with the brewery, in a managerial role.

You cannot even buy any of the Chimay products from the abbey. The Ferme des Quatre Saisons which is just over the crossroads as you join the Riezes to Chimay road sells the full Chimay range – not just beers and glasses, but also the aperitifs, cheeses, ham, sausages

Indulge yourself in the total Trappist experience: cheese, sausage and pâté – the perfect accompaniments for Chimay beers.

and pâtés as well as the obligatory souvenirs. One of the cheeses, Chimay à la Bière, has a rind steeped in a hop mixture and is designed to accompany Chimay beers. You may have to get in quickly to sample the meat products as we understand the abbey's meat processing plant is currently up for sale.

CHIMAY BLANCHE / CINQ CENTS

8% alc/vol. 33cl crown corked and 75cl corked bottles.

KNOWN INGREDIENTS: Pale, amber and crystal malts. Yakima and Hallertau hops. Spices are added, but type and quantity are kept secret.

APPEARANCE: Amber with a creamy, head.

NOSE: Hops slightly dominate a pleasant, gentle maltiness.

PALATE: Bitter, with a citric lemon note enhancing a slight peppery edge to a distinctive hoppiness. Minimal maltiness in the background and a few alcohol notes. KBR: Has an odd, but pleasant, flowery/herby character.

FINISH: Very mouthdrying with a distinctly hoppy bitterness and a hop tang in the distance. Some alcohol burn on the tongue (KBR) or the throat (JDW).

OVERALL: An accomplished ale, full in taste yet surprisingly delicate for a Trappist brew. Larger quantity of Hallertau hops used than in other Chimay beers which accounts for its stronger hop character. KBR: Has an elusive complexity which has to be worked on to find.

GENERAL: Sold as Cinq Cents (literally translating as 500, referring to its first appearance in large bottles to celebrate the 500th anniversary of the town of Chimay) in 75cl corked bottles. First brewed in the 1960s. Like the other Chimay beers it should be stored upright (both 33cl and 75cl). Best drunk at 6-12 months old. Only 10% of Chimay's production is of the Blanche.

JDW: 9 / 7 KBR: 8 / 8

CHIMAY BLEUE / GRANDE RÉSERVE

9% alc/vol. 33cl crown corked and 75cl corked bottles.

KNOWN INGREDIENTS: Pale, amber and crystal malts. Yakima and Hallertau hops. Spices are added, but type and quantity are kept secret.

APPEARANCE: Rich, ruby amber with a creamy, head.

NOSE: Rich, vinous fruit and a little malt which gets fuller with age.

PALATE: A very full mouth of taste. Dark, vinous, quite sweet and malty with a strong alcohol element. JDW: Good balance of sweetness and bitterness. KBR: Surprisingly bitter undertones.

Finish: Strong, lingering malt. Initial peak of bitterness which subsides to leave hints of molasses and raisins. Pronounced alcohol notes.

Overall: Accomplished "top of the range" Trappist ale which falls slightly short of the Rocheforte and Westvleteren benchmarks unless aged well in a cellar (preferably in its 75cl bottled version) – a process which also eliminates the Bleue's tendency towards over-fizziness when young. After two or three years you will be rewarded with a noble, smooth, rounded and warming beer which further complements its rich and vinous character. Our marks are for an aged Bleue.

General: Sold as Grande Réserve in 75cl corked bottles. Although both bottle sizes are vintage dated, we would heartily recommend that any serious drinker should age it in its larger guise. Vintage Bleue is occasionally offered in better bars (usually as Grande Réserve), but you will probably face a hefty bill for such a luxury. First brewed in 1948, it should be stored upright. Chimay Bleue accounted for over half the output of the brewery in 1995.

JDW: 9 / 9 KBR: 9 / 9

CHIMAY ROUGE / PREMIÈRE

7% alc/vol. 33cl crown corked and 75cl corked bottles.

Known Ingredients: Pale, amber and crystal malts. Yakima and Hallertau hops. Spices are added, but type and quantity are kept secret.

Appearance: Dark amber with a good, creamy head.

Nose: Predominantly a fruity malt. JDW: With a few hops.

Palate: Malty and fruity with some bitterness and a little pepperiness from the hops that are just evident.

Finish: Dry and bitter with roasted malt. Lingering peppery hop tang which develops with age.

Overall: A good, rounded fruitiness redeems what could otherwise be quite a disappointingly ordinary beer. Has an intrusive fizz, even when aged for a few years.

General: Sold as Première (in recognition of it being the first beer from the original brewery) in 75cl corked bottles. The brewery states it is best drunk between 6 and 12 months old.

JDW: 8 / 7 KBR: 7 / 6

BARS & CAFES RECOMMENDED BY THE BREWERY

FERME DES QUATRE SAISONS, Rue de Scourmont 8b, 6464 Forges-Chimay.

LE CASINO, Place des Ormeaux, Chimay.

All cafes in Grand Place, Chimay.

SHOPS RECOMMENDED BY THE BREWERY

DELHAIZE, Chimay.

MATCH, Chaussée de Mons 17, 6460 Chimay.

UNIC, Rue de Bourlers 1, 6460 Chimay.

Brasserie Abbaye des Rocs

✉ Chaussée de Brunehault 37, 7387 Montignies-sur-Roc, Hainaut.
☎ 065 75 99 76
Mon-Fri 0800-1800.
Pre-arranged only. At least 30 days notice. No charge.
SHOP Cases, bottles and glasses.
660hl (in 1995).
→ Coming from Quievrain and Audregnies the brewery is on the right hand side of the road just before the village turn-off to the left. The most obvious thing to look out for is a large green and black bottle-shaped sign at the roadside.

The use of the name Abbaye des Rocs by the brewery is perhaps a little confusing as it is neither located in an abbey nor does it brew on behalf of one. In fact the beers are not even in the traditional abbey style (though the owner describes his Abbaye des Rocs beer as an abbey beer and La Montagnarde as a triple). Despite this anomaly we would heartily recommend that anyone searching for characterful beers should take the trouble to track these down.

The brewery was started in 1979 by Jean-Pierre Eloir, a tax inspector who enjoyed home brewing, and commenced operations in his garage as Brasserie Eloir-Bertiau. This was in response to a challenge from his father-in-law, who had been the production director for Brasserie Cavenaile in Dour, to make more of his hobby skills.

Things have come a long way since then. His daughter, Nathalie, has joined the business and even taken over the role of brewer. There has also been a succession of extensions built on the end of the previous building in the grounds of his home. In fact it seems that every time we visit the brewery Jean-Pierre is mixing concrete or tiling a new roof.

The buildings themselves are tastefully constructed, in keeping with the local architecture, and Jean-Pierre has used material from the ruins of the original Abbaye des Rocs (from which the brewery takes its name), and features attractive arched windows inside. It certainly looks nice – but there again it has to when your kitchen window overlooks it!

The brewery's beers most definitely have a Wallonian character and all are spiced. Perhaps the most fascinating aspect of their production is the amount of different grains used in some of the brews – six types of barley are used in Abbaye des Rocs and oats, wheat and barley are used in Blanche des Honnelles. We believe this to be the main reason for the amazingly full tastes of Abbaye des Rocs beers.

A sign to watch for on the road.

Although you might find others on the shelves of beer shops, there are in fact only the four staple products from the brewery. The others may be differently-labelled versions of these (such as La Schaerbeekoise which is Abbaye des Rocs relabelled for the Beer Museum at Schaerbeek) while there are occasional one-off brews for specific occasions (such as Trans-frontalière to celebrate the twinning of Tournai with Bethune in Pas de Calais, France). The mainstay of the brewery's output is Abbaye des Rocs and La Montagnarde at 220hl each.

Like many good breweries, Abbaye des Rocs produces an informative leaflet about how to appreciate its beers. It recommends a serving temperature of between 8° and 12°C for its strong brews and 4°C for Blanche des Honnelles. It also advises that its beers can be laid down in a cool cellar, away from light, for up to three years (though it states that all the beers are mature after six months). If you do decide to "lay them down", you should keep them in the upright position.

The first Abbaye des Rocs label.

While visiting Abbaye des Rocs it would be a shame not to take the 6-8 km car drive to Restaurant Le Baron in Gussignies (just over the unmarked border into France) to sample the excellent range of beers from Brasserie Bailleux, which are more akin to the Wallonian style than the bières de garde of the surrounding area.

ABBAYE DES ROCS

9% alc/vol. 75cl and 33cl bottles (magnums & jeraboams on request), corked & crown corked.

KNOWN INGREDIENTS: Six types of malt. Three types of hop. Spiced with ginger, sweet and bitter orange peel, liquorice and dandelions.

APPEARANCE: Dark, copper amber colour with a large, solid head.

NOSE: Clean malt with dry, spicy notes. Hints of caramel.

PALATE: Initially there is sweet, fruity

malt which quickly develops a harsher dark flavour with hints of butterscotch before giving way to a herbal, spicy dryness. Vinous, full-bodied and beautifully balanced with some bite. Sediment mellows the taste.

FINISH: Burnt malt tang with sherry notes, developing a dry, fruity tang at the back of the throat. Long, warming and satisfying finish.

OVERALL: Good complex beer with enough complementary tastes to keep you interested from the nose through to the lingering finish. Has abbey beer qualities with the added interest of lots of typically Wallonian spice.

GENERAL: The labels shows the coat of arms of the old abbey (founded 1757). This beer has been sold as **La Shaerbeekoise** and **Le Saint Lenderik**. First brewed in 1979.

JDW: 8 / 7 KBR: 8 / 9

ABBAYE DES ROCS SPÉCIALE NOËL

9% alc/vol 75cl and 33cl bottles (magnums & jeraboams on request), corked & crown corked.

KNOWN INGREDIENTS: Six types of malted barley. Three types of hop. Spiced with vanilla.

APPEARANCE: Deep reddy-brown with a lively, lasting head and nice lacework

NOSE: Dark, rich, malty with a little spicy hop. Dry, roasted promise.

PALATE: Rich roasted malt with a pronounced dry burnt tang. Very full tasting if a little over-vinous. Hints of oats with a strange "aged" character. JDW: Alcohol warmth increases with age.

FINISH: Dry, bitter and gloriously warming. Rich, deep, malty and satisfying.

OVERALL: Wonderful Christmas beer which, as the name suggests, is essentially an Abbaye des Rocs with the addition of a higher proportion of chocolate and black malt in the mash. Beautifully smooth and creamy.

GENERAL: Has the normal Abbaye des Rocs label with the addition of the special neck label shown above. Usually available from the end of November. First brewed in 1984.

JDW: 8 / 8 KBR: 10 / 9

BLANCHE DES HONNELLES

6% alc/vol. 75cl and 33cl bottles (magnums & jeraboams on request), corked & crown corked.

KNOWN INGREDIENTS: Barley, wheat and oats. Spiced with orange peel, coriander and juniper.

APPEARANCE: Orangey, old gold colour with large fluffy head which lasts well.

NOSE: Dominated by a peppery spice with some hints of orange. Grainy background, mostly wheat. Deeper and less fresh than most commercial white beers. Sediment dulls the nose and adds mustiness.

PALATE: Initial hit of spice with a pronounced grainy taste (predominantly wheat but you can certainly taste others) and a citric bite. Nice balance of sweet, sour and bitter which gives a very full taste. Sediment makes it spicier, increasing the orange peel character.

FINISH: Dry, slightly bitter wheat with a bittersweet tang and a general bitterness. Many different layers give it a complex finish.

OVERALL: One of the most complex artisanal white beers – multi-faceted and rewarding, which makes it a good summer quencher yet interesting enough to drink anytime. Very original and refreshingly different. Equally good with or without sediment to the point that we recommend trying it both ways to see which suits your particular preference. KBR: So many tastes that some may find it difficult to cope with – not most people's concept of a white beer.

GENERAL: Named after the locality of the brewery. The label depicts local poet Emile Verhaeren (1855-1916). First brewed 1990, originally for the association "Les Amis du Verre à Bière".

JDW: 8 / 8   KBR: 7 / 8

LA MONTAGNARDE

9% alc/vol. 75cl and 33cl bottles (magnums & jeraboams on request), corked & crown corked.

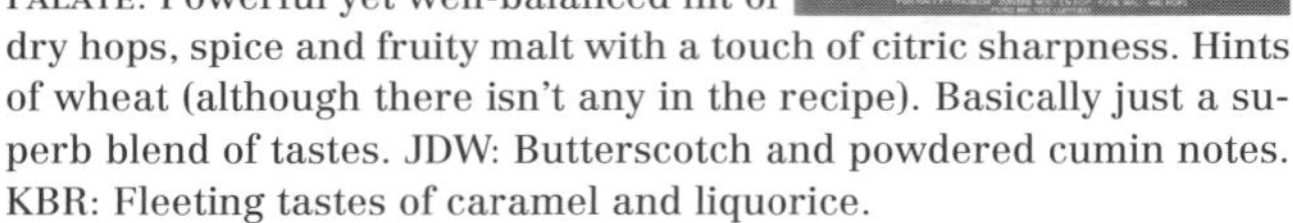

KNOWN INGREDIENTS: Two types of malt. Two types of hop. Spiced with cumin.

APPEARANCE: Golden orange-amber colour with a large, lasting creamy head.

NOSE: Excellent, complex, hop aroma with a subtle blend of fruity malt. Some spice and flowery notes.

PALATE: Powerful yet well-balanced hit of dry hops, spice and fruity malt with a touch of citric sharpness. Hints of wheat (although there isn't any in the recipe). Basically just a superb blend of tastes. JDW: Butterscotch and powdered cumin notes. KBR: Fleeting tastes of caramel and liquorice.

FINISH: Alcohol comes to the fore with a sherryish character alongside a lingering hoppiness and fruity bitterness. Dry spice counters the vinous qualities. JDW: Occasional pear drop notes. KBR: Some toffeeish character.

OVERALL: A very accomplished beer with a deep and complex character. Ageing the beer enhances the fruitiness and depth. Excellent, quite thick texture with just enough fizz to prevent cloying.

GENERAL: A "Montagnarde" is an inhabitant of Montignies-sur-Roc and the label shows the town's coat of arms. First brewed in 1980.

JDW: 9 / 10   KBR: 10 / 10

BARS & CAFES RECOMMENDED BY THE BREWERY

CAFÉ DE L'ENSEIGNEMENT, Chausée de Lodelinsert, Gilly.
DE PIKARDEN, Cotthemstraat 6, Sint-Lievens-Houtem (E. Flanders).
L'EXCELSIOR, Grand Place 29, Mons.
MUSÉE DE SCHAERBEEK, Rue Louis Bertrand, Schaerbeek.
TAVERNE DU CHÂTEAU, Place, Montignies-sur-Roc.

BEER SHOPS RECOMMENDED BY THE BREWERY

BIÈRES ARTISINALES, Chausée de Wavre 174, Brussels.
DRINK HOLEMANS, Langdor Sewteenweg 117, Aarschot.
DURIGNEUX, Rue de l'Église, Dour.
VANUXEEM, Rue d'Armentières 150, Ploegsteert.

Brasserie d'Achouffe

✉ Rue du Village 32, 6666 Achouffe, Luxembourg.

☎ 061 28 81 47 Fax: 061 28 82 64.

🕓 Mon-Sat 1030-1200, 1400-1800.

Pre-arranged only. 3 months notice. In French, Flemish or English. 150 Bfr charge.

SHOP Cases, bottles, glasses.

7,000hl (in 1994).

➔ See article.

Brasserie d'Achouffe, nestling in the beautiful Ardennes countryside close to Houffalize in the province of Luxembourg, is a real microbrewery success story. It has a portfolio of just two regular and two seasonal beers but has also brewed under contract for clients such as drinks shop owners and trade organisations. Its beers are marketed in a professional manner and, despite the hefty price tags, there seems to be an ever-increasing demand for its products.

As many as 10,000 "tourists" visit the brewery and its busy bar (built on the back of the brewhouse) per year and this accounts for almost 20% of the brewery's total sales, no doubt taking advantage of the emergence of the Ardennes as a popular holiday area.

Unlike most microbreweries, which depend largely on very local allegiance to their products, Achouffe has found that around 50% of its output is destined for export – surprisingly, even to countries such as Russia and Lebanon!

In the late 1970s brothers-in-law Chris Bauweraerts and Pierre Gobron decided they wanted to run a brewery and sell their own beer and eventually founded Brasserie d'Achouffe in 1982 with the first brew, 49 litres, on 17th August. Initially the brewery was run very much as a serious hobby with 1983 seeing a total production of just 40 hl. However, in March 1984 things took an upward swing when Pierre gave up his job as production manager of an ice-cream factory to work full-time at the brewery. That year it produced 240 hl and also changed its brew plant for one of 700 litre capacity.

The business went from strength to strength. In 1986 it bought the farm which currently houses the brewery and production had increased to 900hl. In 1988 Chris left his computer engineer job to help push the production to 2,000hl and this year saw its first export order go to Canada.

The brewery bar was opened in April 1990 and more investment came in 1991 with a new brew plant of 5,500 litre capacity. This was fully operational in 1992 and production that year climbed to 5,000hl. The final part of the story took place in June 1993 when the new fermenting room was completed.

Their two best known beers – La Chouffe and McChouffe – have a very impressive, exceptionally clean taste and are both also quite spicy. A lot of the taste can be put down to the water used which comes from a local spring, one of the highest in Belgium. The spicy character is surprising considering McChouffe has no added spice and La Chouffe contains only coriander.

So what is a chouffe? A red-hatted, long-bearded gnome of course. You can't miss them – they are everywhere, forming the focus for all the brewery's marketing including the large one on the silo beside the farmhouse. Gnomes are apparently a popular part of the local folklore and they have served Achouffe well by giving them an easily recognised identity and powerful marketing tool.

To find the brewery you will have to travel well into the Ardennes in Luxembourg province, leaving the A26 at junction 51 to Houffalize and heading north on the N30. A short distance from the town you take a left turn in the direction of Achouffe and Wibrin. Achouffe is the first village you come to, and the brewery is unmissable.

In addition to the four stock beers, the brewery has also produced a number of special beers which are not for sale at the brewery as they are brewed under licence and the client has sole selling rights. **La Vieille Salme** is the only special beer currently produced (8.3 alc/vol.) – an excellent, interesting and quaffable ale with a strong apple character, which is well worth seeking out from certain outlets in the town of Vielsalm and at the taverne/restaurant at the brewery.

Chouffes everywhere – on the silo and on the new Patachouffe beer cheese label.

CHOUFFE BOK 6666

6.666% alc/vol. 75cl corked and crown corked bottles (may also be available in 150cl bottles).

Known Ingredients: Pilsener malt. Styrian Goldings and Saaz hops. Brown candy sugar.

Appearance: Copper coloured with a good head and lacework.

NOSE: JDW: Distinctive hop aroma. KBR: Dutch bock beer character with added herbs and spices.

PALATE: JDW: A pleasant mix of hops and malt with a touch of spicy fruit at the end. KBR: Very malty and strong in alcohol.

FINISH: Strong, hoppy bitterness. KBR: Warming.

OVERALL: JDW: Good hop character. KBR: Obviously brewed in the Dutch style with a strong malty bitterness, a little shallow.

GENERAL: Available in limited quantities. Brewed for the American market (180hl produced and called simply **Chouffe Bok**) where it is sold from March to May and for the Dutch market (360hl) to be sold in October. First brewed in 1991. Unusually short-lived for an Achouffe beer, this is apparently best drunk at three months old and keeps for only six months.

JDW: 7 / 7 KBR: 7 / 5

LA CHOUFFE

8% alc/vol. 75cl corked & crown corked bottles and daught. In 1.5 litre bottles it is called **Big Chouffe**.

KNOWN INGREDIENTS: Pilsener malt. Saaz and Styrian Goldings hops, white candy sugar. Spiced with coriander.

APPEARANCE: Rich gold with a good white head.

NOSE: Reasonably fresh citric (lime and lemon) hops with a herbal, mainly coriander powder, element. Spiciness increases with age

PALATE: Very spicy (with coriander and pepper to the fore) with lashings of lemon and lime hops. Orchard fruit hints lurk in the background along with some malt and a gentle bitterness. KBR: Has a faint wheatiness.

FINISH: A little dry and hoppy with a few departing spicy notes. Short-lived and tantalisingly faint when young but increases when aged.

OVERALL: Excellent, characterful, refreshing ale which, for a micro-brewery, is very consistent. Amazingly drinkable for its strength. Addition of some sediment increases the graininess of texture and adds to the spice. Has a clinical character about it not usually found in artisanal beers.

GENERAL: First brewed in 1982 and now found in many specialist beer shops throughout Belgium. We have even seen it served with grenadine and called a Chouffe Royale. Best drunk six months old although will keep for two years.

JDW: 9 / 9 KBR: 9 / 9

Mc CHOUFFE

8.5% alc/vol. 75cl corked & crown corked bottles and draught.

KNOWN INGREDIENTS: Pilsener malt. Styrian Goldings hops. Brown candy sugar.

APPEARANCE: Deep copper with a good, lasting creamy head.

NOSE: Unusual blend of fruit and malt with a strong herbal element and spicy notes.

PALATE: Full, rich and complex

with a spicy, herbal character and a strong roasted, chocolate malt taste. JDW: Strong alcohol element which increases with age. KBR: Darker character tends to mask the spice more than the La Chouffe.

FINISH: Fruity roast malt with a long-lingering dry bitterness. KBR: Slightly tannic.

OVERALL: Well made ale with good complexity and character. Fuller, richer and more warming that La Chouffe.

GENERAL: Apparently the idea for McChouffe came from a Scottish friend of the brewers. Interestingly the brewery describes it as an abbey brune. Although it is hardly in the strict tradition of a scotch ale, we like to think of it as a Wallonian spiced equivalent. Also sold as **Cuvée du Tcheste** when labelled for the Confrerie du Tcheste in Neufchateau. First brewed in 1987, best drunk after six months but should keep for up to two years.

JDW: 8 / 8 KBR: 9 / 9

N'ICE CHOUFFE

10% alc/vol. 75cl corked & crown corked bottles (may also be available in 150cl bottles).

KNOWN INGREDIENTS: Pilsener malt. Styrian Goldings and Saaz hops. Brown candy sugar.

APPEARANCE: Deep dark copper.

NOSE: KBR: Very burnt malt and caramel with a little spice. JDW: Rich, fruity Christmas cake.

PALATE: Very strong burnt malt element dominates the rich, vinous fruit. KBR: Figgy hints and some creamy, lactic notes.

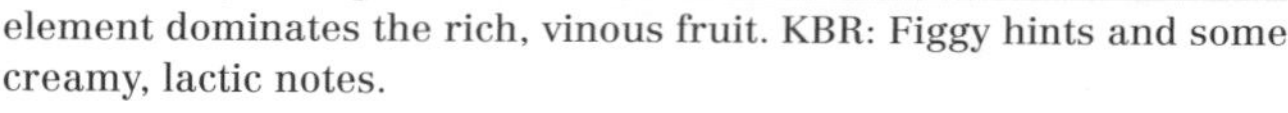

FINISH: Burnt malt. JDW: A long lasting finish of dry, fruity malt heavily laced with alcohol. KBR: Overly burnt, very dry, very bitter

OVERALL: An uncompromising beer that for JDW did not deliver the promise of the nose. The burnt malt element has a tendency to overpower all else.

GENERAL: Achouffe's winter beer, first brewed in 1993, which is best drunk at a year old but will keep up to 5 years. Limited availability as only 360hl is brewed annually. The above picture shows the design which was screen printed onto the bottle of the beers we tasted.

JDW: 7 / 5 KBR: 7 / 5

BARS & CAFES RECOMMENDED BY THE BREWERY

BIER CIRCUS, Rue de l'Enseignement 89, Brussels.
BREWERY TAVERNE, Rue du Village 32, Achouffe.
PETITE FONTAINE, Rue du Village, Achouffe.
HÔTEL ESPINE, Achouffe.
BISTRO LEO, Bastogne.
OUD TEUVEN, Rue du Village 3, Teuven (Province of Limburg).

BEER SHOPS RECOMMENDED BY THE BREWERY

DELHAIZE, certain outlets.
DELEPINE DRINK MARKET, Rue Eugène Cattoir 13, Brussels.
CORMAN-COLLINS, Rue Xhéneumont 1A, Battice.
PAL CENTRE, Route d'Arlon, Oberpallen (Grand Duchy of Luxembourg).

Brasserie d'Ambly

Rue Principale 45, 6953 Ambly, Luxembourg.

084 21 15 78.

Any reasonable hour by arrangement.

Pre-arranged only. 7 days notice. In French, or English by appointment. 60 Bfr charge.

Cases, bottles and glasses.

300hl (anticipated for 1996).

See article.

The newest, and smallest, of the trinity of breweries around the town of Rochefort is Brasserie d'Ambly, set in the tiny village of that name in the heavily forested foothills near Nassogne of the Ardennes.

Young Pierre Jacob is justifiably proud of the operation which started in 1996 in the converted barn behind his parents' farmhouse, which looks out onto a yard complete with wandering calves.

After a few unrelated jobs Pierre, a keen home-brewer for years, took the plunge and set up his own professional outfit after a month's intensive course in the art of brewing.

The barn conversion and construction of the brewplant was done by Pierre and his brother to a surprisingly good standard for such a small, self-built affair. The tiered design of the plant takes advantage of the generous height of the barn, leaving a good amount of spare floorspace allowing scope for any future expansion.

The brewery that Pierre built . . . with help from his brother.

The brewplant essentially consists of two multi-functional vessels, one above the other, with a series of steps and platforms from which to work. An old gas-fired steam boiler (recycled from a mayonnaise factory) is used to pump the water and liquor to the top vessel, enabling a good use of gravity in the rest of the operation. The overall set-up is well thought out and makes very efficient use of the space.

Bottling, corking and crowning is all done by hand and the barn has a warm room in one corner.

There is currently just the one beer produced, but Pierre is developing a brown beer which he hopes to sell in the near future.

To find the brewery, head into the centre of Ambly (a village of just 400 inhabitants) off the N889 north west of Nassogne and find the small monument in the middle of a road junction. The farm, number 45, is on the south-east corner of the junction. You will have to park on the gravel at the front and announce your presence at the farmhouse. There are no signs on either the road or the farm and the brewery is not visible from the road

LA SAINT-MONON

7% alc/vol. 75cl corked & crown corked bottles.

KNOWN INGREDIENTS: Pale, amber and caramel malts. Brewers Gold hops.

APPEARANCE: Reddy amber with a good fluffy head.

NOSE: Very hoppy with a peppery dry promise. KBR: Some background fruit with distinct tannic notes. Very pleasant and inviting. JDW: Rich, mellow malt. Slight spiciness.

PALATE: Distinct hop character and a little too much caramel. KBR: Instantly dry with a tannic, fruity malt – doesn't have the expected bitterness. JDW: Very tangy taste with a sharp alcohol edge.

FINISH: Dry and bitter with leftover fruity tannins which develop into a slightly cloying tang after a few mouthfuls. JDW: Lightly roast malt with an abundance of alcohol warmth.

OVERALL: Promising maiden ale from a new, young brewer. An odd hoppiness for a Belgian ale, but this helps to balance the fruit and tannins. The beer seems to want to deliver more yet stops short all the way through.

GENERAL: Saint-Monon was apparently a monk who came to the area from Scotland to spread the evangelist word in the 7th century. He is the patron saint of Nassogne. The beer should be served at 10-12° and Pierre believes it will improve with age if kept well.

JDW: 7 / 7 KBR: 8 / 7

BARS & CAFES RECOMMENDED BY THE BREWERY

LE RELAIS ST MONON, Nassogne.
L'ESTAMINET, Forrières.

BEER SHOPS RECOMMENDED BY THE BREWERY

Bottles of La Saint-Monon can only be bought from the brewery at present.

Brasserie La Binchoise

Faubourg St Paul 38, 7130 Binche, Hainaut.

032 64 33 61 86 Fax: 032 64 33 61 86.

Mon-Fri 0900-1730 and by appointment.

Pre-arranged only. 1 week's notice. In French, Flemish and English. 90Bfr charge. Tasting available.

Cases, bottles, glasses.

800hl (in 1995).

See article.

Situated on the plains of Hainaut between Mons and Charleroi, Binche has had a long and interesting history. Unusual for the area, most of the town's formidable ramparts survive in surprisingly good condition and it is at the foot of these walls, in the cobbled south-west old quarter, that the Brasserie La Binchoise is found.

From Binche's Grand Place you take an exit from the corner opposite the link road to the main shopping street of Avenue Charles Deliege and descend a suspension-testing cobbled road called Rue Saint Paul before taking a right turn into Faubourg Saint Paul where the brewery's industrial brick façade is found to your left after 50 metres.

The building is an old brewery and maltings and, although we have no information regarding the date of its construction, it is presumably over 100 years old and oddly placed in between houses.

Most of the brewing plant appears to be recycled from previous establishments which gives an old rustic air, in keeping with the rest of the interior. In March 1995 Binchoise celebrated the official opening of its new sampling room, tastefully converted from the old maltings and with some of the defunct equipment still in place. Called "La Malterie des Remparts" it also serves as a bar and function room, forming the focal point of the brewery's 'open doors' weekend in September. For this occasion it brews two more beers – a Spéciale Blonde and Rose des Remparts.

The business, started in 1989 by André Graux and Françoise Jauson, has evolved into a successful enterprise which exports to Canada and, unusually for an artisanal Wallonian brewery, does a healthy trade in Flanders with its Binchoise Blonde relabelled as Fakir (it considered the change in name and label necessary to promote the beer without its obvious Wallonian identity and, incidentally, was given the title of André's childhood nickname). The Blonde now accounts for almost half of the brewery's total output.

The adventurous range (all non-filtered and top fermented) now contains five beers, some of which may be relabelled for local fête and carnival use, although this is usually only done with its Blonde and Brune. All its beers should be stored on their side and peak at six months with the exception of Spéciale Noël which peaks at 12 months.

Until 1995 the brewery produced a contract honey beer called Le Pavé de l'Ours – latterly brewed by Silenrieux – but now produces its own brew called Bière des Ours (Bear Beer), relabelled as Berenbier for Flanders, to a similar recipe.

The Blonde and Brune sport beautifully printed silver labels bearing the Binche coat of arms and two masks in recognition of the famous "Masque de Gille", a carnival which has taken place in the town since 1860. The addition of orange peel in the recipes of many of its beers reflects the traditional throwing of orange blossom at the carnival. Its Bière de Pâques shares, with Oleye's Brassin de Pâques, the honour of being the only Easter beers from Wallonia.

BIÈRE DE PÂQUES

7% alc/vol. 75cl corked bottles.

KNOWN INGREDIENTS: Pilsener and aromatic malts. Saaz and Goldings hops.

APPEARANCE: Beautiful rich copper/amber.

NOSE: Intense hoppiness when first poured but settles to a nice mellow aroma of fruity malt and hops.

PALATE: Predominantly mellow malt with some citric hop highlights and a gentle bitterness. Sediment gives it a grainy taste and removes the citric element. JDW: Nice herbal elements develop with age.

FINISH: Dry herbal tang with a little bitterness. Sediment makes it drier and more bitter.

OVERALL: An interesting brew which doesn't really live up to its "special" beer status. Enough taste to keep you interested and a bitter finish which entices you to drink more. KBR: Has a somewhat over-fruity tang which can grow tiresome. JDW: At 18 months it is a superb mellow tasting ale.

GENERAL: Tasteful label shows three geese, entitled "Friends". Best served 8-10°C. First brewed in 1991. Sold as **1549** in the USA.

JDW: 8 / 8 KBR: 6 / 7

BIÈRE DES OURS

9% alc/vol. 75cl corked bottles.

KNOWN INGREDIENTS: Spiced with honey.

APPEARANCE: Honey gold colour.

NOSE: Fairly neutral with hints of musty hops and a trace of spiced honey.

PALATE: Reasonably sweet with an intense honey, a pronounced hop bitterness and a tangy pale malt.

FINISH: Full mouth of lingering honey bitterness with a satisfying grainy base. Some spicy notes which are exaggerated with the addition of sediment.

OVERALL: An accomplished beer which oozes quality yet retains a small brewery taste. Addition of sediment makes a marked difference, derogatory in our view, adding spice and a cloying tanginess.

GENERAL: Name translates as Bear Beer. Sold as **Berenbier** (Flemish for Bear Beer) when sold in Flanders, although at the time of going to press we do not know how different the label will be. The brewery suggests it should be served at 8-10°C.

JDW: 9 / 7 KBR: 10 / 9

BLONDE

6.5% alc/vol. 33cl crown corked and 75cl corked bottles.

KNOWN INGREDIENTS: Orange peel.

APPEARANCE: Light gold with a good, fluffy head.

NOSE: Clean, almost sharp, citric hops with a little orange. KBR: Distant pale malt. When first poured has a pronounced orange aroma.

PALATE: Relatively sweet with a strong clean and fresh citric hop above a gentle pale malt base. Faint lemon hints.

FINISH: Initial suggestion of sweetness gives way to a drier, more bitter pale malt with lingering citric notes.

OVERALL: Great straight from the fridge (although the brewery states is should be served at 8-10°C) as it loses a little of the freshness when it warms. Has a good texture and a lovely citric quality. KBR: This is the blonde to which others should aspire.

GENERAL: Sold as **Fakir** in Flanders and Canada. Also relabelled as **La Molagnarde Blonde**. First brewed in 1989.

JDW: 9 / 8 KBR: 9 / 9

BRUNE

8.5% alc/vol. 33cl crown corked and 75cl corked bottles.

KNOWN INGREDIENTS: Orange peel.

APPEARANCE: Dark brown with red highlights. Large, fluffy head makes a nice contrast to the beer.

NOSE: Rich and spicy malt with initial bitter orange hints before developing a darker character with an underlying sweetness and dryish hop promise.

PALATE: A very hoppy bite with a rich, fruity, dark coffee character and a pronounced bitterness. JDW: Some sharp notes enhance the character.

FINISH: Dry and bitter with a taste reminiscent of plain chocolate. Seems to want to deliver a roasted character but doesn't quite succeed. Nevertheless, still satisfying and long lasting.

OVERALL: Rich, very malt-based beer with strong roast and coffee notes. Wonderfully smooth, creamy texture. Has a surprising spicy hop character for a brune, giving it an extra dimension.

GENERAL: Also relabelled as **La Molagnarde Brune**.

JDW: 9 / 7 KBR: 9 / 8

SPÉCIALE NOËL

8.5% alc/vol. 75cl corked bottles.

KNOWN INGREDIENTS: Orange peel.

APPEARANCE: Rich amber brown with a slight head.

NOSE: Rich fruity spiced malt. Sediment produces some hop notes. KBR: Sherry notes with whiffs of dark roast coffee. JDW: Hints of butterscotch.

PALATE: Very rich, fruity, roast malt with quite a lot of bitterness. KBR: Dark spices and coffee notes. A little butterscotch and a suggestion of dark candy sugar.

FINISH: Dry and bitter with a mouthful of burnt malty fruit. JDW: Lots of bitter butterscotch which lingers and intensifies.

OVERALL: Classic, warming winter spicy ale with plenty of depth in its character. JDW: Let down a little by an excess of roasted character

GENERAL: Brewed in November for European consumption but there is a batch brewed in July specifically for export to the Canadian market due to the transport/delivery time. An attractive new label (shown) was introduced in 1995, replacing the somewhat dated old one.

JDW: 8 / 7 KBR: 9 / 9

OTHER BEERS

Rose des Remparts and **Spéciale Blonde** – Apparently made for the occasion of the brewery's 'open door' weekend. At the time of going to press we have no further details on these beers.

BARS & CAFES RECOMMENDED BY THE BREWERY

CHEZ BOULE, Rue Saint Paul 13, Binche.
PHILIPPE II, Avenue Charles Deliege 18, Binche.
LA CHAMADE, Grand Place 44, Binche.
L'EXCELSIOR, Grand Place 29, Mons.
TAVERNE BINCHOISE, Grand Place 41, Binche.
HOP DUVEL, Rokerelstraat 10, Gent (East Flanders).

BEER SHOPS RECOMMENDED BY THE BREWERY

BINCHE BOISSONS, Route de Merbes 396, Buvrinnes.
CORA, Rue de la Franco-Belge, La Louverie.
CORMAN-COLLINS, Rue Xhéneumont 1A, Battice.
DELBERGHE, Rue d'Herchies 37, Ghlin.

Brasserie de Blaugies

✉ Rue de la Frontière 435, 7370 Dour (Blaugies), Hainaut.

☎ 065 65 03 60 (fax also).

🕓 Mon, Tue, Thur, Fri 1700-1830. Wed, Sat 0900-1300.

Pre-arranged only. Minimum 15 people. 15 days notice. In French or English. 50 Bfr charge. Tasting available

SHOP Cases, bottles, glasses.

500hl (in 1994).

➔ Once you have found the village of Blaugies (south east of Dour) there are numerous "La Moneuse" signposts to guide you.

Brasserie de Blaugies is located in an extension on the side of the attractive 18th century farmhouse, typical of the area, in the small, sprawling village of Blaugies near the French border, south west of Mons. The storage and refermentation warm room could be mistaken for a garage at the bottom of the garden.

Opened in 1987 the brewery is still essentially a family and friends affair, owned by the Carlier-Pourtois family. Virtually all the equipment is modern and purpose-built in stainless steel. The brewer hopes to expand a little more in the near future and, although the brewhouse is small, it could take a couple more vessels before needing another extension. The introduction of a new brew, Saison d'Epeautre, in 1994 would seem to indicate that the brewery is flourishing and its penchant for producing unusual, adventurous beers is undiminished.

Its bottling plant suffers, as do others, from the problem of the slightly varying sizes of 75cl bottles from different sources. The equipment, being modern, expects a little more uniformity. On one of our visits the brewer was sporting a well-bandaged hand after an accident attempting to free a bottle which had jammed in the mechanism!

The family dog knows a warm place to sleep!

Like other small Wallonian breweries, it has a great affinity with its locality. This is expressed is in the naming of its two principal beers – La Moneuse and Darbyste.

La Moneuse is named after infamous local villain and gang leader A. J. Moneuse (1768–98), an ancestor of the brewer's family, who had a reputation for extracting the whereabouts of his victim's money by placing their feet in the fire at their homes!

Darbyste is named after a preacher from England who followed the temperance teachings of a priest called Darby (hence Darbyste). After his parishioners suffered many sermons extolling the virtues of abstinence he was happy to see them drinking a "soft drink" they said was fig juice. This drink, however, bore an uncanny resemblence to alcohol in its effects! Blaugies Darbyste actually contains fig juice – not as you might expect from its taste, fresh green fig juice, but dark and sticky syrup extracted by centrifuge from reconstituted dried figs.

Saison D'Epeautre is, as the name suggests, made with spelt in addition to Pilsener malt which we take to be a welcome sign that Blaugies is still being adventurous in its development of new beers.

The brewery states that its beers will last indefinitely if stored on their sides in a cellar but they are at their best after six months. In our experience Blaugies beers develop a more sour character when they are stored for over a year – so if you prefer a cleaner, fresher taste we would advise you to drink them young. Darbyste and Saison should be served chilled, the others at cellar temperature.

DARBYSTE

5.8% alc/vol. 75cl corked bottles. Occasionally available on draught.

KNOWN INGREDIENTS: Pilsener malt and wheat. Saaz hops. Fig juice.

APPEARANCE: Cloudy wheat colour with a massive head.

NOSE: Somewhat neutral but figgy hints come out eventually when worked on.

PALATE: Gently grainy with a figgy fruitiness. Starts a little sweet with almost a suggestion of sourness before a gentle bitterness comes through.

FINISH: Dry and grainy with a few bitter herbs and a touch of fruit.

OVERALL: An unusual but characterful brew. Although it is quite light in colour it gives the impression of being a dark beer.

GENERAL: The brewery describes Darbyste as a fruity white beer, but we would add that it is certainly not in the classic white beer style. First brewed in 1990.

JDW: 8 / 8 KBR: 8 / 8

LA MONEUSE

8% alc/vol. 75cl corked bottles.

KNOWN INGREDIENTS: Pilsener and Munich malt. Saaz hops.

APPEARANCE: Golden with a good head.

NOSE: Good hop aroma which almost succeeds in masking delicate hints of apricots and peaches. KBR: Some caramel and peppery notes.

PALATE: Fails to deliver the complexity of the nose. Strong hops and tangy bitterness lifted by some fruit and sharp lemon. Astringency and alcohol are evident. A little fizz-burn on the tongue lessens the appeal. JDW: Spiciness from hops.

FINISH: Long lingering dry and bitter finish with a touch of tannin and hints of fruit. Strong alcohol element.

Overall: A reasonably interesting beer with a lovely nose but marred by the excessive fizziness which prevents the taste coming through.

General: Described, quite accurately, by the brewery as an old, artisanal saison beer. **JDW: 6 / 6 KBR: 5 / 6**

LA MONEUSE SPÉCIALE NOËL

8% alc/vol. 75cl corked bottles.

Known Ingredients: Pilsener, Munich and Caramunich malt. Saaz hops.

Appearance: Copper amber colour with a large, lasting head.

Nose: Abundance of hops with a spicy character. KBR: Malty with a hint of tartness. JDW: Fresh fruit including apricots and lemon.

Palate: Warming, with a bitter hoppy kick. KBR: Malty with a touch of tart citricity. JDW: Some lemon.

Finish: Quite dry with some hop bitterness. KBR: Richer, caramelly malt coming through. JDW: A tart tang.

Overall: Not as dark and rich as you would normally expect a Christmas beer to be, although certainly deeper and darker than the others in the Blaugies range. Starts off almost refreshing and summery but gives way to a more pronounced winter warmer quality.

General: This Christmas version gives a deeper, more complex character absent in the regular Moneuse. **JDW: 8 / 9 KBR: 8 / 7**

SAISON D'EPEAUTRE

6% alc/vol. 75cl corked bottles.

Known Ingredients: Pilsener malt and spelt.

Appearance: Light golden wheat colour with a good head.

Nose: Dry yeasty aroma with a little lemon and wheat.

Palate: A wishy-washy taste consisting mainly of a creamy wheat with some strong citric notes and a gentle bitterness with a dry, peppery element.

Finish: Dry with bitterness deep in the throat. KBR: Creamy wheat.

Overall: Distinctive but disappointing beer with texture dominant until the bitterness in the finish takes over.

General: Spelt (a close relative of wheat) gives the beer its peculiar, creamy but watery wheat character. **JDW: 7 / 6 KBR: 7 / 6**

BARS & CAFES RECOMMENDED BY THE BREWERY

FERME DES TEMPLIERS, Rue Ropaix 169, Dour.
"DA SALINE", Rue Ropaix 39, Dour.
L'EXCELSIOR, Grand Place 29, Mons.

BEER SHOPS RECOMMENDED BY THE BREWERY

CASH BATTARD, Grand Rue 234, Basècles.
CASH BATTARD, Rue des Viaducs 287, Nimy (Mons).
CASH BATTARD, Rue Neuve Chaussée 139B, Péruwelz.
DELHAIZE, Grand Rue, Quiévrain.

Brasserie de Brunehaut

✉ Rue des Panneries 17-19, 7623 Rongy, Hainaut.

☎ 069 34 64 11 Fax: 069 34 64 12.

🕓 Mon-Fri 0800-12.30 and 1400-1700.

Pre-arranged only. 7 days notice. In French and English. 60Bfr charge.

SHOP Cases, bottles, glasses.

1,500hl (in 1995).

→ From Howardries and the west, take the first left as you enter Rongy. The brewery is found on the right. Rongy is almost on the French border, south-west of Bléharies.

Brasserie de Brunehaut owes its existence to the enthusiasm of Guy Valschaerts and his wife, both of whom were trained in the science of brewing in Zaire, West Africa. Guy was born in Zaire and has spent most of his life there but was keen to move to Belgium, mainly for his children's education, but was also hoping to fulfill a long-time ambition to run his own small brewing business.

The peace and tranquility of the rolling countryside in the far west of Wallonia was a far cry from Guy's previous employment in a Unibra facility where he helped make Skol for African beer drinkers, but it was here that he started on the road to make his dream come true.

His first point of contact in Belgium was to Joseph Groetembril, owner of the faltering Allard and Groetembril brewery in Guignies (established in 1891), with whom he discussed possible investment to keep the family business viable. At that time negotiations broke down but, on hearing later that the brewery was going bankrupt, he seized the opportunity to buy it and started a new operation at nearby Rongy, completing the new brewery building in 1992. The first brew was produced in September 1992.

The philosophy of Brasserie de Brunehaut is to use the best of both the modern and the traditional in brewing its products. Modern is certainly one word which must be used when describing the brewplant which is all new with an emphasis on scrupulous cleanliness and hygiene. The plant includes a flash pasteuriser and a complete bottle washing, filling, labelling and crating machine with special mention needing to be made regarding its integrated cleaning-in-place (CIS) system. For a brewery with an annual output of just 1500hl this shows

A look inside the brewery reveals the mix of modern and traditional plant.

an amazing amount of investment. The traditional ethic comes from the fact its beers, although filtered and pasteurised, are top-fermented and go through a secondary fermentation in the bottle. It is also proud to declare that no chemical additives are used.

The brewery's modern yet traditional philosophies, themselves fundamentally conflicting, are reflected in the character of its beers. Such modern plant can often produce very consistent products with an inherent clinical quality, which means that ingredients need to be chosen carefully to give the beer some depth and personality. It is interesting to see the latest offerings from Brunehaut have departed from the original "basic" malt and hops recipes and the range now includes a blanche, an interesting dark roasted brew and a beer spiced with juniper berries.

Guy has recently returned to Africa but has left the brewery in the capable hands of his wife who runs it with the help of a brewery manager.

Brunehaut says its beers are best stored upright for one or two weeks after buying or moving and should be served at ±10°C with or without the yeast (we recommend it without).

The local area is well-known for its rose-growing and tree nurseries, and is also home to a famous 4m high standing stone, called the Brunehaut Stone, which has countless accompanying legends. The stone's impact has, however, by lessened by surrounding it with a small hedge and a tree at each corner of the grassed plot, giving it an odd, soulless, man-made environment, more appropriate for a piece of modern sculpture.

The Brunehaut stone.

ABBAYE DE ST. AMAND

7% alc/vol. 33cl corked bottles.

KNOWN INGREDIENTS: Juniper berries.

APPEARANCE: Golden colour with a massive head.

NOSE: Hoppy with gentle, short lived vanilla notes. JDW: Citric, with a rich but refreshing promise. KBR: Wonderful, perfumed aroma with hints of coriander and bubble gum.

PALATE: Huge hop-flower attack with attendant bitterness. JDW: Slightly citric with background fruit hints and a spicy edge from the hops. Excellent balance of sweet and bitter with bitterness coming out on top. KBR: A little sweet at first becoming lactic. The hops kill any delicate herbs which seem to be trying to get through.

FINISH: Dry and bitter with a tongue-tingling hoppiness. JDW: A building tangy bitterness, surprisingly saliva-inducing not mouthdrying. KBR: Some leftover, background herbiness.

OVERALL: A refreshing golden ale with a good complexity, let down by its excessive fizz. KBR: Has a great delicacy which is unfortunately smothered by the overbearing hop.

GENERAL: First brewed in 1996 for the town of St. Amand, just south of the brewery in northern France, famous for its stunning, ruined abbey. Many bars in St. Amand's central square have the beer on sale.

JDW: 7 / 6 KBR: 7 / 7

ALL BLACK

6% alc/vol. 33cl crown corked bottles.

INGREDIENTS: Unknown.

APPEARANCE: Very, very deep red brown that appears black with a minimal head.

NOSE: Lashings of dark, gently roasted, fruity malt. Some hops manage to get through giving it a pleasant balance.

PALATE: KBR: Sharp, almost sweet, very fruity start with a dry and bitter fruit following through and a delicate citric hop note with a touch of pepperiness. JDW: Masses of moderately roast malt with a fair degree of fruit and a good hop element – gently bitter yet surprisingly sweet.

FINISH: KBR: Dry, bitter with a lightly spiced hop and wafts of dark fruit with candy sugar suggestions. JDW: Bitter roast malt with a gentle fruit background.

OVERALL: Not what you would expect from the look and smell. Surprisingly light and hoppy rather than the expected thick, cloying stout.

GENERAL: First brewed in 1995 as a Christmas beer, elevated to regular beer status in mid-1996.

JDW: 6 / 4 KBR: 6 / 6

BIÈRE DU MONT SAINT-AUBERT

8% alc/vol. 33cl crown corked bottles.

INGREDIENTS: Unknown.

APPEARANCE: Light gold with a good rocky head.

Nose: Hoppy with malt and citric lemon notes. KBR: Wheat hints.

Palate: Reasonably sweet with a well balanced and rounded malty taste supported by abundant dry hops. A pleasant thirst-quenching bitterness. JDW: Distinct fruity elements.

Finish: Creamy maltiness with a lasting, dry bitterness. JDW: Lingering fruity tartness.

Overall: A quality beer with a good balance of hoppy bitterness and fruity malt. One to keep the sediment out of.

JDW: 7 / 6 KBR: 7 / 6

BLANCHE DE CHARLEROI

5% alc/vol. 33cl crown corked bottles.

Ingredients: Unknown.

Appearance: Wheat coloured with a good but short-lived head.

Nose: Lovely aroma, based around a distinctly lactic, spicy wheat. JDW: Very perfumed, hints of vanilla. KBR: Some fresh hops.

Palate: Creamy wheat with a light peppery spice element which builds into the finish. Distinct hints of orange and coriander. JDW: Hints of vanilla. KBR: Some herbal notes and a delicate hoppiness imparting a light dryness.

Finish: Very lactic. JDW: Astringent, spicy and peppery with a touch of wheat. KBR: Herbal dryness which lingers after the lacticity has subsided.

Overall: Reasonably complex white beer with a delicate, almost perfumed palate. KBR: Lovely hop character for a white beer.

General: An organic beer (certified by Eco Cert), first brewed in 1996 for the town of Charleroi

JDW: 7 / 7 KBR: 8 / 8

L'ÉCUME DES JOURS

8% alc/vol. 33cl crown corked bottles.

Ingredients: Unknown.

Appearance: Golden with a scummy head.

Nose: Intriguing aroma, not particularly powerful, but with many fleeting elements – hops, a touch of must and fruit. Some earthy and vegetable notes.

Palate: JDW: Subdued after the nose, mellow hop and pale malt with a touch of spice and a tangy vegetable edge, suggests sourness without really delivering. KBR: Tartish, fruity and a little citric.

FINISH: Dry, tangy bitter hop. Sightly astringent with lingering fruit notes. JDW: A touch of spice.

OVERALL: An odd beer with a multi-faceted nose and strong, lasting finish but nothing much between.

JDW: 6 / 5 KBR: 6 / 5

TRADITION

6.5% alc/vol. 33cl crown corked and 75cl corked bottles.

KNOWN INGREDIENTS: Two row Pilsener, Munich and Biscuit malts. Saaz, Styrian Goldings and Target hops.

APPEARANCE: Amber with a large, rocky head.

NOSE: Dull malt. KBR: Some distant dark spice. JDW: Some vegetable notes.

PALATE: A distinctly fruity and winey maltiness with some hop bitterness enhancing a more tangy, earthy malt bitterness.

FINISH: Lightly burnt malt with a lingering, earthy bitterness.

OVERALL: Predominantly fizzy in character, there is an interesting taste lurking in the background. The result is a rather dull ale with the fizz-burn not allowing the tongue and mouth to work on the taste.

GENERAL: Beautiful label printed in full colour on gold foil with a mainly blue background. First brewed 1992.

JDW: 5 / 3 KBR: 6 / 4

VILLAGES

6.5% alc/vol. 33cl crown corked and 75cl corked bottles.

KNOWN INGREDIENTS: Two row Pilsener malt. Saaz, Styrian Goldings and Target hops.

APPEARANCE: Orangey gold with a good, very lively head.

NOSE: A pronounced hoppy aroma. Reasonably citric, sweet, and a touch musty. JDW: Hints of lemon. KBR: Some fruity malt and spice.

PALATE: Very hoppy with sharp acidic hop notes protruding through a very tangy fruity bitterness. KBR: Has a creamy wheat hint.

FINISH: Very hoppy, dry and bitter with an odd wheaty tang.

OVERALL: An odd, but unfortunately bland, beer with both saison and abbey triple characteristics.

GENERAL: Label is mainly green. First brewed in 1992.

JDW: 7 / 6 KBR: 4 / 4

BARS, CAFES & SHOPS RECOMMENDED BY THE BREWERY

None recommended.

Brasserie La Caracole

Côte Marie-Therese 86, 5500 Falmignoul, Namur.

082 74 40 80 Fax: 081 22 06 83.

By appointment only, preferably weekends.

Pre-arranged only. 28 days notice. In French, Flemish and English. Charge unknown. Tastings available.

Cases, bottles and glasses.

186hl (in 1995).

Falmignoul is just south of Dinant on the N95. Enter village and turn right opposite the school. Turn left in the direction of Blaimont (N989) and the brewery is on your right.

For a small brewery La Caracole has an impressive and varied range of beers. Founded in 1990 by two homebrewers in an outbuilding of one of their grandmother's houses, it has seen a steady increase in output to the 1994 total of 90hl – and that was achieved with a brewplant capacity of just 400 litres. Things should be a little easier now, however, as production has recently moved to new premises.

The business is controlled and fronted from an excellent beer shop in the centre of Namur called La Cave de Wallonie (Rue de la Halle 6, 5000 Namur) which offers the entire range of Caracole beers (when available) in addition to a large selection of other hard-to-find Wallonian products.

The ever-increasing demand for their portfolio of six beers has necessitated the acquisition of the new premises and its larger brew capacity. The brewery is in the village of Falmignoul, which is reached via a picturesque drive along the edge of the Meuse valley where it forms a deep gorge south of Dinant. Formerly the Brasserie Moussoux (from the 18th century to 1941) and the Brasserie Lamotte (1941-1971) it was last used to produce a range of table beers. The Moussoux brewery also owned their own maltings, which has since been demolished. The output from the building now, however, has very little in common with table beer.

While many Wallonian breweries produce blonde and brune versions of a stock beer, La Caracole made the decision to brew an Ambrée and a Brune – both first brewed in 1990. Its excellent, truly artisanal white beer joined the range in 1992 followed by two new products – Cuvée de l'An Neuf (an uncompromisingly dark new year beer) and Saxo (brewed for the anniversary of the death of Adolphe Sax, inventor of the saxophone who was born in nearby Dinant) which now appears to be a regular brew.

One of the striking characteristics of Caracole's beers are the beautiful labels adorning its bottles. From the pseudo-Art Nouveau Ambrée and Brune labels to the simplistic line drawings of the Troublette and Cuvée de l'An Neuf (though, sadly, this was "updated" for 1996), the recurring theme is that of spiral snail shells from which the brewery takes its name (apparently the snail is the emblem of Namur and the word for a snail in local Namurois dialect is Caracole).

Occasionally its Brune is used for contract brewing, but the brewery insists that the label carries the Caracole name, e.g. **Caracole des Canaris**, **Caracole du Panier Perce**, etc. Early 1996 saw experiments with 20 litre kegs so many of the beers may be available on draught as well as in the usual 75cl bottles.

CARACOLE AMBRÉE

6.5% alc/vol. 75cl, corked bottles.

KNOWN INGREDIENTS: Orange peel and other undisclosed spices.

APPEARANCE: Dull orange golden amber.

NOSE: Sharp, sweet hops with hints of orange peel and a citric meadow grass element. KBR: Highly aromatic with apples and an odd spiciness.

PALATE: Numerous grain tastes with a distinctly hoppy and a gentle, but increasingly bitter character with some more traditional malty tastes showing through. JDW: Some strong wheaty notes. KBR: Sweet start to dry and bitter hoppiness – a very wide spectrum of tastes.

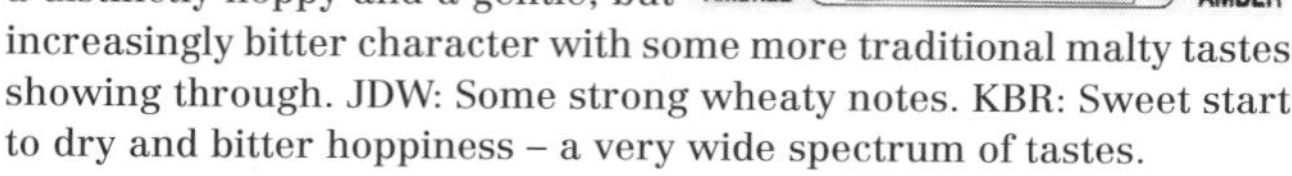

FINISH: Very mouthdrying, dry, bitter hops. KBR: Odd herbal quality lingers long.

OVERALL: Excellent complex beer with a strong hop element and a very full interesting grain and malt taste. Nice smooth texture.

GENERAL: The label is confusingly similar at first glance with yellow details compared, not surprisingly, to the Brune's brown. First brewed in 1990.

JDW: 8 / 9 KBR: 8 / 8

CARACOLE BRUNE

6.5% alc/vol. 75cl corked bottles.

KNOWN INGREDIENTS: Liquorice and other undisclosed spices.

APPEARANCE: Very dark, red tinged black/brown.

NOSE: Pungent, dry and burnt malt with hints of coffee.

PALATE: Powerful burnt malt taste with a touch of fruit and bitterness, not unlike an aged stout. Texture (thick creaminess with tiny, intense bubbles) intrudes into palate. KBR: Has an odd lactic sourness.

FINISH: Gently bitter with burnt malt and a touch of coffee.

OVERALL: Very odd texture spoils an otherwise impressive, if a little overpoweringly burnt tasting, ale. Although medium in body the fizz-induced creaminess gives it a thicker feel – yet still tastes watery.

GENERAL: Like the Ambrée, first brewed in 1990.

JDW: 6 / 5 KBR: 5 / 4

CUVÉE DE L'AN NEUF

8% alc/vol. 75cl corked bottles.

KNOWN INGREDIENTS: Special and roast malts. Many spices.

APPEARANCE: Deep, deep red brown, impossible to see through, with a creamy brown head.

NOSE: Very full aroma of mainly burnt malt with a hint of pepperiness to excite the nostrils.

PALATE: A mélange of gently burnt malt (though less than the nose would suggest) with some coffee and cocoa. The addition of sediment sweetens it slightly.

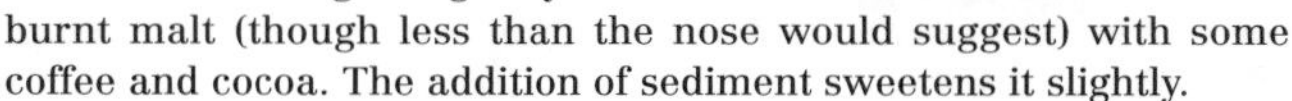

FINISH: Sharp burnt malt and, again, coffee and cocoa. Sediment mellows the sharpness but enhances the lingering burnt taste.

OVERALL: An after-dinner drink with an amazingly smooth and creamy texture. Although we would have to describe it as extremely "stoutish" in character, it has a great deal more depth and complexity than most people's idea of a true stout.

GENERAL: L'An Neuf is colloquial for the New Year and, needless to say, it is made as a winter warmer for sale over the festive season. These notes relate to the 1994 brew.

JDW: 7 / 6 KBR: 7 / 9

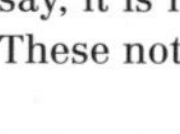

SAXO

6.5% alc/vol. 75cl corked bottles.

KNOWN INGREDIENTS: Pilsener and Munich malts. Saaz hops. Many undisclosed spices.

APPEARANCE: Cloudy, golden wheat.

NOSE: Hoppy with dry spice and a little malt. KBR: Dark roasted notes that belie its colour.

PALATE: Bizarre grainy (wheat and malt) punch of taste preceding hops and waves of flavours whizzing over the tongue. KBR: Peppery herbs and spices. JDW: Quite fruity with a touch of vanilla.

FINISH: Dry hop bitterness and a fruity hop tang. KBR: Some spice lingering on the tongue.

Overall: An odd beer with a complexity somewhat masked by the hops and bitterness.

General: Brewed to commemorate the centenary of the death of Adolphe Sax (1814-1894), the inventor of the saxophone, one of Dinant's famous sons. First brewed in 1994.

JDW: 7 / 7 KBR: 7 / 7

TROUBLETTE

5% alc/vol. 75cl corked bottles.

Known Ingredients: Pilsener malt and wheat. Saaz hops.

Appearance: Milky wheat in colour.

Nose: Intriguing aroma of sweet mangoes and apple peel with a little wheat and yeast in the background.

Palate: Particularly complex; starts off reasonably sweet with mangoes, apricots, citric fruit, wheat, yeast and a suggetion of hop before developing a slight sourness.

Finish: Sourness gives way to a tangy bittersweet fruit and wheat.

Overall: An original and successful approach (along with Abbaye des Rocs' Blanche des Honnelles) to producing a Wallonian artisanal white beer with a great deal of complexity and interest. Mouthfuls of all sorts of tastes wash across the tongue in waves.

General: The beer takes its name from the French word "trouble" which means cloudy or turbid. First brewed in 1992.

JDW: 8 / 7 KBR: 8 / 9

OTHER BEERS

Archiduc (5.2% alc/vol., 75cl. Known ingredients: Amber malt, Saaz hops, spiced with coriander and juniper. First brewed in 1996): This is a saison-style beer which was previously produced by Brasserie Duvieusart in Nivelles. La Caracole have been requested to reproduce it for La Confrerie des Compagnons de Jean de Nivelles. At the time of writing (May 1996) there have only been two 5hl brews.

Caracole au Miel (7.2% alc/vol., 75cl. Known ingredients: Amber malt, Styrian Golding and Hallertau hops, spiced with honey. First brewed in 1996): Only one 4hl brew to date for Les Amis de la Terre for their 20th anniversary. It may well eventually become a regular beer.

BARS & CAFES RECOMMENDED BY THE BREWERY

L'EBLOUISSANT, Rue Armée Grouchy, Namur.

BEER SHOPS RECOMMENDED BY THE BREWERY

BRASSERIE BALLEUX, Rue de Vignée, Beusoniny.
DE HOPDUVEL, Coupure Links 625, Gent (East Flanders).
LA CAVE DE WALLONIE, Rue de la Halle, Namur.
DRINK D'ANNEROIE, Chausée de Namur 60, Anneroie.

Brasserie Caulier

✉ Rue de Sondeville 128, 7600 Péruwelz, Hainaut.

☎ 069 77 24 71.

🕓 Fri 1600-2400, Sat/Sun 1100-2400.

Pre-arranged only. 14 days notice. In French. Free admission.

SHOP Cases, bottles and glasses.

2000 hl (estimated for 1996).

➔ Coming into Péruwelz from the north, on the N60, continue past the main square and gently uphill. At a crossroads (N60 signposted left to Valenciennes) you proceed straight on into a cobbled street – this is Rue de Sondeville. At the top of the hill the brewery is on the right with the car park behind the Caulier greengrocers.

For many years a beer called La Vieille Bon-Secours has been on sale in beer shops and bars throughout Wallonia and rumours persisted about its origins and whether or not it was a label beer. Finally, and surprisingly, Brasserie Caulier – whose name has always been on the bottle – has commenced brewing and the elusive, phantom brewery of Peruwelz is now a reality.

The aesthetically-minded may find the location a little "unartisanal" – sharing the same site as a drive-in drinks market, a greengrocers, a garage forecourt and what appears to be the trailer park for the wholesale beer operation. However, when Roger Caulier decided to expand his business to include a brewery and tavern it obviously made sense to use the existing buildings. Standing in the car park it is possible to see two colossal coppers through the windows, making you wonder just how big this new venture might be.

The tavern itself is tastefully done with a spacious, airy feel thanks to the large windows down one side and a centrepiece bar made from an old brewing kettle. Fish pools and a waterfall help to break up the large floor area covered in tables and chairs and one end of the room is dominated by the impressive copper kettles.

For a brewery which had only been operational for two months at the time of our visit the kettles seemed to suggest that Caulier was perhaps a little over-optimistic in its ambitions. However, a look through a door in the brick wall base revealed a more realistic 40hl capacity stainless steel mash tun and kettle hiding behind them – a wonderful design concept, also saving a piece of Belgian brewing history (the kettles used to belong to the De Neve brewery in Schepdaal).

Adjacent to the coppers are some open fermenters visible behind glass panels which, again, are part of the "museum" show and are not used in the operation. The real fermenters and maturation tanks are in a vast room behind the wall where, for such a small brewery, there is a mind-boggling amount of stainless steel vessels. Plans are afoot for an automatic cleaning system for the tanks and a bottling plant was about to be built on the ground floor behind the drinks market. With this amount of investment it is obvious that Caulier has plans to increase output in the near future.

La Vieille Bon Secours, named after the French border village of Bon Secours a few kilometres to the south, was previously brewed by Riva but now the full production is done at Caulier and is widely available at specialist beer shops. At first the brewery made just the standard Bon Secours, but this has now been joined by an Ambrée and a Brune.

The quality of the brewing is due mainly to a Monsieur Lebeau, the head brewer, who works for De Keersmaeker in the week and Caulier at weekends. He has had years of experience in the brewing trade, although by producing Mort Subite (a sweet, Lambic range of fruit beers and gueuze) he admits he has hardly been at the forefront of the traditional beer revival. However, he has been developing a 100% Lambic Kriek beer for Caulier which is refermented in the bottle and has an impressive complexity. This is one beer to look out for in the near future – it will probably be marketed under the name Rouge Gorge (robin in English), in keeping with the proposed strategy of naming all new beers after wild birds.

On our visit the brewery tavern was serving Bon Secours on draught along with two other beers which they do not plan to bottle.

LA VIEILLE BON SECOURS

8% alc/vol. 33cl crown corked, 75cl corked bottles and draught.

Known Ingredients: Two-row spring and Caramunich malts. Saaz hops.

Appearance: Bright golden with a massive rocky head.

Nose: Wonderfully fresh, citric hops with a lightly malty background. An initial touch of must.

Palate: Lashings of lemony hops giving a clean, fresh taste. A good full palate despite being only lightly malty, The alcohol stops just short of being intrusive.

Finish: Lingering dry, slightly bitter pale malt with some hop citricity holding over from the palate and a gentle alcohol warmth.

Overall: Quality, full yet clean-tasting, hoppy ale with a lovely texture after the initial fizz. Unsurprisingly, it is very similar to the old Riva version

General: First brewed in 1995 at Caulier. Peaks after six months.

JDW: 8 / 9 KBR: 8 / 7

LA VIEILLE BON SECOURS AMBRÉE

8% alc/vol. 33cl ceramic stoppered bottle.

Ingredients: Unknown.

APPEARANCE: Orange amber with a ludicrously large head.

NOSE: Yeasty, tart hints. JDW: Lots of exotic fruits, sweetish, suggestions of marzipan. KBR: Tannic, fruity malt with a light, almost perfumed, hop when first poured.

PALATE: Tart, fruity malt with some citric notes. JDW: A strong yeast-induced character with a slightly yeasty taste and hints of toffee. KBR: Surprisingly light with a pleasantly sweet, yet bitter, taste with some tannic notes.

FINISH: KBR: Mouthwatering fruity acidity vies with a hoppy bitterness – complex with plenty of interest.

OVERALL: An intriguing fruity, tart, bitter ale presented in a very impressive and distinctive, high-necked ceramic stoppered bottle.

GENERAL: First brewed in 1996.

JDW: 7 / 7 KBR: 7 / 8

LA VIEILLE BON SECOURS BRUNE

8% alc/vol. 33cl ceramic stoppered bottle.

INGREDIENTS: Unknown.

APPEARANCE: Light chestnut brown with a good fluffy head.

NOSE: Dark roasted malt with a pronounced, strange hop aroma. KBR: Initially very hoppy but soon goes, leaving just a fruity, roast malt. JDW: Hints of chicory.

PALATE: Distinctly sharp, tart, fruity edge to a lightly roasted, dark fruity malt with a little bitterness. Surprisingly sweet with a fair whack of alcohol throughout. JDW: Starts sweet with liquorice and aniseed notes, but builds to a full palate with surprisingly delicate layers of taste.

FINISH: Long lingering and warming. Reasonably sweet with a little liquorice. KBR: Some leftover tart fruit with a little aniseed.

OVERALL: Wonderful beer with the elusive mix of a clean, professional taste with a complex, artisanal character. Nicely balanced sweetness and bitterness though the sweetness can be stronger than you expect.

GENERAL: First brewed in 1996. Comes in the same shaped bottle as the Ambrée.

JDW: 8 / 7 KBR: 9 / 9

OTHER BEERS

Scoubidou (7% alc/vol.): Very unusual beer with a tart apple character and some gueuze-like traits. Highly original and a great summer quencher.

BARS & CAFES RECOMMENDED BY THE BREWERY

TAVERNE DE LA BRASSERIE, Rue de Sondeville, 132, Péruwelz.
LE MÉNESTREL MUSE LA BIÈRE, Grand Place, Péruwelz.

Brasserie Devaux

✉ Rue de l'Eglise Saint Philippe 1, 5600 Philippeville, Namur.

☎ 071 66 63 47.

🕒 Mon-Sat 0900-1100 and 1400-1600.

No tours. No tasting facility.

SHOP Cases and bottles.

125hl of Schwendi (in 1995).

➔ In the north west corner of the main square (la Place d'Armes) of Philippeville, near the church.

Brasserie Devaux is a long-established, family-owned brewery that has historically concentrated on supplying the very local area with table beers. Everything about the operation, not least the presentation of the beers themselves, suggests an air of rusticity.

The brewery was founded around 1860 in its current location in a corner of the main town square, near the church, and is still owned by the Devaux family. There is nothing on the front of the house or on the gate to say that a brewery is round the back, but by venturing through the gates you will find a courtyard with old whitewashed buildings and a collection of crates in one corner next to the brewhouse. They also appear to supply other beers.

The Devaux beers all used to be presented in 75cl swing-top ceramic stoppered bottles which originated from all sources as evidenced by the variety of brewery names etched or raised in the glass. Old age was beginning to tell on these bottles, and many of them would surely have a few tales to tell. This is changing though. Schwendi is being marketed a little more seriously with new bottles sporting the more familiar cork in place of the swing top. Perhaps this change was necessitated by the scarcity of the old bottles and the fact that many Schwendi bottles were not returned as they appealed to a farther-reaching market. The table beers are still sold in the more characterful bottles which presumably need to be returned.

The operation is low-key and you get the impression they would rather carry on as a very local supplier of table beers. Foreign visitors are greeted with a little suspicion but if you want to sample the beers you must call in.

DEVAUX BLONDE

2% alc/vol. 75cl ceramic stoppered bottles.

APPEARANCE: Pale gold with little or no head.

NOSE: Initially a gentle hop aroma, but it doesn't last.

PALATE: Quite sweet with a lightly hopped bitterness. Like an ale with lots of lemonade added,

FINISH: A slight hop dryness.

OVERALL: A reasonably bland, quaffable table beer for when you want something to quench your thirst without having to think about it.

JDW: 6 / 5 KBR: 5 / 2

DEVAUX BRUNE

2% alc/vol. 75cl ceramic stoppered bottles.

APPEARANCE: Dark amber with little or no head.

NOSE: Just a faint hint of malt.

PALATE: Very sweet – almost sickly – with a cloying, gently malty, syrupy base.

FINISH: Very mouthdrying with loads of saccharin and just a hint of malt. The aftertaste (which is not particularly pleasant) lingers for a long time.

OVERALL: We find it difficult to think of any occasion when one might want to drink a 'beer' like this. But, to be fair, dark table beers (sometimes known locally as "caramels") all tend to be cloying, sickly sweet products.

JDW: 3 / 2 KBR: 3 / 1

SCHWENDI

6.5% alc/vol. 75cl corked bottles.

KNOWN INGREDIENTS: Pilsener and amber malt. Hallertau hops.

APPEARANCE: Copper amber in colour with a small, compact head.

NOSE: A gentle, musty fruit. KBR: Enticingly dry, with some tartness.

PALATE: Strangely sour but predominantly fruity. KBR: Has an almost lambic quality. JDW: Crabapples with some hops and a wheaty element.

FINISH: Long, dry and fruity. KBR: Climaxes with a hit of sour red berries. JDW: Tangy crabapples.

OVERALL: A strange but enjoyable, complex ale. Refreshing and quenching. Defies all attempts to categorize.

GENERAL: For a small table beer brewer to introduce such an interesting new product in 1991 shows a good deal of commitment to their expansion into mainstream beer production. Although it does not taste like it, the beer is actually filtered but the brewery states that it improves with age, peaking at one year old. Label displays an old medal depicting the first mayor of Philippeville and the town's coat of arms.

JDW: 7 / 7 KBR: 6 / 7

BARS, CAFES & SHOPS RECOMMENDED BY THE BREWERY

Devaux's beers are only available at the brewery.

Brasserie du Bocq

✉ Rue de la Brasserie 4, 5530 Purnode, Namur.

☎ 082 61 37 37 Fax: 082 61 17 80.

Mon-Fri 0800-1600.

Pre-arranged only. Tasting available.

Cases, bottles and glasses.

60,000hl (in 1995).

➔ Purnode is on the N937 Spontin to Yvoir road, most easily found from junction 19 of the E411 (Brussels to Luxembourg). The brewery is easily seen on the north side of the road as you enter the village. Turn right at the crossroads into Rue de la Brasserie.

Brasserie du Bocq is a long-established brewery which just about manages to walk the thin line between brewing traditional Wallonian beers and running a successful, commercial enterprise in today's highly competitive marketplace. It is living proof that breweries can survive without brewing bland Pilseners and pale ales.

The village of Purnode nestles in a hollow on a plateau north-east of Dinant and the Meuse valley, and the brewery is unmissable as you descend the hill on a cobbled road into the village. It is an imposing collection of white-washed buildings which would not look out of place in many parts of Germany.

Founded in 1858 in its current location, it is still owned by the Belot family, and has built up quite a large market share throughout Wallonia as well as having some success in Flanders and other countries.

The portfolio is pretty awesome, but with so many beers there is a certain amount of overlap between ranges – for instance the St. Benoit and La Gauloise brands which, to us, seem to be chasing the same market. The brewery, however, considers the La Gauloise range its traditional flagship brews and describes the St. Benoit beers as being in the abbey-style, thereby appealing to a different drinker.

Du Bocq is often criticised as being a prodigious label beer producer, a practice which still continues. The etiquette versions listed are from our own information and numerous other sources.

La Gauloise was originally introduced around 1930 in its potent brown guise. Presumably the continued success of this beer prompted

Du Bocq to launch the new range of La Gauloise beers in 1994. Previous to this St. Benoit Triple (launched around 1970 and more usually seen with its Triple Moine or Deugniet labels on) was joined by two other St. Benoits in 1988.

Even the brewery can't be certain when Saison Regal was first brewed (before 1940) but it is now almost certainly the easiest "Saison" beer to find. Du Bocq acquired both Saison Regal and Regal Christmas through the takeover (in 1967) and subsequent closure (in 1983) of Brasserie Marbaix-la-Tour.

Blanche de Namur, named after an historical figure rather than just being a white beer from Namur (which it isn't) is also quite a newcomer, being launched in 1990 with availability becoming widespread in a very short time. Its Christmas stablemate, Blanche de Noël, is an adventurous brew with a unique palate.

According to the brewery all its products (except the wheat beers) are filtered and do not benefit from ageing, therefore you are best drinking them young. Most of its beers are also available on draught.

With regards to tasting, JDW found (as with many in the Silly range) an odd "vegetable" element in some of Du Bocq's beers. KBR can't experience the same – this is the benefit of joint tastings.

BLANCHE DE NAMUR

4.3% alc/vol. 75cl corked and 25cl crown corked bottles. Also available on draught.

KNOWN INGREDIENTS: Pilsener malt and unmalted wheat. German and Slovenian hops. Spiced with coriander and bitter orange.

APPEARANCE: Murky wheat colour with little or no head.

NOSE: Principally wheat with a floral lemon element and a little sourness. KBR: Some lactic notes. JDW: Slightly musty with a little ground coriander.

PALATE: Masses of wheat following a strong lemon start. KBR: Subdued bitterness lurking in background. JDW: Sharp acidity is everpresent, as is a peppery coriander which is enhanced by addition of sediment.

FINISH: Mostly wheaty with a slight citricity. KBR: Odd watered-down cream taste. JDW: Sediment adds a spicy element.

OVERALL: Very refreshing white beer with an interesting character, quite different to the Flemish whites. Much better with sediment, as it adds spiciness and herbiness. Wonderful texture.

GENERAL: Drink it very young as mustiness can set in. Serve at 4°C. First brewed in 1990. **JDW: 7 / 7 KBR: 7 / 7**

BLANCHE DE NOËL

4% alc/vol. 25cl crown corked bottles (there may also be other sizes).

KNOWN INGREDIENTS: The brewery did not wish to disclose ingredients.

APPEARANCE: Cloudy orange amber with a slight, scummy head.

NOSE: Spicy wheat with some orange notes. Coriander and other herbal hints. KBR: A gorgeous nose. JDW: Distinctive and unusual.

Palate: Very distinct, original, wheaty taste. Herbal, slightly sweet start with a light dryness. JDW: Slightly tart wheat dominant with some orange and a touch of powdery spice.

Finish: Lingering bitter herbiness. KBR: Strangely lacking in anything else. JDW: Dry with a slightly tannic wheat tang.

Overall: A notable departure from the usual Christmas style, it is more of a heavily spiced wheat beer rather than a white beer. KBR: Interesting beer which unfortunately does not live up to the promise of the nose. JDW: As a Christmas brew I would have expected it to be more exciting.

JDW: 6 / 5 KBR: 7 / 7

LA GAULOISE AMBRÉE

6.5% alc/vol. 33cl crown corked and 75cl corked bottles. Also on draught.

Known Ingredients: Pilsener, Munich and Caramunich malts. Slovenian and German hops. Spiced with liquorice, coriander and ginger.

Appearance: Amber/copper coloured with a disappointing head.

Nose: Caramel malt and spice with suggestions of toffee.

Palate: KBR: Very dry, burnt caramel which fills the mouth. JDW: Burnt malt with a gentle malty bitterness following a surprisingly sweet start.

Finish: Very dry, mouthdrying, tangy, burnt caramel bitterness.

Overall: Totally uncompromising – a roast and burnt taste from start to finish. The added spices are completely lost to the caramel.

General: Has the same label design as the other La Gauloises but has a different colour (Ambrée is green) and neck label. Serve at 6°C. First brewed in 1994.

JDW: 5 / 3 KBR: 5 / 5

LA GAULOISE BLONDE

7% alc/vol. 33cl crown corked and 75cl corked bottles. Also on draught.

Known Ingredients: Pilsener malt. English and German hops. Spiced with sweet orange peel and liquorice.

Appearance: Light gold with a soft, creamy head.

Nose: Strong aroma, mostly citric hops with pale malt and a touch of wheat. JDW: An intriguing blend of pale malt, hops and herbs.

Palate: Citric lemon comes through a muddied grainy (pale malt and wheat) hop background. A little sweet but also some bitterness.

Finish: Light, dry bitterness with some lingering lemon notes. KBR: Quite complex and spicy. JDW: Cloying and tangy.

Overall: JDW: A bit of a muddled beer which seems to be trying to be a number of things and not really succeeding. Too cloying and tangy with a taste that is not clean enough. KBR: Quite characterful beer which makes a good summer refresher. Not dissimilar in some respects to a St. Benoit Blonde.

General: Has the same label design as the other La Gauloises but has a different colour (Blonde is yellow) and neck label. Serve at 6°C. First brewed in 1994.

JDW: 6 / 5 KBR: 7 / 7

LA GAULOISE BRUNE

9% alc/vol. 33cl crown corked and 75cl, 150cl and 300cl corked bottles. Also on draught.

KNOWN INGREDIENTS: Pilsener, Munich and Caramunich malts. English hops. Spiced with sweet orange peel and aniseed.

APPEARANCE: Dark reddish brown with a scummy head.

NOSE: Dark malt with strong chocolate, cocoa and a hint of coffee.

PALATE: A full mouthed, dry, fruity, roast malt. JDW: Hints of cocoa.

FINISH: Dry with a gentle roast malt bitterness and some coffee. KBR: Tannic and burnt.

OVERALL: A dark abbey-style beer with saison overtones. Very dry and roasted throughout, but not "forced" like the Ambrée.

GENERAL: Prior to the introduction of the range, this was the only La Gauloise (without the "Brune" tag), and there may well still be a few old bottles around. Now has the same label design as the others in the range but has a different colour (Brune is red) and neck label. Serve at 6°C. First brewed around 1930. **JDW: 7 / 5 KBR: 7 / 7**

REGAL CHRISTMAS

9% alc/vol. 25cl crown corked and 75cl corked bottles.

INGREDIENTS: Unknown.

APPEARANCE: Deep red amber.

NOSE: Lightly spiced malt with solid fruity background and a distinct herbiness. KBR: Hints of liquorice.

PALATE: Very clean tastes – roasted barley, herbs and spices. Warming and quite complex. Cloying burnt sugar in the background develops with age.

FINISH: Dry and spicy against a strong background of lightly burnt caramel and alcohol. Just a little bitterness.

OVERALL: A warming and relaxing beer – not one to quaff. Adding sediment increases the spice but mellows the roastiness and the herbs. KBR: The burnt/roast element seems strangely distant from the rest of the taste. Serve at 7°C. **JDW: 7 / 7 KBR: 7 / 7**

SAISON REGAL

5.5% alc/vol. 25cl crown corked and 75cl corked bottles. Also draught.

KNOWN INGREDIENTS: Pilsener and Munich malts. English and German hops. Spiced with liquorice, aniseed and sweet orange peel.

APPEARANCE: Copper coloured with a slight, short-lived head.

NOSE: Strong, very spicy hop, slightly sweet malt with some mustiness. KBR: Dry with some fruit. JDW: The hop element is well balanced with the malt.

PALATE: A well balanced yet strongly spiced hop and malt taste with fruity notes and some bitterness. Lashings of peppery spice.

Finish: Dry and bitter fruity malt. KBR: A formidable thirst slaker.

Overall: An excellent introduction to Wallonian beers. Well balanced and very full taste, with a character to suit any occasion. The 75cl version is heavily sedimented but best drunk without as it adds graininess to the texture and an unpleasant tang.

General: First brewed around 1940.

JDW: 8 / 9 KBR: 9 / 8

ST. BENOÎT BLONDE

6.5% alc/vol. 33cl crown corked and 75cl corked bottles. Also draught.

Known Ingredients: Pilsener malt. Slovenian and German hops. Spiced with sweet orange peel and coriander.

Appearance: Pale gold with minimal head.

Nose: Flowery hops with a little spice in the background. KBR: Distant, dull herbiness.

Palate: Lots of hops with a sweetly sharp, saliva-inducing lemon bite. Just a touch of bitterness and a little malt in the background.

Finish: Pronounced hop bitterness with some spice and citric notes.

Overall: Refreshing but not particularly inspiring Wallonian blonde. Perhaps too sharp for most tastes.

General: First brewed in 1988.

JDW: 6 / 6 KBR: 7 / 6

ST. BENOÎT BRUNE

6.5% alc/vol. 33cl crown corked and 75cl corked bottles. Also draught.

Known Ingredients: English hops. Spiced with liquorice, sweet orange peel and coriander.

Appearance: Reddish amber brown.

Nose: KBR: Heavily roasted malt and liquorice masking a dark spiciness. JDW: Hint of spice set against a mixture of liquorice, malt and some odd vegetable aroma.

Palate: KBR: Roast malt and liquorice, so powerful it is difficult to detect anything else. JDW: Extremely odd vegetable-like taste with sharp citric notes.

Finish: Dry, roasted malt with a surprisingly strong alcohol warmth for its strength. JDW: Distinct citric zing in the mouth.

Overall: KBR: If you are not a heavy roast malt fan, give this beer a miss. Suspiciously similar to Gauloise Ambrée. JDW: Very odd beer reminiscent of the now defunct l'Gayette.

General: First brewed in 1988.

JDW: 4 / 3 KBR: 5 / 5

ST. BENOÎT TRIPLE

6.5% alc/vol. 33cl crown corked and 75cl, 150cl and 300cl corked bottles. Also draught.

Known Ingredients: Pilsener malt. English, Slovenian and German hops. Spiced with sweet orange peel and coriander.

APPEARANCE: Light gold with a generous, firm, rocky head.

NOSE: Lovely, full, fresh hop aroma. KBR: Touch of peppery spice.

PALATE: Strong, reasonably clean hops giving a gentle bitterness which is penetrated by a sharp, citric lemon. KBR: A hint of sweetness with soft, spicy notes.

FINISH: Good kick of hop bitterness which passes and leaves you with a gentle, long lingering bitter tang. KBR: Some alcohol burn.

OVERALL: Very pleasant, very hoppy, crisp-charactered beer. Satisfying, quenching and easy to drink. Better without the sediment (the 75cl version is heavily sedimented). Hardly in the strict abbey triple style, we would describe it as more of a strong saison.

GENERAL: Serve at 7°C. A beer which Du Bocq consider worthy of at least two other labels – namely **Triple Moine** and **Deugniet**, both of which are widely available. First brewed around 1970.

JDW: 8 / 8 KBR: 8 / 8

OTHER BEERS

La Bergeotte: A contract beer.

Corsendonk Agnus (8% alc/vol.): A contract beer which is one part of the abbey beer duo, along with Corsendonk Pater. Agnus is the blonde. A very hoppy beer from the nose through to the palate and well into the finish. Not unlike St. Benoît Triple.

Cuvée San Antoine (8% alc/vol.): A contract beer. Amber coloured ale with a pronounced roast malt character. JDW: Odd vegetable tang. Too much burnt malt.

Kelottes White (5% alc/vol.): A contract beer brewed for Brasserie Koo, a distributor in Verviers.

Super des Fagnes (8% alc/vol.): A contract beer brewed for Brasserie Lauvaux-Couvin (a distributor). Very full pale malt with a hop fruitiness cutting through the malt.

Cuvée "Li Crochon" Blonde and **Cuvée "Li Crochon" Brune** are label beers. The brewery would not disclose the original beers but we suspect they are St. Benoît Blonde and Brune.

BARS & CAFES RECOMMENDED BY THE BREWERY

LA BESACE, Rue du Centre, Crupet.
LA COURONNE, Rue Sax 1, Dinant.
LE CHEVAL BLANC, Chaussée de Dinant, Spontin.
LE MÉTROPOLE, Rue Émile Cuvelier, Namur.

BEER SHOPS RECOMMENDED BY THE BREWERY

None recommended.

Brasserie Dubuisson

✉ Chaussée de Mons 28, 7904 Pipaix, Hainaut.

☎ 069 66 20 85 Fax: 069 66 17 27.

🕓 Mon-Sat 0800-1200 and 1300-1700.

Pre-arranged only. At least 10 days notice. In French, Flemish and English. 50 Bfr charge. Tasting available.

SHOP Cases, bottles and glasses.

18,500hl (in 1995).

➔ Prominent, large white and green buildings on the right hand side of the N50 between Tournai and Mons, near the turn-off to Pipaix. From Tournai you can't miss the sign at the depot end.

Brasserie Duibuisson has a long and distinguished history. In 1994 it celebrated its 225th anniversary, brewing a beer – Bush 7% – to mark the occasion. The brewery claims to be the oldest Wallonian brewery still in ownership by the family and is determined to stay independent. It works hard to promote its products and boasts the fact that over 3,000 people from many different countries visited the brewery in 1993. In 1994, when it had an open event to mark its anniversary and to inaugurate its new reception hall, more than 7,000 joined the two-day celebration.

The brewery started in 1769 when Joseph Leroy, a maternal ancestor of the Dubuisson family, became a farmer-brewer. He built the brewery on his own land and supplied farmworkers and local villagers.

The products we know today were developed as a direct result of Alfred and Amedée Dubuisson opting to be brewers rather than farmers in 1931. At this time British beers were becoming fashionable to Belgian drinkers so, in 1933, Alfred developed a high alcohol beer with both Belgian and British characteristics. The name given to this powerful brew – Bush Beer – is indicative of its "Britishness" in that Bush is the English for Dubuisson. Over the years it has become the mainstay of the brewery, winning many medals at exhibitions around the world and in 1994 accounted for almost 90% of the brewery's total output.

1991 saw the launch of Bush de Noël, a Christmas beer (brewed every year since), which heralded an end to the years of Bush Beer being Dubuisson's sole product.

Discounting Trappist beers, Bush Beer must be the most well-known of all Wallonian beers, and it has a very high profile on the export market where it is sold in many countries as **Scaldis**. The word Scaldis is Latin for "bush" and the name change was necessitated to avoid confusion with products from Annheuser-Busch the US giant brewing conglomerate (how anyone could possibly confuse a 12% alc/vol. ale of this quality with a mass-market American beer is beyond us!). Bush de Noël is likewise known as **Scaldis de Noël** but, to date, we have not heard whether Bush 7% will follow the same trend and become Scaldis 7%. Some 14% of the brewery's production was exported in 1993.

The Dubuisson range still exudes a certain British character about it and, as such, is quite unique among the Wallonian beers. Drinkers of strong English barley wines will be familiar with the warming, fruity malt but they will also experience a lightness and dryness with a less cloying texture.

Today the brewery is in the hands of Vincent and Hugues Dubuisson, the eighth generation, and employs 25 people. As well as the brewing operation they also run a beer wholesaling business with two drive-in drink markets, one behind the brewery buildings (although this tends to sell only mass-market brands) and another in Tournai. This side of the business has also been going for some time – it was one of the first suppliers of Stella Artois in 1926!

All Dubuisson beers are filtered so, although they will undoubtedly keep for some time without significant deterioration, they are not likely to improve. Unlike the majority of Wallonian breweries Dubuisson only supplies its beers in 25cl crown corked bottles, which is probably a good thing bearing in mind the strength of Bush 12!

BUSH BEER 7%

7.5% alc/vol. 25cl crown corked bottles.

INGREDIENTS: Pilsener and Caramunich malts. Styrian Goldings hops. Spiced with coriander.

APPEARANCE: Golden with a lovely, light and fluffy head.

NOSE: Fresh and clean hops abound with a lightly fruity pale malt base.

PALATE: A little sweet and quite bitter with generous helpings of hops and pale malt. JDW: Pronounced alcohol character. KBR: Pleasantly fruity.

FINISH: Dry with a strong, lasting, tangy hop bitterness.

OVERALL: Strong, golden and hoppy ale which is distinctive and typically "Bush". JDW: Perhaps too much tangy hop for its own good.

GENERAL: Thankfully, now you don't have to endure 12% of alcohol to enjoy a Bush Beer. First brewed in 1994.

JDW: 6 / 4 KBR: 6 / 5

BUSH BEER 12%

12% alc/vol. 25cl crown corked bottles.

INGREDIENTS: Pilsener and Caramunich malts. Kent and Styrian Goldings hops.

APPEARANCE: Deep, dark gold with a firm, lasting head.

NOSE: KBR: Dry, fruity and powerfully alcoholic malt. JDW: Sweetish, fruity pale malt.

PALATE: Masses of warming, if not burning, alcohol almost hides the fruity malt. KBR: A full-mouthed fruitiness. JDW: Reasonably sweet but also bitter.

FINISH: Immense glow of warming alcohol with lashings of fruity malt. KBR: Subsides to reveal a long, slightly herbal, aftertaste with a dry tang. JDW: Lasting tangy bitterness.

OVERALL: Totally uncompromising beer with a pleasant, surprisingly light, texture. KBR: Warming and satisfying, a beer for sipping. JDW: An excess of alcohol taste.

GENERAL: First brewed in 1933. Sold in some export markets as **Scaldis**.

JDW: 9 / 4 KBR: 9 / 8

BUSH DE NOËL

12% alc/vol. 25cl crown corked bottles.

INGREDIENTS: Pilsener and Caramunich malts. Kent and Styrian Goldings hops.

APPEARANCE: Deep amber with a generous, short-lived head.

NOSE: Sweetish, bitter, candied malt with a strong suggestion of alcohol. KBR: Pear drop hints.

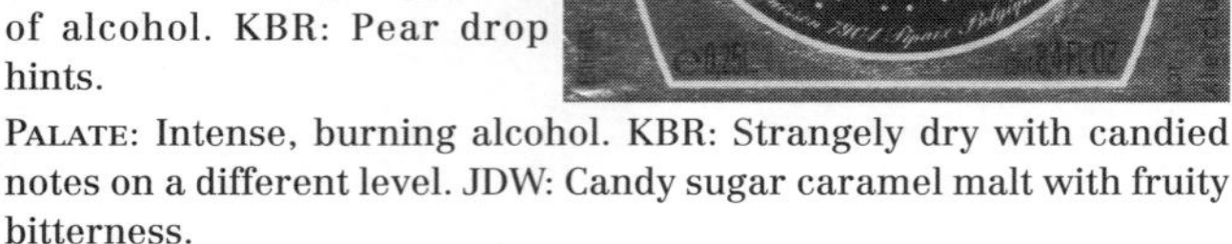

PALATE: Intense, burning alcohol. KBR: Strangely dry with candied notes on a different level. JDW: Candy sugar caramel malt with fruity bitterness.

FINISH: Dry with a tangy fruit bitterness.

OVERALL: Very similar in character to Bush 12% but fuller taste and body. KBR: The fuller body of this beer helps to soften the fruity alcohol most will find so uncompromising in the Bush 12%.

GENERAL: Although the same malts are used as in Bush 12% there is a higher proportion of Caramunich in the recipe. First brewed in 1991. Sold in some export markets as **Scaldis de Noël**.

JDW: 7 / 4 KBR: 8 / 7

Brasserie Dupont

✉ Rue Basse 5, 7904 Tourpes, Hainaut.

☎ 069 67 10 66 Fax: 069 67 10 45.

🕓 Mon-Fri 0900-1200 and 1300-1700. Sat 0900-1300.

Pre-arranged only. 8 days notice. In French, Flemish and English. 60Bfr charge. Tasting available.

SHOP Cases, bottles and glasses.

6,500hl (in 1994).

➔ On the N526 from Leuze-en-Hainaut towards Beloeil the brewery is signposted right as you enter the village of Tourpes. Taking the first left (signposted) it is found on the left after 200-300m.

Brasserie Dupont produces a range of beer which, to many people, epitomises the concept of a Wallonian saison brewery. But to pigeonhole all of its products as being in the saison style would, however, not do justice to the depth and variety of its range.

It is an industrious, quite small, farmhouse brewery which has been in the family since Alfred Dupont bought the farm and brewing concern in 1920. Previous to this it had been Brasserie Rimaux which was established around 1850. The brewery is now run by the grandchildren of the founder (Marc Rosier and his two sisters) along with some of his great-grandchildren. Not content with just farming and brewing, the family also operates a winter maltings, a bakery, a fromagerie (well worth a visit for the excellent aged Moinette cheese) and a soft drinks business.

An annual production of just 6,500hl is surprising for a brewery with such a large range and also when you take into account that more than half the beer brewed is Moinette Blonde.

Saison Dupont Vieille Provision has been produced since the brewery was founded and must be regarded by most as a classic of the style. Its second oldest beer still in production is, ironically, Rédor Pils – introduced in 1950 and today accounting for 1,500hl annual production. Around 1960 the Moinette beers and its New Year beer, Avec Les Bon Vœux, joined the range.

In 1990, Dupont took the brave and commendable decision to commence production of what it claims were the first organic beers in Belgium. These "biologique" versions of its Saison and Moinette Blonde received their official stamp of recognition from *Nature et Progrès* – a European association for organic agriculture and hygiene – but only after verifying the authenticity of the malt and hops to be used and regular checks on its well water. For such a small brewery to gain this recognition, while still maintaining the quality and production of its substantial range of "normal" beers is no mean feat. The introduction of Biolégère in 1992 completed the trio of organic products and the brewery appears to be promoting them strongly with a new set of labels and plenty of multi-lingual marketing leaflets.

Dupont's staple product, Moinette Blonde, is the beer with which the brewery identifies itself and is the easiest of the Dupont brews to obtain in bars and shops – although easy is perhaps not the right word to use due to its very local availability. The name Moinette comes from the Rosier's farm which was once part of an abbey estate.

The brewery does a good trade in contract beer supplying and, although other products are used, most "etiquette" beer is Moinette Blonde and the new label will incorporate an "Abbaye de la Moinette" seal somewhere in the design. Some other contract beers, for instance Vieille des Estinnes and Cervoise de Leptines (for Brasserie Wanderpepen, which ceased production of its own beer in 1941) and Cervesia (for a nearby archeological site) are unique brews.

All 75cl bottles should be stored horizontally where they develop a distinct sediment stripe which sticks well to the inside of the bottle even while pouring. After transportation, care should be taken to make sure the stripe is on the underside of the bottle when storing as it will have formed over several weeks. Positioning the stripe at the top or bottom and gently pouring into glasses in one action (i.e. not standing the bottle between pours) provides the right mix of sediment and beer, giving a slight hazy bloom to an otherwise bright beer. KBR prefers to pour with the stripe at the bottom, JDW with it uppermost – the former method resulting in slightly more sediment in the beer.

Dupont beers are an excellent introduction for newcomers to Wallonian beers with the added benefit that, unlike those of Du Bocq, they tend to exude a true artisanal character

AVEC LES BONS VŒUX DE LA BRASSERIE

9.5% alc/vol. 75cl corked bottles.

KNOWN INGREDIENTS: Pale malt. Kent hops.

APPEARANCE: Dull golden with a massive, lasting head.

NOSE: Strong spicy hops with some estery notes. JDW: Some sweetness. KBR: Distinct alcohol promise.

PALATE: An instant mouthful of hops, though not overly bitter. Slightly malty with a pleasant, smooth wheat and oats texture. A distinct white pepper spiciness and a warming alcohol.

FINISH: A lasting, strong hop bitterness with alcohol warmth.

OVERALL: A very full tasting, well balanced beer – typically Dupont, typically Wallonian – with lots of spicy hops. Gets smoother with age. KBR: Alcohol impinges on an otherwise satisfying winter warmer.

GENERAL: New year beer originally given as gifts to favoured clients but now available to all. The name translates as "With the best wishes of the brewery". Ageing for over a year greatly enhances the beer making it smoother and mellower.

JDW: 9 / 9 KBR: 8 / 8

LA BIÈRE DE BELŒIL

8.5% alc/vol. 75cl corked bottles.

INGREDIENTS: Unknown.

APPEARANCE: Dull copper with a good head.

NOSE: Strong slightly spicy hops predominate with a little spice. KBR: Some creamy maltiness. JDW: Some light citric notes.

PALATE: KBR: Very malty with a peppery sweetness and dark, bitter fruit tastes lurking behind the excessive fizz. JDW: Very hoppy with a few sharp citric notes coming through a harsh bitterness that is well balanced by a little pale malt.

FINISH: Tannic with a good deal of bitterness. KBR: Some coffee notes. JDW: Hints of fruit.

OVERALL: Promising characterful beer spoilt by its excessive fizz.

GENERAL: Although a regular Dupont beer, it is named after the Château de Belœil, an impressive and popular tourist attraction, 5km from the brewery. The organic malt used in the "biologique" beers comes from the maltings at Belœil.

JDW: 7 / 7 KBR: 7 / 6

BIOLÉGÈRE

3.5% alc/vol. 25cl crown corked bottles.

KNOWN INGREDIENTS: Organic pale malt. Organic Kent hops.

APPEARANCE: Golden colour with a good head.

NOSE: Nicely blended wheat, spice and hops.

PALATE: Quite a sharp, hop taste with something else a little less pleasant lurking in the background. Adding sediment produces a wheatier taste.

FINISH: Extremely mouthdrying with a very strong tang of grain plus an unpleasant "chemical-like" element.

OVERALL: Very light and smooth with an interesting taste but an unpleasant tang. May appeal to some pils drinkers.

GENERAL: Translating literally as "organic light", the lightest of the organic trio. Although we commend Dupont's foray into "green" beers, we find them to have a character very different and less appealing than the non-organic beers in the range.

JDW: 5 / 2 KBR: 5 / 2

CERVESIA

6.4% alc/vol. 75cl corked bottles.

KNOWN INGREDIENTS: Barley and wheat malt. Kent hops. Spiced with apple, bay leaf, coriander, cumin, ginger, green pepper, juniper, lemon balm, orange peel plus others (unspecified).

APPEARANCE: Straw coloured with a large fluffy head.

NOSE: Dry spicy hops with a little pale malt. KBR: Some damp hay with pronounced herbal notes and odd menthol/eucalyptus hints. JDW: Distinct but undefinable, exquisite herbal element.

PALATE: Very herbal with a sharp citric bite and loads of hop taste with accompanying bitterness. Strong, distinct herbal tang in the background. JDW: Strong, spicy edge to the herbal element.

FINISH: Mellow citric bitterness and a quenching pale malt graininess which soon subsides. KBR: Lingering, fascinating herbal notes.

OVERALL: Very interesting beer with, possibly, a unique character. Wonderfully refreshing and easy to drink. Addition of sediment gives it a lovely smooth, slightly grainy herbal hop taste.

GENERAL: Brewed in the ancient Gallic style for the archeological site of Aubechies (about 2km from the brewery), a living iron age museum. The beer is only obtainable from there. Brewery states it peaks at six months old.

JDW: 9 / 10 KBR: 9 / 9

MOINETTE BIOLOGIQUE

7.5% alc/vol. 25cl crown corked and 75cl corked bottles.

KNOWN INGREDIENTS: Organic barley malt. Organic hops.

APPEARANCE: Golden with a ridiculously large head. Pour carefully.

NOSE: Massive bouquet. Very spicy with malt and wheat. JDW: Sharp hop aroma.

PALATE: KBR: Bitter with a wheaty tang. Spicy and dry. JDW: Quite sweet with strong citric notes to the dominant hoppiness. Some light malt lurking in the background.

FINISH: Spicy, dry hop bitterness.

OVERALL: Like the Saison Biologique this is much less complex and satisfying than the "real" version and, although to a lesser degree, it still has the characteristic organic malt tang shared by the Biolégère.

GENERAL: The strongest of Dupont's organic trio. Peaks at six months old.

JDW: 7 / 6 KBR: 7 / 5

MOINETTE BLONDE

8.5% alc/vol. 25cl crown corked, 75cl and 150cl corked bottles.

KNOWN INGREDIENTS: Pale malt. Kent hops.

APPEARANCE: Orange tinged hazy old gold with a large, well-formed head.

NOSE: Very hoppy with lots of musty spice and hints of dry fruit.

PALATE: Masses of strong, flowery, citric, spicy hops with some gentle malt in the background.

FINISH: Satisfying layers of taste. Dry, fruity, hoppy, spicy and herbal. Has a suggestion of tartness without the acidity which usually accompanies it.

Overall: Amazingly full flavoured, fresh and complex brew. Would suit almost any occasion. Becomes more mellow and sweet, but spicier, with the sediment.

General: Virtually the flagship of the brewery and the one chosen for the numerous label beers. Dupont believes it peaks at six months, but we believe it improves up to a year.

JDW: 9 / 9 KBR: 9 / 10

MOINETTE BRUNE

8.5% alc/vol. 25cl crown corked and 75cl corked bottles.

Known Ingredients: Pale malt. Kent hops.

Appearance: Dark copper with a short-lived head.

Nose: Roast malt and dry hops. JDW: Pear drop hints.

Palate: A slightly vinous and creamy, full-mouthed taste. JDW: Malty, lots of alcohol and a herbal bitter tang.

Finish: Little more than a creamy lightly roasted malt. JDW: A dry, herbal tang.

Overall: Lacks the quality and complexity of its blonde stablemate. Somewhat of a disappointment for a Dupont beer.

General: Brewery states that it peaks at six months but, again, we believe it will improve up to a year.

JDW: 6 / 5 KBR: 6 / 6

RÉDOR PILS

6.5% alc/vol. 25cl and 33cl crown corked and draught.

Known Ingredients: Pale malt. Styrian Goldings hops.

Appearance: Pale gold with a good head.

Nose: Pretty neutral apart from some sweetness.

Palate: A little sweet with a grainy (wheaty) taste and distinct hop notes.

Finish: Very clean and extra dry with a typical pils tang.

Overall: Excellent creamy texture and an interesting taste give it a surprising amount of character for a pilsener, but still a little bland.

General: Label states it is a smooth and creamy, bottom fermented beer – and we certainly wouldn't disagree with that. The slightly higher alcohol content is presumably a throwback to the days when beers were usually stronger than today's brews.

JDW: 7 / 5 KBR: 8 / 5

SAISON DUPONT BIOLOGIQUE

5.5% alc/vol. 25cl crown corked and 75cl corked bottles.

Known Ingredients: Organic malt and hops.

Appearance: Light gold with a good head.

Nose: Yeasty with a pronounced light malt and a little spice which disappears with the addition of sediment.

Palate: Quite dry, though a touch sweet, with a very tangy, bitter, hop taste marred by a slight metallic note. Sediment reduces the tangy bitterness and the metallic element. KBR: Very malty with some wheat. JDW: A yeasty citric taste.

FINISH: Dry with a metallic bitter tang.

OVERALL: Like a normal Saison Dupont with the flavours turned down. Has the unfortunate, characteristic organic tang throughout.

GENERAL: Sold in Britain under the name and label of Belgo, as the house beer of the Belgo bars in London. Peaks at three months old.

JDW: 5 / 5 KBR: 4 / 5

SAISON DUPONT VIEILLE PROVISION

6.5% alc/vol. 25cl crown corked and 75cl corked bottles.

KNOWN INGREDIENTS: Pale malt. Kent hops.

APPEARANCE: Golden yellow with a firm rocky head.

NOSE: Lightly yeasty with some spice and fruit. Citric hints. KBR: Some wheaty notes.

PALATE: Sharp citric bite and loads of hops. Lightly spiced with a strong, earthy, pale malt base. KBR: A truly artisanal character.

FINISH: Long, dry finish. Distant herby hints. JDW: Powerful bitter hop tang with a gentle astringency. KBR: Hoppy with a pleasantly light, quenching bitterness.

OVERALL: Wonderful example of a Walloon saison style with enough interest for the connoisseur yet accessible enough for the beginner. Definitely a beer that benefits from ageing in spite of the brewery recommending six months as the optimum age. KBR: A four-year-old example, although losing some of its freshness, was exquisite.

GENERAL: By virtue of the "I" on the label it is regarded by the brewery as the "bière ordinaire" in the saison beer trinity along with Moinette Blonde (II) and Avec Les Bons Vœux (III).

JDW: 9 / 9 KBR: 10 / 9

OTHER BEERS

Vielle Des Estinnes (7.5% alc/vol.): Brewed for Wanderpepen. A superb beer, very hoppy throughout with a little fruit in the palate. Easily quaffed.

Cervoise de Leptines (8.5% alc/vol.): Excellent full tasting, easy drinking beer with loads of malt nicely balanced by a citric sharpness.

BARS & CAFES RECOMMENDED BY THE BREWERY

CAVES DUPONT, Rue Basse, Tourpes.
LA FORGE, Place, Tourpes.

BEER SHOPS RECOMMENDED BY THE BREWERY

DRINK DEFOREST, Chausée de Willemeau 207, Tournai.
Ets JACQUET, Rue de Sondeville, Peruwelz.
SUPERETTE LINDA, Place, Tourpes.
DRINK DELEPINE, Rue Eugène Cattoir 13, Brussels.

Brasserie Ellezelloise

✉ Guinaumont 75, 7890 Ellezelles, Hainaut.

☎ 068 54 31 60 Fax: 068 54 37 16.

🕓 Mon-Sat 0800-1900, Sun 0900-1200 and 1500-1900.

Pre-arranged only. 7 days notice. In French. 50Bfr charge.

SHOP Cases, bottles and glasses.

1,000hl (in 1995).

➔ See article.

New Year's Day 1993 saw a few people raise a glass to celebrate the launch of a new brewery – Brasserie Ellezelloise – on the outskirts of Ellezelles, a small village near the Flemish border.

The setting verges on the idyllic – very rural with a pleasant outlook over the surprisingly hilly countryside on the southern edge of the area known as the "Flemish Ardennes" – and the brewery building fits in perfectly. The impressive conversion of an old barn now houses the small but well laid out brewery along with a tastefully decorated sampling room built into the roof space overlooking the kettles. There is also space for the room in which Ellezelloise's beers undergo a 10-day lagering process in oak casks, bought in from Germany, prior to bottling.

The operation, run by Philippe Gerard and his son, was launched with just one stock beer, Quintine, presented in a swing-top bottle. The range has since been expanded to include Hercule and Quintine Ambrée. At Christmas, Quintine de Noël complements the regular brews, although this is essentially Quintine with added caramel malt.

The swing-top bottle marketing ploy is all too often hiding the inadequacies of a very ordinary beer – but Quintine is certainly an exception to the rule. Lovers of beer glasses will also like the dedicated Quintine glass which is distinctive and substantial.

Witchcraft features prominently in the folklore of the Ellezelles area and this is reflected in the fact that most of the present day festivals and fêtes take on the theme. To perpetuate this tradition, the brewery has named its beer after a legendary, local, broomstick-wielding witch called Quintine. Before the sad demise of the Brasserie Voisin in nearby Flobecq it, too, exploited the witches and wizards legacy in its beer names.

The brewery, however, is not easy to locate. The best approach is to find the main square and take the road signposted Brakel. Go past a church and one bank, then turn right at the second bank (the road does not have a name) which should take you out into open country-

The upstairs drinking room where you can watch the brewer at work.

side. The first turn left (which looks like a farm track) should be signposted to the brewery which is found behind the white farmhouse approximately 100 metres up the track. Signs have been made, but at the time of our last visit the brewery was still trying to obtain permission to put them up.

Although Ellezelloise's products are unfiltered, the brewery does not believe they improve with age.

HERCULE

9% alc/vol. 33cl ceramic stoppered bottles.

KNOWN INGREDIENTS: Torrified malt. Goldings hops.

APPEARANCE: Very dark – almost black – with a good head.

NOSE: Fairly neutral, just a faint alcohol note which gets more noticeable as the beer warms.

PALATE: A full but simple taste with an abundance of dark malt and liquorice balanced by some nice hops. KBR: Spicy hops lift it from the expected black hole.

FINISH: Bitter, dark roasted malt.

OVERALL: A very well balanced stout with a lovely texture. KBR: Has a good, thick, warming richness – but the taste could prove a little tiresome after a glass or two.

GENERAL: Introduced in 1995, it now appears to have become a regular brew.

JDW: 6 / 5 KBR: 8 / 7

QUINTINE

8.5% alc/vol. 33cl ceramic stoppered bottles.

KNOWN INGREDIENTS: Pilsener malt. Mixture of hops including Goldings and Styrian Goldings hops.

APPEARANCE: Orange gold with a good, creamy head.

NOSE: Pleasant mix of hops and fruit with a distinct citricity. JDW: Possibly some apricot notes and a faint spiciness. KBR: Spicy hops with fruity malt relegated to the distance.

PALATE: Grainy with a good helping of dry, hoppy bitterness. JDW: Fruity (orchard fruits). KBR: Hoppy, but building to a fruity maltiness.

FINISH: Dry, hoppy and very bitter. KBR: A fruity malt tang.

OVERALL: Characterful, very dry and hoppy ale with a nice soft texture, although some may find it a little uncompromising. KBR: Quaffable for its strength, but malt tang prevents it being a good quencher.

General: "La Bière des Collines" translates as The Beer of the Hills. First brewed in 1993.

JDW: 7 / 6 KBR: 7 / 7

QUINTINE AMBRÉE

8.5% alc/vol. 33cl ceramic stoppered bottles.

Known Ingredients: Caramel malt. Goldings hops.

Appearance: The perfect amber colour with a good head.

Nose: Strongly malty with an odd vegetable hint. JDW: Candy sugar and caramel with a faint hop. KBR: Fruity with an aromatic hop.

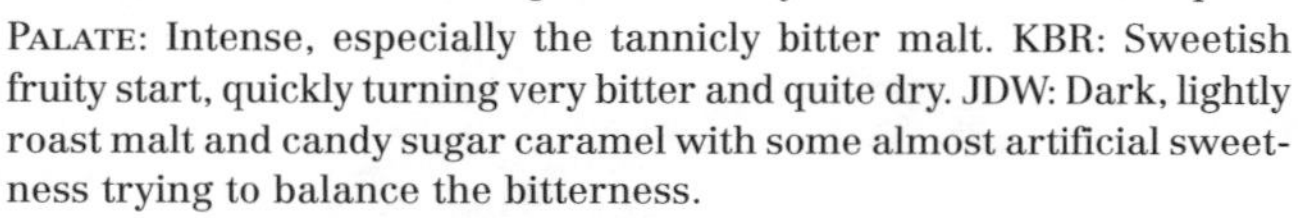

Palate: Intense, especially the tannicly bitter malt. KBR: Sweetish fruity start, quickly turning very bitter and quite dry. JDW: Dark, lightly roast malt and candy sugar caramel with some almost artificial sweetness trying to balance the bitterness.

Finish: Mostly tannic bitterness and dryness. KBR: A little lingering fruit. JDW: An excess of cocoa.

Overall: One dimensional with an overbearing tannic malt. KBR: Like a pale ale with the tastes turned up too much. JDW: Too candied.

General: First brewed in 1996.

JDW: 4 / 3 KBR: 5 / 4

QUINTINE DE NOËL

8.5% alc/vol. 33cl ceramic stoppered bottles.

Known Ingredients: Pilsener and caramel malts. Mixture including Goldings and Styrian Goldings hops.

Appearance: Deep copper brown with a nice tight head.

Nose: JDW: Rich, slightly vinous, bitter chocolate malt. KBR: Dark roast malt with fleeting spicy fruit notes and some candy floss hints.

Palate: Not as strong as the nose suggests. Slightly sweet start turning bitter with rich, roasted malt and suggestions of fruit. JDW: Some caramel. KBR: Hops struggle to get through.

Finish: Dry and bitter roast malt. JDW: Candy sugar hints. KBR: Rich in fruit and alcohol with a clean, almost clinical quality.

Overall: Essentially the same as ordinary Quintine with darker malts. Just what you would expect from a Christmas version. Its rich, full finish makes it quite a good after dinner beer.

General: First brewed in 1993.

JDW: 6 / 5 KBR: 7 / 8

BARS & CAFES RECOMMENDED BY THE BREWERY

None recommended.

BEER SHOPS RECOMMENDED BY THE BREWERY

Widely available, not thought appropriate to specify individual shops.

Brasserie Fantôme

✉ Rue Preal 8, 6997 Soy, Luxembourg.

☎ 086 47 70 44 (fax also).

🕓 Mon-Sat 1000-2000.

Prearranged only. At least 7 days notice. In French, Flemish and English. 100 Bfr charge. Tasting available.

SHOP Cases, bottles and sometimes glasses.

400hl (in 1995).

→ Soy is a small village on the N807 between Hotton and Erezée (north-east of Marche-en-Famenne). Approaching from Hotton the brewery is on the left as you leave Soy, the last building before a field, and then a petrol station.

April Fool's Day is normally associated with acts of a light-hearted nature, but in 1988 it was the day chosen by Dany Prignon to found one of Belgium's finest, truly artisanal breweries. Dany works in the local tourist office and it was largely a desire to have more to offer the tourists that encouraged him to start the brewery and its attached small bar after many years of amateur brewing.

The brewery itself (sometimes referred to as Brasserie Prignon, even on the bottle labels) is in a spartanly converted barn which is easily dismissed as just another farm building when you drive through the village of Soy. Even when you do find it, things may not get any easier, as Dany's "real" work commitments can mean he is a hard man to track down. If you happen to turn up and find the brewery closed, you may see a notice pinned to the door directing you up the road to his father's house. Providing he is in you should be able to sample and buy some of Fantôme's extraordinarily characterful beers.

Given Dany's elusiveness, the Fantôme referred to in the name of the brewery and its main beer could well be the brewer – but in fact it is Berthe, a well known ghost who is reputed to haunt the ruins of the nearby château of La Roche-En-Ardenne.

As with many of the artisanal Wallonian breweries, funding is somewhat limited and development of the property has to take place at a leisurely pace. There is a small bar tacked on one end of the barn where you can drink the beers at weekends and evenings in summer, but Dany is currently turning a much larger room upstairs into a suitable venue for parties or large groups visiting the brewery.

The beers are very hard to come by – even in the surrounding towns and villages – but have such individual tastes and are generally of such quality that any self-respecting beerhunter or connoisseur should be prepared to put up with any inconvenience to try them.

Only one of the beers can be said to be regular, and that is Fantôme, being made all year round to the same recipe. The other stock brews are Fantôme de Noël at Christmas and the truly seasonal series of four beers called Saison d'Erezée (named after the season in which they are brewed, i.e. Printemps, Été, Automne and Hiver).

The Saisons d'Erezée are flavoured with the plants and flowers of that particular season – a concept unique in commercial Belgian brewing, and perhaps around the world. Many brewers use herbs and plants but none, to our knowledge, regularly produce four beers each year with the genuine aroma and taste of particular seasons. To add an extra dimension to their exclusivity, Dany finds it necessary to vary the recipe each year according to which plants are ready to be picked at the time he is ready to brew. As a result of this, a Saison d'Erezée of the same season will differ to some degree from one year to the next, especially in the character imparted by the herbs and flowers.

Dany has a preference for young beer with a fresh taste, and this is what he aims for when brewing. Whilst many beers noticeably improve with age, Dany states that this is not the case with Fantôme beers and, to experience them at their best, they should be drunk within the first year. We believe the Saisons should be enjoyed within a few months of production, before the aromas and tastes of the herbs lose their delicate edge.

In addition to the brewery's stock beers, Fantôme produces a vast amount of one-off and annual specials for fêtes and organisations. Usually the person requesting the beer will say roughly what characteristics they want it to have and Dany will come up with a recipe and produce the beer for them. This can be anything from five to 50 hectolitres. There will often be some of these specials awaiting despatch from the brewery and, providing it was not brewed for a charity, you might be able to buy a bottle or two – we would advise you to do so, as they are all unique brews and all worth sampling.

FANTÔME

8% alc/vol. 75cl corked and crown corked bottles and draught at the brewery tap.

Known Ingredients: Pilsener malt. Hallertau and Goldings hops. Spiced with special (but secret) ingredients including two fruit juices and two herbs.

Appearance: Golden orange in colour with a variable head.

Nose: Intriguingly fruity, floral and sweet aroma. KBR: Various herbs, spices and suggestions of tropical fruits. JDW: Various whiffs of the following: orange, apricot, melon, lemon, passion fruit and mango. Whatever combination they come out in, it is exquisite.

Palate: Many layers of complexity, although it tends to vary slightly even from bottle to bottle. KBR: A beautiful balance of fruity but very light malt and a bittersweet herbiness. Distinct tropical fruit and pear notes. JDW: A good balance of sweet, bitter and sour. A grainy, lightly hopped taste with lots of fresh fruit (mostly apricots) and herbs. A warming alcohol sensation occasionally comes through.

Finish: Complex, long-lingering and very interesting. KBR: Deep, herb and tropical fruit bitterness with a slight, tart dryness. A cacophony of tantalising herbs round off an altogether enjoyable experience. JDW: Mouthdrying grainy tang with slight bitterness and a few tart notes plus exotic elements all around.

Overall: Absolutely gorgeous, complex summer refresher with enough interest to drink all year round. Multi-layered and exuding great depth of character. KBR: Perhaps some beer drinkers will find Fantôme just *too* complex and *too* unique – but those looking for a beer of extraordinary depth and complexity need look no further.

General: Like most of the Fantôme products it can be variable, but rarely fails to impress. Definitely better drunk young as the herbal ingredients seem to go through a "breaking down" process and the beer has a tendency to develop a tart character as it gets older. The palate becomes more mellow and grain-based and the exquisite nose loses its cleanliness.

JDW: 10 / 10 KBR: 10 / 10

FANTÔME DE NOËL

10% alc/vol. 75cl and 150cl corked and crown corked bottles.

Known Ingredients: Pilsener and roast malt. Goldings hops. Spiced with honey, caramel, coriander, black pepper, plus other secret ingredients.

Appearance: Very dark brown with cherry highlights. Good, creamy head.

Nose: Odd herbal aroma with distant dark fruit notes. KBR: Whiffs of chicory and a roasted (but, strangely, not necessarily malt) character. JDW: Hints of malt.

Palate: Wonderfully rich and warming dark fruit, malt and herbs. Slightly burnt malt imparts some coffee notes. Surprisingly both sweet and bitter but is well balanced. KBR: A certain tartness.

Finish: Dry and quite bitter with oodles of bittersweet fruit and some herbal touches. Leaves a wonderfully satisfying complexity in the mouth and throat for absolutely ages.

Overall: Beautifully warming with an amazing, almost overwhelming, depth of character. Well balanced bittersweet, fruity ale which must surely be the ultimate winter warmer.

General: Difficult to obtain due the fact that only 10 hectolitres is brewed each year, but well worth the effort to seek out. The label pays homage to a famous Belgian cartoonist in its drawing style in its depiction of Berthe.

JDW: 10 / 10 KBR: 10 / 10

SAISON D'EREZÉE RANGE

The Saison d'Erezée beers vary from year to year as the ingredients are dependent upon what is available at the time of brewing, this is particularly true of the flowers used. As a basis, the beers use Pilsener malt and Hallertau hops. Examples of the "extras" added are dandelion flowers, lime tree leaves, cherries and apples. The following notes are produced after sampling the 1994-6 vintages (plus some earlier examples) and are intended as a guide to the style you can expect, though the specifics may change. To give an indication of just how much they can vary from year to year, we have included tasting notes on both the 1994 and 1996 Printemps.

The Saisons are available on draught to special order and are recommended by the brewery as being at their best after just two months.

All the Saisons are brewed in very small quantities and the brewery sells out of them very quickly – especially in the seasons when tourists call in on their way through the Ardennes. This exclusivity serves to heighten the anticipation and appreciation when they are savoured after such a long, eventually successful search, making them elusive but obligatory additions to any beer connoisseur's "must-have" list.

SAISON D'EREZÉE AUTOMNE

7.5% alc/vol. 75cl corked and crown corked bottles and draught at the brewery tap.

APPEARANCE: Golden with a good head.

NOSE: Predominantly fruity (pineapple, apricot, orange and lemon) with a little pale malt and a distant herbal layer.

PALATE: Great depth of flavour and fresh tastes. Very herbal and flowery with hints of camomile. Also fruity with a slight bitterness and some distinct citric (lemon and lime) elements.

FINISH: Mouthdrying, tangy, fruity bitterness with other flavours hiding in the background.

OVERALL: Excellent refreshing drink which is very floral in character. The sediment definitely detracts from this particular beer.

GENERAL: Automne is French for autumn. **JDW: 8 / 8 KBR: 8 / 9**

SAISON D'EREZÉE ÉTÉ

8% alc/vol. 75cl corked and crown corked bottles and draught at the brewery tap.

APPEARANCE: Chestnut brown with an excellent lasting head.

NOSE: Very spicy and herbal over a full malt base. KBR: Dry and hoppy

PALATE: Very powerful palate. Dominated by a very herbal element. Dark fruit and spice contribute to a wide ranging palate that has an additional tartness. JDW: Distinctive alcohol element.

FINISH: Masses of warming alcohol dominates the herb tastes. KBR: Tart acidity blends wonderfully with the herbs. JDW: Long lasting with the herb element growing.

OVERALL: The Été from 1996 was definitely not what most would expect from a summer beer. Despite its great complexity and interest, it had a distinct, dark winter brew character – but perhaps this will prove to be an anomaly in comparison to future years' brews. The Été is the most difficult to obtain due to its popularity with tourists.

GENERAL: Été is French for summer. **JDW: 8 / 8 KBR: 10 / 10**

SAISON D'EREZÉE HIVER

8% alc/vol. 75cl corked and crown corked bottles and draught at the brewery tap.

APPEARANCE: Orange brown with a large cream head.

NOSE: Dark yet clean and fresh. Very herbal with a faint sharp hop, a grainy base and peppery spice notes.

PALATE: Excellently different. Darkly sweet in the start, developing a richer, fruitier and herbal palate which stops short of the expected sicklyness to be a beautifully balanced beer. Hints of roast malt and an "old brown" tartness. KBR: Has a woody element. JDW: Quite a lot of peppery spice and masses of sharp alcohol. A good helping of hops and malt add to the impressiveness of the palate.

FINISH: Christmas-cakey and warming, yet balanced enough to allow the delicate, lingering herbal qualities to be appreciated. Very long lasting spicy warmth. JDW: Peppery, spicy alcohol with just a touch of malt.

OVERALL: Very warming winter beer with an exceptional palate of multi-layered herbs and spices over pleasant hop and malt elements rather than the usual heavy malt.

GENERAL: Hiver is French for winter **JDW: 9 / 10 KBR: 10 / 10**

SAISON D'EREZÉE PRINTEMPS

6.2% alc/vol. 75cl corked and crown corked bottles and draught at the brewery tap.

GENERAL: Printemps is French for spring.

1994 VINTAGE

APPEARANCE: Amber with a variable head.

NOSE: Slightly spicy light malt. KBR: Dried fruit and herbs. JDW: Some wheaty hop notes.

PALATE: KBR: Delicate layers of herbs and meadow plants (the taste conjurs up visions of dandelions and daisies!) and a very complex character, although I found the rich, sweet and sickly fruity tang a little too much. JDW: Rich, spicy, fruit cake-like taste overlays a complex malt with hints of caramel. Sediment makes is smoother and more mellow

FINISH: KBR: Completely dominated by an intensely fruity malt tang. JDW: Very fruity with some malt. Slightly spicy with sediment.

OVERALL: KBR: A beer of immense character and quality which, personally, I found too tangy. Others may like the tang, so this is reflected in my marks for the beer. JDW: Excellent, complex, fruity beer which gets better with the sediment. **JDW: 9 / 9 KBR: 9 / 6**

1996 VINTAGE

APPEARANCE: Orangey colour with a variable head.

NOSE: Slightly floral (mostly pineapple) with a thick, sweet background.

PALATE: Starts sweet and thick with a strong herb and fruit taste which develops into a distinct pineapple fruit with some yeastiness and a growing herbal bitterness.

FINISH: Strong, lingering herbal bitterness.

OVERALL: Suggests sweetness but in fact delivers a very strong herbal bitterness. A good deal of interest but does not have the deep complexity of the 1994 vintage.

COMMENTS: KBR: Without of the 1994's herbal tang I found it far easier to drink yet noticed the comparative lack of depth – especially in the spicing – this was far more herbal. JDW: In spite of the prominent pineapple elements I found it lacked the darker complexity of the 1994 vintage and was significantly less satisfying.

JDW: 7 / 6 KBR: 8 / 7

OTHER BEERS

The brewery is also a prolific producer of beers to order. Generally these are all different and some of the brews may never be repeated. Here are a few of the other beers we have found on our visits.

Bière des Jumeaux (8% alc/vol.): Loads of bittersweet fruit, oranges, lemons, malt and spices with a slightly sour tang. Lingering citric fruit in the finish.

La Fayimi Blonde (7% alc/vol.): Easy drinking beer with a surprising amount of character. A nice blend of wheat, hops, light citric notes and a touch of sourness.

La Pellainoise (6.5% alc/vol.): Bizarre floral pineapple aroma precedes a very fruity, pineapple and sweet apple taste with a slight citric sharpness and a distinctly wheaty grain base. KBR: Works well as a summer quencher.

L'Hélianthe (8% alc/vol.): The name translates as sunflower, which is presumably what it is flavoured with, giving it a distinct herbal tang.

Bir del Gat' – Similar pineapple qualities to La Pellainoise but with a darker character.

Cisse-Leuze (8% alc/vol.): Brewed regularly for the twinning of Somme-Leuze and Cisse (in France). Brews vary considerably but are generally full of fresh exotic fruits, like a sweeter Fantôme.

Pissenlit (6% alc/vol.): Translating literally as "piss in bed" (but actually meaning a dandelion) it is flavoured with dandelion flowers, giving a very bitter, herbal quality.

BARS & CAFES RECOMMENDED BY THE BREWERY

LE BRONZE, Place du Bronze, La Roche-en-Ardenne.

L'ARCADE, Rue Principale, Erezée.

RELAIS DU VIEUX PONT, Place, Durbuy.

LE COMME CHEZ SOY, Place Troquet, Soy.

BEER SHOPS RECOMMENDED BY THE BREWERY

Fantôme beers are available only in bars or from the brewery.

La Ferme au Chêne

✉ Rue Comte d'Ursel 1115, 6940 Durbuy, Luxembourg.

☎ 086 21 10 67 (fax also).

🕓 Mon-Sun 1000-2400. Brewery: 1000-1800 (closed Wednesday).

Pre-arranged if possible, not Wednesday. 15 days notice. In French. No charge. Tasting available.

SHOP Cases, bottles and glasses.

80hl (in 1995).

➔ Durbuy is on the N833 running north from Hotton to Ouffet, on the River Ourthe. It is a large restaurant with a front car park, and is on the left going into Durbuy from the south.

La Ferme au Chêne (Oak Tree Farm in English) is a restaurant and bar situated on the edge of the pretty and historic village of Durbuy, perched on a rocky outcrop over the Ourthe valley, north-west of Marche-en-Famenne.

Founded as a "brewpub" in July 1989 it remains a very small scale affair which also serves as a well-visited tourist attraction. The small room which constitutes the brewhouse is aimed squarely at the holidaymakers with a video display in French, Flemish and English which lasts around five minutes, promotional leaflets and the actual "business" area of the brewery being boxed in with glazed panels. Brewing in the height of the tourist season must be like working in a goldfish bowl.

The operation is run by two brothers – Jacques and Michel Trine – who own the restaurant, although there appears to be some kind of tie with Brasserie Fantôme as we have found Fantôme corks in Ferme au Chêne bottles and vice versa. One of the brewery's leaflets even states that its beers are brewed in collaboration with Daniel Prignon (the Fantôme brewer). Nevertheless, its beers are made on site with its own equipment and, despite being somewhat pricey, they are certainly worth seeking out.

The tiny brewhouse surrounded by glass.

Its staple product, Marckloff, named

after a family brewing business which existed in Durbuy in the 16th century, and is available all year round.

In 1995 the brewery offered a "special" for St. Valentine's Day which proved such a success that it is likely to become an annual feature. Being released for the end of February it has winter beer qualities which make it appropriate for the time of year.

The beers are only available at the brewery and restaurant which also sells local produce such as honey.

MARCKLOFF

6.5% alc/vol. 75cl corked & crown corked bottles and draught.

Known Ingredients: Pale malt. Goldings hops.

Appearance: Murky wheat colour with a good creamy head.

Nose: Distinctive wheaty, malty, yeasty aroma, like a saison.

Palate: Slightly sharp citric edge to a strong tangy wheat plus, among other tastes, a lightly roasted wheat and a distinct herbal layer. KBR: Some fruity bitterness.

Finish: Grainy, tangy, dry tannic bitterness.

Overall: A pleasant, reasonably characterful Wallonian style ale with enough taste to drink year round, yet performing well as a summer quencher.

General: The draught has a far mellower character than the bottled version, the latter being drier and more bitter. Only about 10% of production is bottled. First brewed in 1989.

JDW: 7 / 7 KBR: 7 / 7

MARCKLOFF ST. VALENTIN

6.5% alc/vol. 75cl corked & crown corked bottles.

Ingredients: Unknown.

Appearance: Deep dark copper red with a minimal head.

Nose: Very herbal, flowery and deeply fruity with a little malt. KBR: Some tropical fruit notes.

Palate: Very warming from a sharp, alcohol fizz-induced zing with a peppery heat. Numerous herbal tastes and layers of rich dried fruit. There is a slight bitterness around the edge and a suggestion of dandelions. KBR: Some sweet and spritzy tart notes.

Finish: Gloriously full and warming, slightly spiced and herbal.

Overall: A superb winter beer: Unbelievably full tasting for its strength. Very warming with plenty of interest from the spices and herbs. Quite reminiscent, perhaps even a lighter version, of Fantôme de Noël. A little more "wintry" character than you might expect for St. Valentine's Day.

General: First brewed in 1995.

JDW: 9 / 9 KBR: 9 / 9

BARS, CAFES & SHOPS RECOMMENDED BY THE BREWERY

The brewery's beers are only available at the brewery and restaurant.

Brasserie Friart

✉ Rue d'Houdeng 20, 7070 Le Rœulx, Hainaut.

☎ 064 66 21 51 Fax: 064 67 67 30.

🕓 Drinks market: Mon-Sat 0900-1800.

Pre-arranged only. 7 days notice. In French and English. No charge.

SHOP Cases, bottles and glasses.

20,000hl (in 1995).

➔ Call at drinks market (see article).

Brasserie Friart was originally founded in 1873 and brewed continuously until it ceased operation in 1977. The grandchildren of the previous brewer, Benoit and Dominique Friart, started brewing again in 1988 to complement the drinks market business they run on the edge of Le Rœulx. In the intervening period, the St. Feuillien name did not disappear from the marketplace as Brasserie Du Bocq took over the contract brewing of the range.

Friart specialises in the marketing of its beers in large capacity bottles and now offers a range of sizes up to 15 litres, although some of the larger sizes need to be specially ordered. The available bottle sizes are: magnum (1.5l), jeroboam (3l), rehoboam (4.5l), methuselah (6l), salmanazar (9l), balthazar (12l) and nebuchadnezzar (15l). It should be noted, however, that the cost of these large bottles is very high – even before any beer is put in them.

The range of bottle sizes at Brasserie Friart is very impressive.

Perhaps the most unusual aspect of its beer production, and a system unique to this guide, is its arrangement with Du Bocq to produce the St. Feuillien beers in the 25cl, 33cl and 75cl bottle sizes, leaving the Le Rœulx brewery to concentrate on the 1.5 litre and larger versions. Grisette is only produced at Du Bocq. The reason for this contract is mainly due to the fact that Friart cannot keep up with demand from its own plant.

The mash tun at the brewery has recently been restored to its former glory.

Although the recipes are the same, the water used at the two sites is obviously different and the St. Feuillien Blonde and Brune both come out at 0.5% alc/vol higher from Friart. It is also a factor that bottle-conditioned beers mature differently (arguably better) in larger bottles. With these points in mind, we did a comparison test and found the Le Rœulx beers on the whole to be a little more complex and, to our palates, definitely preferable.

The brewery was purpose built and bought by the Friart family in the last century. Despite having been in the family for so long it has probably never looked quite as good as it does today. It is a classic red brick tower brewery built around a central courtyard which incorporates the living quarters and is currently nearing the end of a long process of cleaning, painting and renovation.

You probably won't find anyone at the brewery itself as the administration of the business is run from the drinks market, located on the right hand side of the road into Le Rœulx from junction 21 of the E19/E42, where you can buy the Friart range along with other beers.

St Feuillien refers to an abbey founded by disciples of an Irish monk of that name in 1125. The abbey and its brewery thrived until it was closed down by French revolutionaries. Products bearing the St Feuillien name have been made by the brewery for many years although the current Blonde and Brune versions were introduced in 1950 and the Cuvée de Noël followed in 1974.

GRISETTE

4.5% alc/vol. 25cl crown corked bottles. Also availabe on draught.

INGREDIENTS: Unknown.

APPEARANCE: Golden amber.

NOSE: KBR: Hoppy, musty and dry. Metallic and malty with a touch of spice. JDW: Sweet and lightly fruity with just a slight hint of lime.

PALATE: Sweet start with a lightly hopped dry bitterness. KBR: Metallic notes.

FINISH: A gentle bitterness that lingers long before ending in a tannic tang. KBR: Particularly clean in character.

OVERALL: Pleasant enough drink but with a "safe" and unexciting character. Pretty ordinary by Belgian standards.

GENERAL: Brewed by Du Bocq. First brewed in 1988.

JDW: 4 / 4 KBR: 6 / 5

ST. FEUILLIEN BLONDE (Du Bocq)

7.5% alc/vol. 25cl and 33cl crown corked and 75cl corked bottles.

KNOWN INGREDIENTS: Pale malt.

APPEARANCE: A pleasant golden colour with a good, creamy head.

NOSE: A full aroma of sweetish, clean, spicy hops with a hint of lime. Just a little pale malt in the background.

PALATE: Predominantly hoppy with attendant bitterness but has a nice, overall balance. A touch of peppery spice and the odd citric note with an underlying soft maltiness.

FINISH: Very dry and bitter. KBR: Softly malty with a light but lingering dry spice. JDW: A distinctly hoppy tang.

OVERALL: An accomplished wonderfully hoppy blonde ale. Noticeably fizzier than the Friart version. First brewed in 1950.

JDW: 8 / 7 KBR: 8 / 8

ST. FEUILLIEN BLONDE (Friart)

8% alc/vol. 150cl and larger corked bottles.

KNOWN INGREDIENTS: Pale malt.

APPEARANCE: Pleasant dark golden colour with a good head.

NOSE: Lightly spicy and malty with a dry hoppiness and a bitter promise. KBR: Some interesting lactic notes.

PALATE: Sweet, spicy hops with a hint of malt and a fair degree of bitterness. Adding sediment gives a slightly orangey taste and even more bitterness.

FINISH: Masses of hops with a formidably dry bitterness. KBR: Some leftover lacticity. JDW: An acid hop tang in the back of the mouth.

OVERALL: Sweeter and smoother than the Du Bocq version with a less clean and clinical, but more artisanal, taste. Hop character is also noticeably different.

GENERAL: Front labels are the same for Blonde and Brune except for the outside border which is gold on the Blonde and dark brown on the Brune. First brewed in 1988.

JDW: 9 / 9 KBR: 8 / 8

ST. FEUILLIEN BRUNE (Du Bocq)

7.5% alc/vol. 25cl and 33cl crown corked and 75cl corked bottles.

KNOWN INGREDIENTS: Special and roast malts.

APPEARANCE: Rich chestnut brown.

NOSE: KBR: Spicy with a good, sweet fruit character with a rich, dark promise. JDW: Hop tinged malt with pleasant fruity notes.

PALATE: Lots of roast chocolate malt with fruit and a herbal spiciness. KBR: Lashings of caramel. JDW: A reasonable amount of bitterness manages to come through the roast malt.

FINISH: Dry roast malt with a gentle bitterness. KBR: A lingering lightly spiced fruitiness. JDW: Sediment introduces a spicy hint and a more tangy roast malt.

OVERALL: Distinctive dark abbey-style beer with a pronounced roast malt character (JDW: Perhaps too much roast malt). Addition of some sediment imparts more spicy flavours and a little more interest.

GENERAL: First brewed in 1950. **JDW: 7 / 6 KBR: 7 / 7**

ST. FEUILLIEN BRUNE (Friart)

8% alc/vol. 150cl corked bottles.

KNOWN INGREDIENTS: Special and roast malts.

APPEARANCE: Deep chestnut brown with a good, lasting head.

NOSE: Lashings of roast chocolate malt underlying a strong, rich dark fruit.

PALATE: Powerful, deep chocolate malt with a complex and complementary spicy hop and dark fruit. Sediment makes it more mellow and adds spice. KBR: Quite sweet with hints of coffee which adds interest to the otherwise overpowering roast malt.

FINISH: Dry, rich, burnt malt. KBR: Gorgeously rich, yet still allows fleeting dark spices to flow through. JDW: Quite bitter.

OVERALL: Although overtly dark roast malt in character it is fuller and has a greater depth than the Du Bocq version, mainly due to the fact that more fruit and spice came through. Addition of some sediment adds still greater depth and makes it mellower and creamier.

GENERAL: First brewed in 1988. **JDW: 8 / 6 KBR: 9 / 8**

ST. FEUILLIEN CUVÉE DE NOËL (Du Bocq)

9% alc/vol. 25cl crown corked and 75cl corked bottles.

KNOWN INGREDIENTS: Special and roast malts.

APPEARANCE: Rich red highlighted amber brown with a massive, rocky head that soon disappears.

NOSE: KBR: Deep, dark roasted malt with a touch of spice and distant hints of molasses. JDW: Sweet, estery, rich and overtly fruity. Candy fruit with hints of rum. Slightly marzipanish. A little spice became evident towards the end of the bottle.

PALATE: Dark, rich and smooth with a powerful roasty bite. Some tannic notes. JDW: Candy fruit tastes and a little bitterness.

FINISH: KBR: Lashings of lovely roast malt with lingering bitterness, smokiness and, perhaps, wood. JDW: Mostly roast caramel, tangy fruit and tannin. A little bitter with strong alcohol notes.

OVERALL: It starts off surprisingly, and offputtingly, fizzy but settles down to be a pleasant warming dark ale with a character which certainly lives up to most drinkers' idea of a Christmas beer.

GENERAL: Having tried an eight-year-old bottle that was stored well in a proper cellar we would not recommend anyone keep it so long! First brewed in 1974.

JDW: 7 / 6 KBR: 9 / 8

ST. FEUILLIEN CUVÉE DE NOËL (Friart)

9% alc/vol. 150cl and 300cl corked bottles.

KNOWN INGREDIENTS: Special and roast malts.

APPEARANCE: Rich dark ruby brown with little head.

NOSE: Rich fruity, slightly roasted malt with some hops. Slight bitter notes with some fruit. KBR: Surprisingly hoppy through the dark roast and quite vinous. JDW: Plummy.

PALATE: Very full taste of darkly rich, fruity, roast malt. Rich and warming with a vinous quality. JDW: Liquorice. KBR: A good mix of bitter and sweet with a touch of tartness in the background, becoming a little sickly towards the end of the glass.

FINISH: Warming alcohol and fruity roast malt. JDW: Burnt, a little spicy at the start, very long lasting. KBR: Treacley, bittersweet malt with some sherry hints.

OVERALL: Excellent example of a dark and warming winter beer. Very rich, full and fruity. JDW: Considerably more accomplished than the Du Bocq version which tasted almost artificial in comparison. KBR: Well balanced at first, becoming sickly and cloying towards the end but has hop and herb qualities missing from the Du Bocq version.

GENERAL: First brewed in 1988.

JDW: 9 / 9 KBR: 9 / 8

OTHER BEERS

Jean de Nivelles (7.5% alc/vol): Fruity malt is dominant throughout, although the finish is spicy with a strong, fruity tang. Only available locally to Nivelles.

BARS & CAFES RECOMMENDED BY THE BREWERY

AU COMMERCE, Place de l'Église, Le Rœulx.
AU PASSE-PIERRE, Place de Béguinage 6, Mons.
LA GRIMAUDIÈRE, Place de l'Eglise, Le Rœulx.
LA TOUR GLACÉE, Route Baccara 4, Ronquières.
LE RAPIEUR, Grand Place 14, Mons.
LE TYBERCHAMPS, Place des Alliés 6, Seneffe.

BEER SHOPS RECOMMENDED BY THE BREWERY

Available at most large stores in Wallonia.

Brasserie Gigi

✉ Grand Rue 96, 6769 Gérouville, Luxembourg.

☎ 063 57 75 15 (fax also).

🕓 Saturday on request 0900-1700.

Pre-arranged only. 30 days notice. In French. 80BFr charge. No tasting available.

SHOP Cases, bottles and glasses.

1500hl (in 1995).

➔ See article.

Previously known as Brasserie d l'Étoile you could be excused for thinking that Brasserie Gigi is named after a film star, a pet or something similar. It is in fact the surname of the family that bought the business in 1888 when it was already 46 years old.

Like other breweries which concentrate mainly on table beer production, the beers from Gigi are particularly hard to find – as is the brewery itself – but they do have a strong local following. This is just as well because the brewery doesn't like to advertise, preferring to rely upon its reputation.

That reputation was, until recently, based on its table beers – in fact Gigi brewed little else until 1991 when it started to brew the La Gaumaise range previously made by the now defunct Maire brewery. Although the beer range may be changing, there is a lot of tradition left at Gigi. The brewing method is as it was at the turn of the century and the brewery still delivers directly to its clients.

The village of Gérouville is on the N88 Florenville to Virton road. If you arrive from the west, Grand Rue is the road to the left of the large, open, rough surfaced area before you get to The Lime (the large grassed area either side of the road). No. 96 is not immediately

Don't worry – it's not orange and lemon beer. Gigi offer the complete service to the community, including soft drinks.

Gerouville's lime tree – the symbol adopted by Brasserie Gigi as its logo.

obvious, especially if you are looking for a brewery! Grand Rue has a terrace of small houses up one side of it and about half way up there are two large garage-type doors with No. 96 to their right. This very ordinary façade (which is the living quarters and bottling plant) is also very deceptive as it hides away the large collection of buildings to the rear which makes up the rest of the Gigi brewery.

Gigi's table beers are perhaps the fullest-tasting and most characterful of all in the genre and should be sampled even if you would normally choose a stronger brew. Due to their strength they make wonderful summer quaffers and are far preferable to many soft drinks or shandies. The 33cl bottles are of an interesting, multi-sided shape, but the 75cl bottles have a more standard, modern design.

The symbol adopted by the brewery is all that is left of a legendary lime tree, supposedly one of the four planted by a monk when Gérouville was founded in 1258. The last survivor, having grown enormous, fell in 1877, after which event a massive branch was hollowed out and put on show in various cities. In 1923 it was returned to Gérouville and set in concrete next to the road, even being given a thatched roof. This area is now known as The Lime and is much frequented by the village youth.

DOUBLE BLONDE

1.2% alc/vol. 33cl crown corked and 75cl screw top bottles.

KNOWN INGREDIENTS: Pilsener malt. Sugar.

APPEARANCE: Pale watery gold.

NOSE: Gentle hop aroma with a touch of malt in the background.

PALATE: Very subdued, not surprisingly, with light hops and a little malt, giving a lemonade-like element. There is a bit of a hop tang which continues into the finish, giving it a pleasant bite. KBR: Sweet in the start with a refreshing maltiness.

FINISH: KBR: A slightly sickly sweet malt. JDW: A touch dry and tangy with some hops and a hint of bitterness.

OVERALL: Surprisingly good table beer. Very light, very easy to drink with a definite ale character.

JDW: 8 / 6 KBR: 8 / 4

LA GAUMAISE BLONDE

5% alc/vol. 25cl crown corked bottles.

INGREDIENTS: Not disclosed.

APPEARANCE: Golden amber with a non-existent head.

Nose: Some pale malt and light hops with a spicy/herbal background.

Palate: Lightly malty with a hoppy spiciness. JDW: There is a herbal element and a sharp edge to the palate that verges on sourness.

Finish: Dry, hoppy bitterness.

Overall: Unsensational beer with a distinct Wallonian character but little to make it stand out. Strange, but pleasant, herbal quality which tries but doesn't quite get through.

General: Previously brewed by Brasserie Maire until it closed. First brewed by Gigi in 1991. The name refers to the area around the brewery, known as the "Gaume".

JDW: 4 / 3 KBR: 5 / 4

LA GAUMAISE BRUNE

5% alc/vol. 25cl crown corked bottles.

Ingredients: Not disclosed.

Appearance: Reddish amber with a non-existent head.

Nose: Dark and malty. KBR: Yeasty with a dry, sourish promise. JDW: Nice mix of malt and fruitcake.

Palate: Sweet and malty with hints of spice. JDW: Cocoa notes.

Finish: KBR: Saccharin and malt. Disappointingly bland. JDW: Lightly fruity cocoa tang in back of the throat.

Overall: KBR: Bland and chemical version of the Blonde. JDW: Nose promises more than is delivered, but a pleasant beer that grew on me as I drank it.

General: Has the same label as La Gaumaise Blonde but has a brown background instead of white. First brewed by Gigi in 1991.

JDW: 6 / 5 KBR: 5 / 4

SPECIALE

2.5% alc/vol. 33cl crown corked and 75cl screw top bottles.

Known Ingredients: Pilsener malt and unspecified spices.

Appearance: Pale gold with no real head.

Nose: Nice, gently aromatic spice against a creamy hop and malt base.

Palate: Surprisingly strong hops with a delayed but pronounced malt character. Has an intriguingly spicy quality, including an almost peppery tingle of the tongue.

Finish: KBR: An unfortunate saccharin taste lingers with the sweet, spicy malt from the palate. JDW: Hint of dryness, powdery spice, a touch of hop bitterness and definite hop notes.

OVERALL: KBR: Tastes quite artificial, especially in its sweetness. JDW: Good quality table beer, easy to drink with an amazing taste for its category and a very unusual level of spicing.

GENERAL: First brewed 1960. **JDW: 8 / 5 KBR: 5 / 3**

SUPER BRUNE

1.17% alc/vol. 33cl crown corked and 75cl screw top bottles.

INGREDIENTS: Not disclosed.

APPEARANCE: Dark chestnut.

NOSE: A slightly herbal malt extract with suggestions of dandelion and burdock.

PALATE: Very sweet, sickly, saccharin "brown" taste.

FINISH: A little cloying with a saccharin tang.

OVERALL: Disappointingly sweet and sickly with little beer character.

JDW: 2 / 1 KBR: 3 / 2

UNIC BEER

3.5% alc/vol. 33cl crown corked bottles.

KNOWN INGREDIENTS: Pilsener malt and unspecified spices.

APPEARANCE: Golden with little head.

NOSE: Light hops. KBR: Quite spicy with a faint malt background. JDW: An odd herbal element.

PALATE: Sweet with nicely balanced flowery hops and malt. Like a watered down saison. JDW: Surprisingly full tasting with many different elements. KBR: Delicately complex herb/spice tastes.

FINISH: Lightly dry with a gentle hop bitterness.

OVERALL: A little strong for a table beer but stands head and shoulders above most others.

GENERAL: First brewed in 1970. **JDW: 8 / 6 KBR: 8 / 5**

BARS & CAFES RECOMMENDED BY THE BREWERY

AU COEUR DE LA GAUME, Rue Dr Hustin 51, 6760 Ethe.
LA CIVANNE, Rue de la Civanne 285, Rossignol.
RELAIS D'ESTELLE, Place des Chasseurs Ardennais 14, 6740 Etalle.
THE PARADISE, Place du Tilleul, 6769 Gérouville.

BEER SHOPS RECOMMENDED BY THE BREWERY

BORN J. P., Rue de Stembert 185, 4800 Verviers.
LA PETITE BOUTIQUE, Place de l'Eglise, 6769 Gérouville.
LE PANIER DU PAYS, Rue du Parc 3, 6850 Offagne.
TERRELUX, Rue du Monument 4, 6730 Ansart.

Brasserie Artisanale du Hameau

✉ Rue d'Erbaut 10, 7870 Lens, Hainaut.

☎ 065 22 52 92.

🕓 Monday, Tuesday, Thursday, Saturday 0900-1800.

Pre-arranged only. 14 days notice. In French. No charge. Tasting possible.

SHOP Cases, bottles and glasses.

2.4hl (in 1995).

➔ Coming into Lens from the north take the road to the right (Rue Thy), direction Baudour on a left hand bend. Take the second left, with a big farm on the corner. This is Rue d'Erbaut. Number 10 is a few houses down the road on the left.

Brasserie Artisanale du Hameau (hameau means hamlet in English) can only be described as a true cottage industry, well worthy of its artisanal tag. The owner, Olivier Goudelouf began home brewing in 1987 and decided to go commercial on 1 September 1993.

The whole operation is run from his house in the outskirts of the village of Lens, on the plains between Mons and Ath. The porch on the back of the house contains the tiny mash tun and an array of small plastic fermentation vessels which gives a good insight into the size of the operation and the amount of labour intensive work which goes into the production of the beers. When we visited, we were invited into the kitchen to sample Olivier's wares surrounded by yet more plastic fermenters (apparently other rooms frequently have various products fermenting away merrily).

The present small-scale facilities are likely to continue until Olivier finds more outlets for his beers – as of December 1995 he was supplying beer to the Delhaize supermarket in Soignes and was hopeful of a successful completion to negotiations to serve his products at the Petite Pise bar in Lens.

Production is currently limited to 150 litres at a time and he tries to brew twice per month. After bottling, the beer spends 15 days in the warm room and at least 30 days in the cellar before being offered for sale. 300 litres of Cuvée de Noël is brewed per year while the regular brews, Bière des Trinitaires and La Dorée de l'Hamio, account for an equal share of the other two hectolitres of annual output. Plans are afoot, however, for a new 9% dark beer in summer 1996.

The house has an adjoining "garage" (we use the term garage loosely as it has not been used as such for quite some time) which has become the brewery shop with numerous racks of beer in its recommended horizontal storing position. Although the operation is small, Olivier is doing a good job of presenting the products professionally with a choice of 75cl or 150cl bottles, three styles of beer glass and various gift packs with or without glasses.

If you visit Hameau in the week you will probably be dealing with Olivier's wife as he is likely to be at his "real" day job, working as a mechanic for NGK Ceramics.

The brewery gets its name from the local area – L'Hameau de Lens – and, although the sign displayed on the front of the garage doesn't contain it, Olivier now prefers to use the "Artisinale" prefix.

BIÈRE DES TRINITAIRES

8% alc/vol. 75cl and 150cl corked & crown corked bottles.

KNOWN INGREDIENTS: Pale malt. Goldings hop cones.

APPEARANCE: Golden amber with a massive, cream coloured, rocky head with impressive lacework.

NOSE: Aromatically spicy hop with a fruity malt. JDW: Excellently balanced. KBR: Has an almost perfumed quality.

PALATE: Full tasting and interesting maltiness (more crystal than pale) with slight grainy spiciness, an odd fruity tang and dry, peppery qualities. Has a moderate hop bitterness which grows into the finish. JDW: Some tartness and alcohol notes. KBR: Has an unfortunate vegetable note.

FINISH: A tangy bitterness with a strong hop character and occasional hints of caramel. Has a pleasing alcohol warmth and some tart/tangy notes. JDW: Complex and quite spicy, particularly when some sediment is added.

OVERALL: Amazingly spicy considering no spice is added. JDW: An accomplished beer with a strong hop character. KBR: Interesting and quite complex ale – darker tasting than its colour implies – as long as you can cope with the unfortunate homebrew character.

GENERAL: The inspiration for the name comes from the fact that Lens had a monastic presence in the 11th century and because the brewer loves Trappist beer.

JDW: 6 / 7 KBR: 6 / 6

CUVÉE DE NOËL

8% alc/vol. 75cl and 150cl corked & crown corked bottles.

KNOWN INGREDIENTS: Munich malt. Goldings hop cones.

APPEARANCE: Slightly hazy light brown with a hint of orange.

NOSE: Gentle aroma of herbal malt and hops with an odd vegetable note. KBR: Distant dark malt with a little dry spice.

Palate: JDW: Nice soft malt with a touch of wheat and a definite bite to the strong hop character that develops as you drink. The hops give a tangy bitterness, strong with some sediment added. There is a strong herbal character and a few zingy notes on the tongue. KBR: Dry and fruity start with some chicory and liquorice notes, then a full mouth of lightly roasted malt. Tastes deeply warming yet is surprisingly light in body.

Finish: Dry with a tangy bitterness above a well balanced hop and malt. KBR: Dry, herbal qualities but distinctly home-brewy.

Overall: An intriguing beer with a nice soft texture and a surprisingly strong herbal character which is enhanced by adding more sediment. Can be of inconsistent quality.

General: First brewed in 1994.

JDW: 5 / 5 KBR: 6 / 6

LA DORÉE DE L'HAMIO

8% alc/vol. 75cl and 150cl crown corked & corked bottles.

Known Ingredients: Pilsener malt. Saaz hop cones.

Appearance: Pale gold with a very slight head.

Nose: JDW: Light, slightly oaty with an acid hoppiness and an odd mustiness. KBR: Quite neutral with just a lightly musty, peculiarly dry hop.

Palate: Good, interesting hoppiness with some citric notes and a mounting mouthdrying bitterness. KBR: Very light for its strength.

Finish: Dry with a strong hop bitterness. KBR: Good balance of light maltiness and hops – not long lasting but quite refreshing.

Overall: Hoppy and lightly malty brew which is unbelievably light and quaffable for its strength. Has a very "small brewery" artisanal quality. Adding sediment gives a fuller but tangy edge in place of the otherwise clean taste.

General: Dorée translates as golden and Hamio is presumably a bastardisation of Hameau.

JDW: 7 / 5 KBR: 7 / 5

BARS & CAFES RECOMMENDED BY THE BREWERY

LA PETITE PISE, Place de la Trinité, 7870 Lens.

BEER SHOPS RECOMMENDED BY THE BREWERY

DELHAIZE, Soignies.

Brasserie Jupiler

- Rue de Vise 243, 4020 Jupille-sur-Meuse, Liège.
- 041 62 78 00.
- Not known.
- Not known.
- Not known.
- 2,200,000hl (in 1994).
- On a large heavy industry estate just off the E25, junction 6, heading north east out of Liège.

A suburb on the outskirts of Liège, Jupille-surMeuse's dubious claim to fame is that it produces (and gave the name to) what is, sadly, Belgium's top selling beer – Jupiler – the signs for which are as much a part of the country's identity as the friterie and the chocolate shop.

One might imagine that dealing with Brasserie Jupiler would be easy as it is part of the huge Interbrew empire and has an army of people involved with the publicity and promotion of their products. In reality, we found quite the reverse.

After writing twice to obtain information for this book we were disappointed to hear nothing. We then visited the site office and were given the name and job title of the man we should deal with, for whom we left a questionnaire and introductory letter at reception due to his being unavailable at the time of our visit. A subsequent phone call (made necessary by the absolute dearth of information again) resulted in a brief conversation with our contact who told us we needed to speak to the marketing manager who is based at the Interbrew head office in Leuven. Having been given the necessary details, we sent off another correspondence pack and, needless to say, we have still had no word to date.

When the concept for this book was first mooted we wanted to let all breweries and their products stand on their own merits and not to let the often stigmatised view – that big (in the world of brewing) means impersonal and characterless – creep in without due cause. Unfortunately, our experience has left us disappointed with the apparent lack of enthusiasm and belief in their own products. On the plus side, we now appreciate more than ever the very personal and welcoming attention given to us by those who are genuinely delighted to find that people from Britain are interested in their beers.

The brewing operation at Jupille-sur-Meuse is of monumental proportions and is now essentially in two halves – the old Piedbœuf brewery (which now looks to be redundant) and the modern building, across the railway, apparently complete with its own sidings. Approaching the complex from the motorway you will first come upon the main transport depot entrance to the new building, with its heavy juggernaut traffic and gatemen's kiosks. The actual administrative part of Jupiler is a good kilometre away, facing the old industrial brickwork façade of the Piedbœuf brewery.

Whereas the new building displays a typically understated modernity with its concrete and galvanised steel, the Piedbœuf structure appears to be in the quaint, architectural angularity of the late art-deco period, with complementary logo and clocks adorning its sides.

We presume that the three Piedbœuf table beers are still produced at Jupille, although only the Blonde and Foncée still carry the words "Brasserie Piedbœuf Jupille" while the Triple says merely "Brasserie Piedbœuf".

Other beers which are reputed to have been made here in the past but which we cannot ratify due to the lack of information are **Jupiler Light**, **Sernia Bock**, **Sernia Pils** and **Vega Pils** – none of which we have seen in either shops or bars in the last two years and might only be produced for sale in other countries where Interbrew operates.

The old Piedbœuf brewery with its cross-street conveyors.

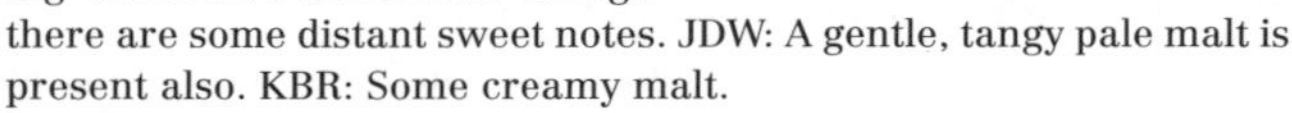

JUPILER

5.2% alc/vol. 25cl crown corked bottles and draught.

APPEARANCE: Pale, watery gold with a scummy head.

NOSE: Gentle grainy hop. JDW: A tangy, almost metallic, hint and a slightly stale sensation. KBR: Dry with a metallic edge.

PALATE: Quite a harsh hop note giving distinctive bitterness though there are some distant sweet notes. JDW: A gentle, tangy pale malt is present also. KBR: Some creamy malt.

FINISH: Dry with a metallic bitterness. KBR: Lingering malt

OVERALL: Bland and easily-drinkable with little reason to analyse it too deeply. Epitomises a mass-market beer which has to suit as many people in its marketplace as possible – if it had any character it might well lose sales from people who simply want a "pils" to quaff. JDW: Tangy, metallic bitterness detracts from any appeal it may have had for me – tastes as though it is out of a can rather than a bottle.

JDW: 5 / 2 KBR: 5 / 2

PIEDBŒUF BLONDE

1.5% alc/vol. 25cl and 33cl crown corked bottles.

KNOWN INGREDIENTS: Saccharin.

APPEARANCE: Watery gold with a slight to good head.

NOSE: Faintly hoppy. KBR: An odd, earthy, maltiness. JDW: Slightly artificial.

PALATE: Watery with hints of hop. KBR: Strangely distant, soft and light malt.

FINISH: A touch dry with faint hop notes and an unappealing metallic character.

OVERALL: Very shandy-like – in common with most table beers – and refreshing but has an artificial edge. Not a bad introduction to the world of table beers nevertheless.

JDW: 7 / 5 KBR: 6 / 2

PIEDBŒUF FONCÉE

1.5% alc/vol. 25cl and 33cl crown corked bottles.

KNOWN INGREDIENTS: Saccharin.

APPEARANCE: Deepish amber brown with minimal head.

NOSE: JDW: Just a hint of malt, otherwise quite watery. KBR: Slight metal notes and very little else.

PALATE: Very sweet and quite malty. KBR: Quite full considering its strength and not unlike a sweet, British keg mild. JDW: A pronounced lemonade-type background but quite malty.

FINISH: A very sugary finish. KBR: Metallic notes grow into the finish. JDW: A touch dry with a hint of malt extract.

OVERALL: Acceptable version of a Brune table beer which, by its nature, is supposed to be very sweet. Has a good deal of fizz which presumably makes it less sticky and a surprisingly full mouth of taste, if a little artificial.

JDW: 4 / 5 KBR: 4 / 3

PIEDBŒUF TRIPLE

3.8% alc/vol. 25cl and 33cl crown corked bottles.

INGREDIENTS: Unknown.

APPEARANCE: Light golden with a good fluffy head.

NOSE: Malty with just the faintest touch of spice.

PALATE: Fuller than the Blonde and Foncée yet, despite having double the alcohol, it still has a weak pils-type character with a gentle hop bitterness and a chemical tang.

FINISH: Dryish with a dull maltiness.

OVERALL: This is not labelled as a table beer even though it is part of the Piedbœuf range. To give a beer like this the name of "Triple" is an absolute travesty and should have Trappist and abbey-beer lovers enraged. Do they not have a Trade Descriptions Act in Belgium?

JDW: 2 / 1 KBR: 1 / 1

Brasserie Lefebvre

✉ Rue du Croly 52, 1430 Quenast, Brabant.

☎ 067 67 07 66 Fax: 067 67 02 38.

🕓 Tuesday-Friday 1400-1800. Saturday 0900-1300.

Pre-arranged only. 15 days notice. In French, Flemish and English. 100BFr charge. Tasting available.

SHOP Cases, bottles and glasses.

13,500hl (in 1995).

➔ See article.

Brasserie Lefebvre is sometimes understandingly overlooked as a Wallonian brewery due to the fact that it lies within the province of Brabant – however, the official Walloon/Flemish border runs just a few kilometres north.

Quenast is quite a large village between Rebecq and Tubize, just west of the N6 Mons to Brussels road. The village and its surrounding countryside bears testament to its importance as a quarrying area and has become very industrialised over the years. The brewery itself was founded in 1846 in the centre of the village but moved to its present site on the upper outskirts at the turn of the century. To find the brewery you should proceed up the hill from the centre of the village, following the road round to the left at the church, where you will see the gates on the right.

The varying architectural styles and the mixture of materials show that there have been numerous additions to the original buildings but it is still, in the main, of brick construction. The latest of these extensions appears to have been the bottling plant and warehouse.

Brasserie Lefebvre is still a family-run business and boasts what at first seems to be an exceptionally long list of beers. In truth there are far more names than there are different beers due to the brewery being a prolific label beer producer. We can appreciate the benefits that come with giving a Wallonian beer a different identity for the Flemish market, but it is hard to justify the confusing amount of other relabelling and the lack of information regarding it.

Some 7,000 hl of the brewery's total output of 13,500 hl is accounted for by its wonderfully hoppy Floreffe Triple (along with its numerous other names). It is also the oldest of the current range of products, being introduced back in 1978. The characterful Saison 1900 joined the range in 1982, followed by another two Floreffe beers – Double and Meilleure – a year later. Following Wallonian trends towards white beers and blonde ales, the brewery introduced Blanche de Bruxelles and Floreffe Blonde in 1990 and 1991 respectively. A recent departure from the range, however, was **Lefebvre Blonde** – a table beer – which ceased production in 1995 due to the falling market.

There is a pilsener-style beer, called La Quenast, which bears the brewery's name but is in fact made by the Flemish brewer Facon.

Interestingly, Lefebvre describes Abbaye de Bonne Esperance as its most important beer – which is backed up by the fact that it is the only product displayed on the exterior walls of the brewery. Considering the beer is just a relabelled Floreffe Triple it leads us to believe that it must sell better under the former's name.

In 1995 the newest of Lefebvre's beer range was introduced – a honey beer called Barbàr.

BARBÀR

8% alc/vol. 33cl crown corked bottles.

KNOWN INGREDIENTS: Two row spring Pilsener malt. Hallertau hops. Spiced with honey.

APPEARANCE: Golden with an orange tinge.

NOSE: Slightly sweet pale malt. KBR: Pronounced honey note when first poured (which tones down later) and a faint spicy hop. JDW: Very much like a blonde.

PALATE: Pale malt with some citric (orange) notes, presumably from the hops. KBR: Very noticeable, but not overpowering, sweet honey with some flowery hints – unfortunately masked by an overtly powerful fizz. JDW: A tangy honey sweetness but only a slight taste of honey.

FINISH: Dry, bitter and tangy. KBR: Excellent balance of dry hop bitterness and sweet honey, the latter lingering long.

OVERALL: A pleasant beer with enough interest to satisfy those looking for something a little special. KBR: The honey is sweeter, but lighter and less likely to cloy than other honey beers, but is too sweet for me. Has an almost perfect balance and, although I can understand the need for some fizz in a honey beer to prevent stickiness, I find it to have far too much. JDW: Could possibly do with more honey to make it really interesting. It drinks its strength.

GENERAL: Beautiful "world art" type label with a tribal African theme which leaves you wondering why it was chosen for a honey beer. Another powerful marketing tool is its impressive, frosted, tankard-shaped glass. First brewed in 1995. **JDW: 7 / 7 KBR: 8 / 8**

BLANCHE DE BRUXELLES

4.2% alc/vol. 25cl crown corked bottles and draught.

KNOWN INGREDIENTS: Pilsener malt. Styrian Golding hops. Spiced with bitter orange peel, coriander and vinegar.

APPEARANCE: Cloudy, pale gold/wheat colour with little head.

NOSE: An earthy wheat aroma, but very little of it.

PALATE: Mostly an earthy wheat with a few citric notes and a little acidity.

FINISH: Principally a citric tang. KBR: Some watery wheat notes.

OVERALL: A different, but hardly inspiring, variation on the white beer theme.

GENERAL: As might be expected from a beer of this name, the neck label depicts the famous Mannekin Pis. Also labelled as **Student**, presumably as a marketing ploy to appeal to the Belgian youth as well as the Bruxellois. First brewed in 1990.

JDW: 4 / 3   KBR: 3 / 3

FLOREFFE BLONDE

7% alc/vol. 33cl crown corked, 75cl corked & crown corked bottles, and draught.

KNOWN INGREDIENTS: Plaisant and Natasha malts. Styrian Golding and Hallertau hops.

APPEARANCE: Orange/golden in colour with a good lasting head.

NOSE: Hoppy with hints of wheat. KBR: Some estery notes with a touch of lacticity. JDW: Some fresh fruit.

PALATE: Hoppy and bitter with a little wheaty malt. KBR: A full earthy character with a distinct peppery hop. JDW: A hint of fresh fruit.

FINISH: Dry, hop bitterness.

OVERALL: Quite characterful for a blonde, with a surprisingly full and hoppy palate. KBR: A little one-dimensional.

GENERAL: Also sold as **Durboyse Blonde** and **St. Léger**. Suspiciously like a now-defunct Lefebvre beer called **Zafke**. Has the same label design as others in the Floreffe range but is predominantly printed in black. First brewed in 1991

JDW: 6 / 7   KBR: 4 / 5

FLOREFFE DOUBLE

7% alc/vol. 33cl crown corked, 75cl corked & crown corked bottles and draught.

KNOWN INGREDIENTS: Plaisant, Munich and Caramunich malts. Styrian Golding and Hallertau hops.

APPEARANCE: Nice rich red brown with a good head of large bubbles which doesn't last.

NOSE: Chocolate malt to the fore. KBR: Sweet promise with coffee and dark spicy notes. JDW: Fruit and a hint of sherry.

PALATE: KBR: Strong, tangy, roasted malt with a nutty dryness and a touch of black pepper. JDW: A watery chocolate malt, although adding some of the sediment gives a more rounded chocolate flavour and more body.

FINISH: KBR: Long lingering dark bitterness with some treacle and hints of molasses. JDW: Light burnt malt.

OVERALL: Oddly described by the brewery as a porter, and certainly not in the style of a traditional abbey double. Excessively fizzy. KBR: Its full taste and dark bitterness lift an otherwise unspectacular dark ale. JDW: Pretty boring – not a beer to write home about, even with the improvement of adding sediment.

GENERAL: Also sold as **Durboyse Brune**. Label is printed predominantly in red. First brewed in 1983.

JDW: 4 / 5 KBR: 4 / 4

FLOREFFE LA MEILLEURE

7.5% alc/vol. 33cl crown corked and 75cl corked & crown corked bottles.

KNOWN INGREDIENTS: Plaisant, Natasha, Munich and Caramunich malts. Styrian Golding and Hallertau hops. Spiced with aniseed and coriander.

APPEARANCE: Deep reddish brown with a reasonable but short-lived head.

NOSE: KBR: Liquorice and aniseed with a dark, treacly roasted base. JDW: Chocolate and coffee.

PALATE: Starts very sweet but develops into a dry, bitter malt with some fruity notes forcing their way through.

FINISH: Surprisingly gentle, lightly roasted malt.

OVERALL: Accomplished, but not – as implied by its name – "the best". Another Lefebvre beer with a tendency towards overfizziness. Very difficult to categorise. Addition of some sediment adds spice throughout and also increases maltiness and tangyness.

GENERAL: Label is printed predominantly in red. First brewed in 1983.

JDW: 5 / 7 KBR: 4 / 5

FLOREFFE TRIPLE

7.5% alc/vol. 33cl crown corked, 75cl corked & crown corked bottles and draught.

KNOWN INGREDIENTS: Plaisant and Natasha malts. Styrian Golding and Hallertau hops.

APPEARANCE: A rounded, golden orange colour with a good, lasting head.

NOSE: A colossal aroma of hop flowers dominates, but with a little malt behind it.

PALATE: A massive attack of hops with the accompanying bitterness – but not too strong – balanced with a little sweetness. Behind all the hops there is a gentle malt with a slight caramel note and a peppery character.

FINISH: More hops, lashings of hop dryness, masses of hop bitterness.

OVERALL: No holding back on the hops with this beer. It is, however, not overdone and there is a pleasant balance which prevents it getting too bitter. An excellent summer thirst quencher.

GENERAL: We believe it is also sold as: **Abbaye de Bonne Esperance**, **Moeder Overste** (Mother Superior in Flemish) and **La Four Chapitre** amongst others. Although the brewery has not admitted this in writing, it was confirmed verbally on one of our visits. First brewed in 1978.

JDW: 9 / 8 KBR: 9 / 8

SAISON 1900

5.2% alc/vol. 25cl crown corked and 75cl corked & crown corked bottles.

KNOWN INGREDIENTS: Plaisant and Natasha malts. Styrian Golding and Hallertau hops. Spiced with ginger.

APPEARANCE: Orange amber with a generous, fluffy head.

NOSE: Citric spicy hops with a pale malt base. KBR: Suggestions of summer flowers. JDW: Hints of thick cut orange marmalade.

PALATE: Starts with slightly sweet fruit and malt but develops into a drier, more bitter, lemony hop with a strong malty background. JDW: A few tangy bitter marmalade notes.

FINISH: A pronounced maltiness with a lovely, thirst-cutting fresh hop.

OVERALL: Excellent summer quaffing beer which is surprisingly light in body. A good introductory saison-style ale for beginners. First brewed in 1982.

JDW: 8 / 8 KBR: 8 / 9

OTHER BEERS

La Quenast (5% alc/vol.): Quite characterful pilsner-style beer with plenty of hop and a positive pale malt element but marred by a metallic edge. Brewed by the West Flanders brewery Facon but sold with a Lefebvre label. Available in 25cl bottles and on draught.

La Seigneurie (7% alc/vol.): Brewed, or perhaps just labelled, for Gusbin, a beer distributor in Erquelinnes. Another, typically Lefebvre, dry and bitter ale which majors on its hop character. Not unlike the Floreffe Blonde.

BARS & CAFES RECOMMENDED BY THE BREWERY

TAVERNE DU MOULIN, Rue Docteur Colson, Rebecq.

Brasserie Mibrana

Place de la Station 2, 5000 Namur.

081 23 16 94 / 081 22 15 09   Fax: 081 22 15 09.

Mon-Sat, 1000-2400. Sun, 1500-2400.

Free visits (ask at the bar). In French, Flemish and English.

SHOP Cases, bottles, glasses.

400hl (in 1995).

In the main square in the centre of Namur. From the railway station, the brewery/bar is opposite and to the left.

Opened in November 1994 in the heart of Wallonia's capital city, Brasserie Mibrana – better known to most as Les Artisans Brasseurs – is the result of months of hard work converting the old Bavaro Belge hotel into a brewpub.

The bar itself is an immaculate, busy, city-centre establishment, entirely in keeping with the fashionable, cosmopolitan image of Namur. As you walk in through the door you can't help but notice the tops of two highly polished copper vessels with gauges, electronic display and pipework, letting customers know that this is not just an ordinary drinking establishment. At the rear of the ground floor bar-room is the bottling plant, encased by glass panels.

The fermenters and maturation tanks are housed in the cellar where an impressive amount of new equipment has been shoe-horned in, taking advantage of every square inch. This is one operation that didn't start small and add bits on every few years – the entire brewplant

The beautifully polished coppers at the entrance to the bar.

has been custom-designed specifically for Mibrana to make the most of the limited amount of space.

The brewpub is owned and run by the Deboot family with the son, Serge, as head brewer. Serge's father worked for some years in Zaire for Unibras and worked alongside Guy Valschaerts (who started Brasserie Brunehaut), sharing the same ambition to one day run a microbrewery back in Belgium. It appears that both potential brewers also shared the same philosophy of starting with brand new, state-of-the-art plant with considerable investment and meticulous business planning.

The beers at Les Artisans Brasseurs, all unfiltered and unpasteurised, make up an adventurous range for such a young brewery. A number of beers – including the regular Cuvée, a strong blonde beer – are only available on draught at the brewpub which makes a good reason for visiting.

At present two of its beers, Blanche and Brune, are relabelled and sold as Bière de Franc Waret, although it should be noted that both come out significantly weaker than the original brews. Two beers are produced for other customers – the 6.5% **Cuvée de Bouillon** for Le Marché de Nathalie in Bouillon and the 6.5% **La Ramée**, though many customers take labelled versions of the stock beers.

One beer is made specifically for the Fête de Wallonie, the annual festival of Wallonia which is held in Namur. This is a dark beer made with wheat, caramel and torrefied Pilsener malts. In 1996, 600hl was produced of which 410hl were consumed between the Friday and the Monday. Mibrana hopes to brew a Christmas beer soon.

One good facility at Les Artisans Brasseurs is the opportunity to buy a "dégustation palette" of three, four or five of their beers in 20cl glasses to sample the different brews. Perhaps other breweries should be encouraged to do the same, although obviously Mibrana is only able to do this because it has draught versions of all its products.

A good range of beer cuisine is also on offer in the bar, including carbonnade, choucroute (sauerkraut) and salmon steamed in beer. A recommended treat is a "sabayon à la bière" – a sort of syllabub dessert flavoured with its Blanche beer.

Downstairs from the bar there is a lot of equipment miraculously shoe-horned into the tiny cellar.

ALDEGONDE BRUNE

8.5% alc/vol. 33cl crown corked bottles and also on draught.

Known Ingredients: Pilsener and Caramunich malts. Saaz and Record hops. Spiced with bitter orange peel.

Appearance: Orange brown.

Nose: Malty with a hint of bitter orange. KBR: Has an unusually dry promise for a brune.

Palate: Intriguingly complex taste. A malty base with a distinctive hoppiness, a herbal element, a strong bitterness and just a touch of sweetness. KBR: A dryish, fruity, bitterness.

FINISH: Tangy, bitter and fruity with a lingering roasted malt. KBR: Surprisingly dry.

OVERALL: Excellent beer, but not what most people would expect as a brune. Distinctive, almost unique, in character. Very malty with a hoppy sharpness and an alcohol warmth. Perhaps slightly over-fizzy. KBR: Drier and more bitter than the classic brunes.

GENERAL: Aldegonde is the patron saint of the village where the brewer was born. Also sold as **Bière de Franc-Waret Brune** at 7.8% alc/vol.

JDW: 8 / 8 KBR: 8 / 7

ALDEGONDE CUVÉE

7.5% alc/vol. Only available on draught at the brewpub.

KNOWN INGREDIENTS: Pilsener malt. Saaz and Record hops.

APPEARANCE: Cloudy wheat colour with a good lasting creamy head.

NOSE: Pronounced herb and spice elements, especially coriander. A dry and bitter promise with a distinct red fruit (probably strawberry). JDW: Rich sweet grape.

PALATE: Wonderfully smooth with a good helping of citric hop and a light maltiness. Barely delivers the spiciness promised by the nose.

FINISH: Lasting, dry quenching hoppiness. KBR: Herbal. JDW: Spicy.

OVERALL: Excellent, easily drinkable beer with a good, full mouth of taste yet light enough to quaff. Exquisite nose.

GENERAL: Same recipe as the Blonde but with two refermentations at 25°C with added sugar.

JDW: 8 / 8 KBR: 9 / 9

ALDEGONDE PRINTEMPS

6.2% alc/vol. Only available on draught at the brewpub.

KNOWN INGREDIENTS: Pilsener malt and spelt.

NOSE: Wonderfully fresh and fruity aroma with a distinct hoppy background.

PALATE: Distinctly fruity, lemony, wheat grain-like taste with some lacticity and hops. There is an interesting, tart edge to the general sweetness.

FINISH: Very drying, hop tanginess with a watery suggestion. General lemon taste.

OVERALL: Pleasant light beer with a slight tendency towards wateriness in the palate. The lacticity is very refreshing when well chilled (as it is on draught).

GENERAL: First brewed in 1996 as an Easter beer but renamed a spring beer in order to extend its season. 1200 litres was produced in 1996 and it sold well, justifying the decision.

JDW: 7 / 7 KBR: 8 / 8

ALDEGONDE SPÉCIALE

8.5% alc/vol. 33cl crown corked bottles and also on draught.

KNOWN INGREDIENTS: Pilsener and roasted malts. Albatros wheat. Saaz and Record hops. Spiced with sweet orange peel.

APPEARANCE: Rich, deep brown.

NOSE: Lashings of earthy, herbal malt. JDW: Some vegetable notes. KBR: Chicory hints and a distant citric hop.

PALATE: Very distinctive with a herbal malt and a sharp, hoppy edge. Gently roasted with some bitterness and a touch of warming alcohol

FINISH: Dry, gently bitter malt. KBR: Darkly dry with a burnt, almost smoky malt.

OVERALL: Very complex and interesting beer with an intriguing herbal character and a good balance.

JDW: 8 / 7 KBR: 8 / 9

LA MARLAGNE BLANCHE

5.5% alc/vol. 33cl crown corked bottles and also on draught.

KNOWN INGREDIENTS: Pilsener malt. Albatros wheat. Saaz hops. Spiced with sweet and bitter orange peel and coriander.

APPEARANCE: Slightly hazy, lemony wheat colour with a good head.

NOSE: Lovely coriander-spiced wheat with hints of orange. KBR: Wonderfully aromatic when first poured, some metal notes creep in later.

PALATE: Full and quite deep taste with a good mixture of sweet and bitter elements. Wheaty with a good deal of coriander and some sharp lemon notes. KBR: Some peppery spice and a distinct lacticity.

FINISH: Leftover wheat with a light dryness. KBR: Some creamy notes.

OVERALL: Excellent example of a Belgian white beer, in the old Hoegaarden style. Very full taste with a good interest from the coriander and orange peels. Spoilt a little by its excessive fizz.

GENERAL: The beer is named after the Marlagne forest, south west of Namur. Also sold as **Blanche de Franc-Waret** at 4.5% alc/vol.

JDW: 8 / 8 KBR: 8 / 8

LA MARLAGNE BLONDE

5.5% alc/vol. 33cl crown corked bottles and also on draught.

KNOWN INGREDIENTS: Pilsener malt. Saaz and Record hops.

APPEARANCE: Light gold with a good, rocky head.

NOSE: Fresh hops with a slight sweetness and only fleeting malty hints.

PALATE: Lashings of clean, sharply citric hops and a good full taste. Slight spiciness to the edge. JDW: Quite rich. KBR: Quite light but has a pleasant fruity dryness.

FINISH: Dry but not overly bitter from the leftover hoppiness. KBR: A shame that little else makes it through the hops.

OVERALL: A good example of a very hoppy blonde with some unusual touches. JDW: Surprisingly full and rich though still clean throughout. KBR: Although very hoppy, it lacks depth – more like a pilsener than any other ale I know – doesn't have enough body to cope with the amount of hopping

JDW: 8 / 8 KBR: 7 / 6

Brasserie d'Oleye

✉ Rue d'Elmette 39, 4300 Waremme (Oleye), Liège.

☎ 019 33 04 35.

🕓 Thursday 0800-1600. Friday 0830-1600.

Pre-arranged only. 7 days notice. In French. 100 Bfr. Tasting possible.

SHOP Cases and bottles.

200hl (in 1995).

➔ See article.

When travelling on the E40 motorway through north-eastern Wallonia you will see a sign on the side of the carriageway informing you that you are now passing through "La Hesbaye". This region is very rural and has gentle rolling countryside with many small rivers, and it is from one of these rivers that the brewery took its name when it first started as Brasserie du Geer.

Originally it produced a range of three beers, all named Hesbaye, in Blonde, Ambrée and Brune guises. The brewery also made a success of brewing contract beers for small organisations and country fairs.

1995 saw the brewery change its name to Brasserie d'Oleye, after the village in which it is situated. We were told this was simply because it felt happier with the new name.

To our knowledge, this is the only Wallonian brewery which has a female brewer. After some time running a beer shop in Liège, Chantal Romain and Didier Cornet finally took the plunge and fulfilled their dream of running their own brewery in April 1994. Chantal now works most of the week at Oleye and Didier joins her at weekends.

The brewery itself used to be part of the village school and the

It might look like part of the school, but the sign in the window gives the game away!

rest of the school buildings are still in use to this day, making it an very unusual location for a brewing operation.

Chantal and Didier initially received a great deal of assistance from Brasserie Fantôme's Dany Prignon and, indeed, much of Dany's old brewing plant is now used at Oleye along with an assortment of recycled dairy industry equipment.

Oleye's range of beers expanded dramatically in 1995 to the point that it is difficult to tell how many will be regulars. Among the new products are a Cuvée de Noël, a Blanche, an Easter beer (**Brassin de Pâques**) and a range of Cuvée Spéciales, some of which are identifiable only by the colour or design of the label. Presumably the range will settle down after seeing how they sell. In addition to the above, Oleye is still a prolific contract brewer and we are told that it makes one particularly successful beer, the 7% **La Pierreuse**, sold door-to-door by a Liègeois youth organisation to raise funds.

The village of Oleye is a stone's throw from the Flemish/Walloon border just north of Waremme (Borgworm in Flemish). The easiest way to find the brewery is to leave at junction 29 of the E40, go to Waremme and follow the signs to Oleye. Once in the village turn left just before the Café du Centre and you will find the school and the brewery at the end of the road on the left.

HESBAYE AMBRÉE

7.5% alc/vol. 33cl crown corked and 75cl corked & crown corked bottles.

KNOWN INGREDIENTS: Pilsener malt. Goldings hops. Candy sugar.

APPEARANCE: Amber with a dull orange tinge.

NOSE: KBR: Clean and fresh with a fruity malt and lightly spiced hop. JDW: Vanilla, malt and hops with suggestions of orchard fruit.

PALATE: Very malty and extremely full-mouthed. Slightly roasted. Butterscotch notes. Strong, warming alcohol throughout. KBR: A little sickly with a pronounced candy sugar taste. JDW: Some hop bitterness enhances the bitterness from the roast malt. A faint spiciness with hints of bitter orange.

FINISH: Very tangy, bitter and long lasting. Butterscotch and alcohol notes. KBR: Overly bittersweet tang with a tendency to cloy.

OVERALL: Just as the aroma promises there is a very full taste but the slightly cloying nature detracts from the appeal the more you drink it. KBR: A bit of a struggle to drink a 75cl bottle by yourself.

GENERAL: First brewed in 1994.

JDW: 7 / 4 KBR: 6 / 5

HESBAYE BLANCHE

3% alc/vol. 25cl crown corked and 75cl corked & crown corked bottles.

INGREDIENTS: Unknown.

APPEARANCE: Pale wheaty gold with no head at all.

NOSE: Peculiar aroma with a yeasty wheatiness and some grapefruit. KBR: Pronounced citricity – mainly grapefruit but other tropical fruits.

PALATE: Lightly wheaty with tart grapefruit. KBR: Very grapefruity but with other citric fruit hints and a tart sharpness. JDW: Slightly sour lacticity.

FINISH: JDW: Tangy grapefruit with a drying, lactic and slightly bitter character. KBR: Pleasantly quenching citric acidity with a light graininess and a grapefruit tang at the end.

OVERALL: KBR: Refreshing, if a little watery. The tartness makes it an odd candidate for a "blanche" tag but gives it that extra character which distinguishes it from the rest. Definitely one to chill.

GENERAL: First brewed in 1995.

JDW: 4 / 2 KBR: 5 / 4

HESBAYE BLONDE

6.5% alc/vol. 33cl crown corked and 75cl corked & crown corked bottles.

KNOWN INGREDIENTS: Pilsener malt. Goldings hops.

APPEARANCE: Orange gold and, like most Oleye beers, a good fluffy head.

NOSE: Fruity (especially apricots), herbal and hoppy with suggestions of honey. KBR: Some musty and woody notes with a distant spice. JDW: Very interesting sweetish mellow aroma.

PALATE: A little sweet with a wonderfully full, fruity, spicy, hoppy and tangy flavour. A bitterness comes through towards the end, as does an alcohol element. KBR: Has a strange appley fruitiness. JDW: Powdered ginger and coriander notes.

FINISH: Drying and bitter with a distinct fruitiness and some definite spicy notes. Good and complex. KBR: A beautiful balance of sweet, bitter, dry and fruity.

OVERALL: An excellent smooth texture complements this impressive, satisfying, complex beer. Deserves to be called something more than simply "Blonde".

GENERAL: First brewed in 1994.

JDW: 8 / 8 KBR: 8 / 8

HESBAYE BRUNE

9% alc/vol. 33cl crown corked and 75cl corked & crown corked bottles.

KNOWN INGREDIENTS: Pilsener and chocolate malts. Goldings hops. Candy sugar. Undisclosed spices, including liquorice.

APPEARANCE: Dark amber.

NOSE: Intriguing and inviting with lots of dark malt and fruit. KBR: Some dry spiciness.

PALATE: Very full and complex. Well balanced malt, fruit, hop and alcohol with a little spiciness. An interesting dark character which delivers subtle hints of various tastes including a sourish element.

FINISH: Lingering fruity malt with hints of spice and hop with a slightly bitter tang.

OVERALL: Rich, fruity and darkly complex. An excellent beer with a good balance, though some may find the malty fruit a little excessive after one glass. The light fizz prevents cloying.

GENERAL: First brewed in 1994.

JDW: 7 / 8 KBR: 8 / 8

HESBAYE CUVÉE SPÉCIALE NOËL

8% alc/vol. 75cl corked and crown corked bottles.

INGREDIENTS: Unknown.

APPEARANCE: Dull orange brown.

NOSE: Earthy with a suggestion that the palate may be sour. JDW: Occasional fruity wafts. KBR: Yeasty.

PALATE: Fruity with a slightly sour edge. Gets more herbal as it warms. JDW: Bitter, grainy and earthy with a persistant tang and lactic notes. KBR: Creamily lactic and very fruity with a sour "twang", but overall it is surprisingly light and refreshing.

FINISH: Dry and bitter. JDW: Astringent, earthy and a touch roasted. KBR: Tarty fruit.

OVERALL: The taste and texture develop as it warms. We would suggest that this may be one to drink very young. When we tried it at one month old we were quite impressed, but at four months (and more) it was consistently delivering the above characteristics. KBR: Definitely an unusual character for a Christmas beer but develops warmth and fullness as you get through the bottle.

GENERAL: First brewed 1995.

JDW: 5 / 4 KBR: 4 / 3

HESBAYE CUVÉE SPÉCIALE NOIRE

7% alc/vol. 75cl corked & crown corked bottles.

INGREDIENTS: Unknown.

APPEARANCE: Very dark, black/brown with ruby highlights.

NOSE: Black malt, very dark with just a touch of hop to add interest. KBR: Nutty dryness. JDW: Roast, almost burnt.

PALATE: Very roasted malt with a tart blackcurrant fruitiness. Little else. Very odd contrast of dry, burnt and tart. JDW: A little nutty.

FINISH: Tart fruit. KBR: Distinct dark roasted fruity maltiness – a little like burnt crabapples. Almost too odd to define. JDW: Lashings of burnt malt. Lingering.

OVERALL: KBR: Not the sort of beer in which to use black malt – the tartness and fruitiness just don't seem to work with dry, burnt malt – almost like an experiment that went wrong. JDW: Like a cask stout with a distinct tartness.

GENERAL: First brewed 1995.

JDW: 5 / 2 KBR: 4 / 3

OTHER BEERS

Oleye have a colossal portfolio of "special" beers, all of which we're told are unique brews. Most are very difficult to obtain, unless you visit the bar/fete/organisation the beer is made for or are lucky enough to find some at the brewery when you visit. The following list gives an indication of what is available.

Hesbaye Blonde Brassin Unique (5% alc/vol.): Very hoppy character with a fair degree of citric lemon and a little tartness.

Poirée (7% alc/vol.): Strong, sweet fruit aroma, pineapples and pears. Bittersweet taste dominated by pineapples.

Hesbaye Cuvée Spéciale (Orange Label) (8% alc/vol.): A beer full of herbal, flower, fruity elements.

La Charlemagne (7% alc/vol.): Brewed for the Confrerie des Discipes du Charlemagne.

La Fayimi Brune (7% alc/vol.).

La Martchotes (7% alc/vol.): Brewed for the Confrerie de l'Hexagone Soumagnard.

La Bière des Moines (8% alc/vol.): Brewed for the Confrerie des Moines Chartreux de Pousset.

Don't let the amateurish appearance of the labels put you off. Some of these beers are well worth a try.

BARS & CAFES RECOMMENDED BY THE BREWERY

CAFÉ DE LA PLACE, Place Albert 1er 2a, Waremme.
LE METROPOLE, Avenue Reine Astrid 20, Waremme.
LE STUDENT, Rue Saint Gilles 182, Liège.
LE VIEUX GUILLEMINS, Rue du Plan Incliné 145, Liège.
TAVERNE DE G.B. DE ROCOURT, Chaussée de Tongres 85, Rocourt.
LE VIKING, Avenue Reine Astrid 2, Waremme.

BEER SHOPS RECOMMENDED BY THE BREWERY

None recommended.

Brasserie Piron

Rue de Battice 93, 4880 Aubel, Liège.

087 68 70 29 Fax: 087 68 79 78.

0800-1600.

Pre-arranged only. In French, Flemish and English. 50BFr charge. Tasting available.

Cases, bottles and glasses.

10,000hl (in 1995, currently non-productive – see article).

See article.

Brasserie Piron is, like Friart, another example of a lapsed family brewing concern being started again, after many years of closure, by members of a later generation.

The original business was founded in 1907 in the town of Aubel, very close to the Dutch border, and was brewing pilsener-style and table beers when it closed in 1969. With the impetus of an approach from the nearby Abbaye de Val-Dieu, the children of the last brewer decided to recommence operations in 1993 and, with their father's help, they now produce a range of three interesting and quite original top-fermenting beers. They form the fourth generation of the family to run the brewery.

The brewery is found on the right hand side travelling north on the N648 just past a roadside industrial zone on the southern outskirts of Aubel. There is a large sign advertising the family drinks market at the entrance of the lane which takes you into a yard with a collection of brown brick buildings, comprising the brewery, office, family accommodation and shop.

Like many Belgian breweries, Piron believes that all abbeys should have a beer associated with them, so it entered into an agreement to brew a blonde and a brune named after, and in association with, the 13th century Abbaye de Val-Dieu which lies just 4km west of Aubel. Amazingly, this arrangement could have come about some 30 years earlier, in 1963, but on that occasion the brewery turned down the offer when it was approached by the abbey.

It should be pointed out, however, that these beers have nothing in common with a widely-available beer called "Triple de Val-Dieu" which is often sold in Wallonian bars alongside the real Val-Dieu blonde and brune by bar owners mistakenly, but understandably, believing it to come from the same stable. To add to the confusion the Triple carries no brewery name on the label, but research has suggested that it is

The range of Piron beers. Note that Triple de Val-Dieu is not among them!

probably a re-labelled "Brigand" from East Flanders brewery Van Honsebrouck which is marketed by distributor Corman-Collins. When you consider that many drinkers buy it because they think it is a Piron product and also that, allegedly, the abbey receives no "licence" money from its sales, one can't help but think that this is one of the worst examples of the unacceptable face of beer-labelling.

Brasserie Piron should be applauded for the brave decision not to take the soft option and produce run-of-the-mill abbey beers. Instead it offers a unique, characterful but complementary range, all of which are well worth looking out for if you want to try something different. With attractive labels and highly marketable gift packs of glasses and bottles, the brewery appears to have done quite well in its short, new life in the marketplace.

Unfortunately, 1996 was not a good year for Brasserie Piron when it experienced major problems with the brewplant. It is unlikely that production will recommence before late 1996.

ABBAYE DE VAL-DIEU BLONDE

6.5% alc/vol. 33cl and 75cl bottles and draught.

INGREDIENTS: "Top secret" recipe which derives from the abbey.

APPEARANCE: Orange tinged gold.

NOSE: Pleasantly hoppy and malty with some sourness. Has an odd herbal and exotic fruit aroma. JDW: Slight vegetable notes. KBR: A distinct citricity.

PALATE: An intriguing taste based on a sharp bittersweet sourness incorporating a number of green fruit tastes like apples and figs. JDW: A basic grainy quality. KBR: Quite acidic.

FINISH: KBR: Some pale malt bitterness finally gets through but has to battle with the lingering fruity tartness. JDW: A sour herbal graininess underlies some tart green fruit.

OVERALL: Verging on being excessively fizzy. JDW: A distinctive beer with a little too much tartness to be really quenching. KBR: Wonderful fruity summer ale with quenching tartness and a great depth of character.

GENERAL: First brewed in 1993. Label is the same as the brune but with slightly different colouring. All Piron bottles have neck labels to identify the product. To be served cool. Brewery does not advise laying it down.

JDW: 7 / 5 KBR: 8 / 9

ABBAYE DE VAL-DIEU BRUNE

8% alc/vol. 33cl and 75cl and draught.

Ingredients: "Top secret" abbey recipe again.

Appearance: Very deep copper brown with a creamy head and lovely lacework in the glass.

Nose: A full, though not too strong, aroma of sweet chocolate malt. KBR: An odd, distant cheesy aroma and a sweet, roasted promise.

Palate: Largely sweet chocolate and roasted malt with layers of rich fruit in the background which imparts some bitterness. An interesting sharp sensation in the mouth.

Finish: Powerful and quite dry roast malt and a fruity bitterness with an intriguing suggestion of sourness.

Overall: An interesting example of something a little different – both sweet and sour – with a fair degree of bitterness from the roast malt. Perhaps there is too much of the latter. KBR: Seems to have the same base as the rest of the range but the roast element masks the subtle layers picked up in the blonde.

General: First brewed in 1993.

JDW: 7 / 7 KBR: 5 / 6

LEGENDE D'AUBEL

7% alc/vol. 33cl and 75cl bottles and draught.

Ingredients: It's top secret again, but an old family recipe this time!

Appearance: Rich deep amber. Good creamy head and nice lacework.

Nose: Complex and enticing mixture of malt and hops with various herbal notes and a dash of sourness. KBR: Chicory element on a fruity malt base.

Palate: JDW: Excellent fruity malt and hop taste with strong herbal tones and a touch of sourness. KBR: Pronounced chicory flavour with a fruity maltiness and some green fruit tartness.

Finish: Dry, very tangy, lightly roasted malt bitterness. JDW: Some bitter chocolate. KBR: Lingering mouthwatering sourness.

Overall: Not as impressive as the nose suggests but still a distinctive beer with an odd sourness throughout. JDW: Excellent nose and palate let down by a too tangy finish. KBR: I found it to have the same base as the Blonde and again the subtleties were drowned out.

General: First brewed in 1993. Despite its name it is the Ambrée of the Piron range which sits squarely between the Blonde and Brune in terms of strength and taste.

JDW: 7 / 7 KBR: 6 / 7

BARS, CAFES & SHOPS RECOMMENDED BY THE BREWERY

None. However, the brewery has a shop on the premises.

Brasserie Artisanale de La Praile

✉ La Praile 3, 7120 Peissant, Hainaut.

☎ 064 77 16 43.

🕓 0700-2100.

Pre-arranged only. 10 days notice. In French and English. No charge.

SHOP Cases, bottles and glasses.

150hl (in 1994).

➔ See article.

It seems strange that some breweries cannot seem to agree on what name to call themselves. The owner of la Praile told us he prefers the name Brasserie Artisanale de la Praile (after the lane in which the brewery is located) but just as often the brewery goes under the title Brasserie Artisanale de Peissant after the nearby village.

Founded in 1991, owner Frederic Navez describes its situation as rural – and he is not kidding! The village of Peissant is a farming community and the brewery is actually situated a few hundred metres to the north in a lane which appears to contain a collection of farmhouses and barns. This is perhaps the most difficult of breweries to find, due mainly to the lack of signposts, so it is advisable to ask in the village square for directions. Peissant is just north-east of the N40 near the town of Erquelinnes.

Current total production is only 150hl which, after seeing the converted garage the operation is run from, is understandable. However, Frederic soon hopes to have a larger brewhouse built in a barn attached to the family farmhouse and, if the new fermentation tank is anything to go by, will mean his output should increase substantially.

Behind the barn there are numerous beehives, kept by his father, which supply Frederic with the honey used in his beer, especially Cuvée d'Aristée (Bière au Miel).

The beers produced by La Praile are certainly interesting and unusual. In 1994 we found that the corks had a tendency to pop violently the moment the wire was released, possibly due to over-priming, with the majority of the range being very effervescent. This also had the effect of agitating the sediment in the bottle so that lumps hung in

Frederick's car has to stand outside all the time – due to the fact that the garage is used as a brewery!

suspension, even after pouring. Whilst obviously detracting from the appearance of the beer it had very little noticeable effect on the taste. By 1995 the sediment problem appeared to have been cured, returning the beers to their original crystal clarity.

Frederic, with the help of his father, looks after the brewery on a part time basis but is hoping that business will develop to such an extent that it can become full time. With ever-increasing interest in his beer (we were told he now exports to Italy) it is advisable to try the range before they lose their artisanal character – but mind where you point the bottle when opening!

BLONDE DE LA PRAILE

7.5% alc/vol. 75cl corked bottles.

KNOWN INGREDIENTS: Pilsener malt. Kent hops.

APPEARANCE: Hazy gold.

NOSE: Slightly sweet, not unlike sweet honey. Some spicy notes. JDW: Whiffs of crabapple.

PALATE: A little sweetness, but also a lemony citric sharpness highlighting a gentle but insistent hop bitterness. Although there is not supposed to be any honey in the recipe the taste suggests otherwise.

FINISH: Moderately mouthdrying with a little hop bitterness and a honeyed tang.

OVERALL: Pretty unspectacular beer at the bottom of the range which can only loosely be categorised as a Blonde. Could do with a bit more depth and interest. Has a nice smooth creamy texture spoilt by one of the most formidable fizzes of any beer we have sampled.

GENERAL: First brewed in 1992.

JDW: 6 / 6 KBR: 6 / 5

CUVÉE D'ARISTÉE (BIÈRE AU MIEL)

9.5% alc/vol 75cl and 150cl corked bottles.

KNOWN INGREDIENTS: Pilsener malt. Yugoslavian hops. Spiced with coriander and honey.

APPEARANCE: Golden honey colour.

NOSE: Honey and a gentle malt.

PALATE: Masses of honey which almost becomes sickly sweet before a pleasant bitterness develops along with moderate hoppiness and a distinct alcohol element.

FINISH: Strong honey and alcohol burn with a lasting bitter honey tang.

OVERALL: Amazingly heavy on the honey. A shared 75cl bottle is about as much as you would really want – going it alone can result in it becoming cloying and sickly. Surprisingly described by Frederic as a "saison".

GENERAL: First brewed in 1991. We believe the recipe has been changed a little for 1996, toning down the character. The tasting notes relate to vintages from 1993 to 1995. **JDW: 9 / 8 KBR: 9 / 8**

CUVÉE D'ARISTÉE SPÉCIALE NOËL

9.5% alc/vol. 75cl corked bottles.

APPEARANCE: Rich dark chestnut brown.

NOSE: Vinous, fruity and malty with a pronounced alcohol element and a touch of tartness.

PALATE: Very full, rich, slightly sweet, slightly roasted, dark malt. KBR: Good balance of roast malt and bitter fruit. JDW: Strong honey tang with attendant spiciness and some prominent, sharp alcohol notes.

FINISH: Wonderful, satisfying warming glow. KBR: A multitude of tastes – all of which complement each other to achieve an excellent balance. JDW: Lashings of lingering bitter chocolate.

OVERALL: Excellent, complex, rich, fruity, warming winter beer. Well worthy of the Christmas tag.

GENERAL: Has the same main label as the Bière au Miel, but carries the above neck label. **JDW: 8 / 9 KBR: 9 / 9**

LA CAMPAGNARDE

9.5% alc/vol. 75cl corked bottles.

INGREDIENTS: Unknown.

APPEARANCE: Rich mid-brown.

NOSE: Predominantly hoppy with a little malt and hints of liquorice. KBR: A touch of spice. JDW: Herbal hints.

PALATE: Alcohol element gives a warmness to a rich, gently bitter maltiness with a little hop and a touch of spice. KBR: Dry and vinous.

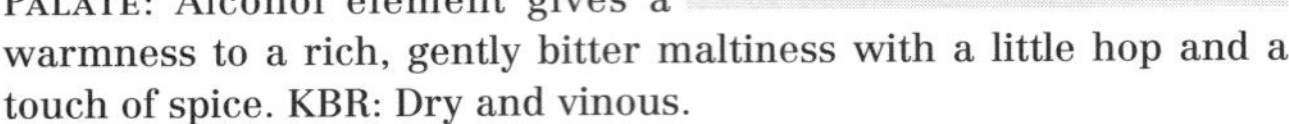

FINISH: Dryish, bitter, burnt malt and warming whisky-like alcohol.

OVERALL: An interesting, powerful but quite palatable beer which is ideal as a nightcap but certainly drinks its strength.

GENERAL: Translates as "The Countryman". **JDW: 7 / 6 KBR: 6 / 7**

BARS & CAFES RECOMMENDED BY THE BREWERY

L'EXCELSIOR, Grand Place 29, Mons.

BEER SHOPS RECOMMENDED BY THE BREWERY

The Cora chain of supermarkets.

Brasserie La Rochefortoise

✉ Rue de Treux 43b, 5580 Eprave (Rochefort), Namur.
☎ 084 37 80 84 Fax: 084 31 84 45.
🕓 0830-1200, 1330-1800.
Pre-arranged only. 7 days notice. In French. 100 Bfr charge.
Cases, bottles and glasses.
1260hl (in 1995).
➔ See article.

Taking its name from the nearest town, Brasserie La Rochefortoise is carving out a good reputation for itself in its relatively short life – and the local Trappists at Saint Remy will be happy to know that the name Rochefort is still synonymous with the brewing of quality ales.

Jos Rezette developed an interest in brewing in 1989 and pursued his hobby enthusiastically for five years before deciding that he would like to do it professionally. This ambition reached fruition in 1994 when he found a suitable site – a disused cow barn – in the small village of Eprave, five kilometres from the town of Rochefort.

With the aid of his son, Thierry, Jos assembled a brewplant from various pieces of dairy equipment along with some secondhand brewing machinery, such as the old Achouffe bottling line. The transfer of water and liquor around the various vats is by a gas-fired steam pump.

The first brew of La Rochefortoise was produced on the morning of 18 March 1995 and the brewery has hardly looked back since. It has aggresively marketed its produce locally, nationally and internationally to the extent that it now exports to five countries and has picked up some contracts, such as the relabelling of its Ambrée as **Ne Janneman** (previously an Achouffe beer). Its latest contract is for the amber 6% **Bière de Mirwart**, produced for a local village.

Officially, the brewery is known as Rezette, after the family name, but it prefers to be known as La Rochefortoise. The current standard range is just its Blonde and Ambrée, but there are plans to introduce a 10% or 12% Christmas beer for 1996.

Nowadays, Thierry has taken on the role of brewer, leaving Jos to concentrate on sales and marketing with the assistance of the charismatic Noël Marsia.

One of the features of the brewery's marketing is the unique and very distinctive glass in which to serve its beer.

Although the operation is set well back from the road behind some other units, it is relatively easy to find as it is signposted in Rue du Treux, the last road on the left as you leave Eprave in the direction of Lessive. The brewery is straight ahead of you up the track which leaves the road on the left.

ROCHEFORTOISE AMBRÉE

8% alc/vol. 33cl crown corked bottles.

KNOWN INGREDIENTS: Secret.

APPEARANCE: Copper coloured with a good head.

NOSE: Distinctly fruity with some earthy herbal qualities and a dark malt in the background. KBR: Some pear drop notes.

PALATE: Very full flavoured, based around a slightly tart, strongly fruity malt with red berry notes. A little caramel with some pear drop hints. JDW: Some apple and pear notes. KBR: Has a subdued start which builds to a very full taste with an aniseed or liquorice quality.

FINISH: A long lasting, herbal fruitiness with a slight astringency. JDW: Tangy fruit. KBR: Quite warming with a lightly dry tartness.

OVERALL: Hugely characterful, very interesting beer with an excellent texture, lifted by its intriguing, pleasant tartness. KBR: Fits the bill as both a quaffing ale and an evening drink to savour.

GENERAL: First brewed in 1994. Also sold as **Ne Janneman**.

JDW: 8 / 8 KBR: 9 / 8

ROCHEFORTOISE BLONDE

6.2% alc/vol. 33cl crown corked bottles.

KNOWN INGREDIENTS: Secret.

APPEARANCE: Wheaty gold with a light fluffy head.

NOSE: Herbal and slightly musty after an initial delicate citric hop. A wheaty creaminess. Some tartness which gives an inviting complexity.

PALATE: A complex taste with a wheaty lacticity and some spicy notes. KBR: An odd mix of sweetness, tartness and herbal/vegetable hints

FINISH: Gently spicy, peppery, lactic wheat with a little astringency. A light, tart acidity and residual citricity.

OVERALL: A beer of great interest and originality which has the lacticity and taste of a wheat beer, but isn't a traditional white beer which would have more coriander and orange. Has a good artisanal character. KBR: More of a Timmermans Wit than a Hoegaarden, and could do with a little more fizz.

GENERAL: First brewed in 1994. Label is same design as the Ambrée but slightly different colours.

JDW: 7 / 7 KBR: 7 / 8

BARS & CAFES RECOMMENDED BY THE BREWERY

BRASSERIE CHEZ LÉO, Place MacAuliffe, Bastogne.
LA TAVERNE, Rue de France, Rochefort.
LE LIMBOURG, Place Albert 1er, Rochefort.
LE LUXEMBOURG, Place Albert 1er, Rochefort.

BEER SHOPS RECOMMENDED BY THE BREWERY

LE CENTRAL, Place Albert 1er, Rochefort.

Brasserie Ruwet

✉ Rue Victor Besme 25-27, 4800 Verviers, Liège.
☎ 087 30 04 36 Fax: 087 44 61 54.
🕓 Not applicable.
No tours available.
110hl (in 1995).
➔ See article.

The town of Verviers has been an important textile town for centuries – it was granted the right to sell cloth back in 1480 – and still is, despite a certain amount of decline in recent years.

One of the inevitable legacies of the European textile recession is the number of redundant buildings left around the town and it is in one of these old textile factories that Brasserie Ruwet is situated, quite close to the centre of the town.

The building itself is owned by the Ruwet family and the brewing plant, built almost exclusively from old dairy equipment, is at the back of the building while the front (shown in the photograph) is used for storage and despatching along with another of the family's sidelines – refurbishment of old fairground rides!

Many Belgian drinkers will have heard of the name Ruwet due to the family's main business of making cider in nearby Thimister. Cidre Ruwet is one of Wallonia's top selling brands and has presumably been an inspiration for Stephane Ruwet in wanting to start his own beer making operation which he did in September 1992.

The brewery is definitely not the easiest to find. A good starting point is the railway station in the centre of Verviers. From here, go down the hill to the right to a set of

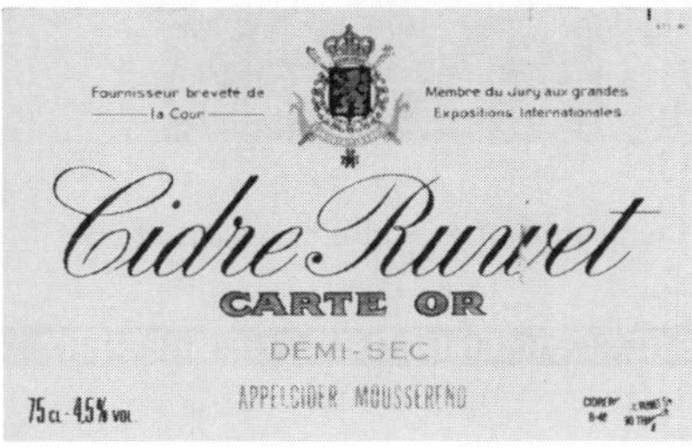

The name Ruwet to most Belgians will be associated with the family's cider business.

traffic lights. Turn right onto a dual carriageway, then take the first left. Follow this road to the end, turn right then, at the end, turn left into a one-way street, up a hill and back on yourself. This is Rue Victor Besme and the building is a couple of hundred yards on the left. However, the effort may not be worthwhile as Stephane doesn't sell beer at the brewery and visits are not available.

Brasserie Ruwet's philosophy is one of "no banks and no debt" so has started small and with low investment. To this end there was, until mid-1996, just the one beer which can be a little difficult to obtain but which is well worth taking the trouble to seek out.

The textile theme is taken further with the name of "La Ploquette" which is named after a piece of machinery from the wool making industry. Stephane told us it is brewed in the style of Duvel which we would have to agree with, although he has imparted a good deal of Wallonian character on it.

LA PLOQUETTE

7.5% alc/vol. 33cl crown corked bottles.

INGREDIENTS: Unknown

APPEARANCE: Bright golden with a good head.

NOSE: Lashings of clean, slightly fruity, hops. KBR: Some spice from the hops.

PALATE: Good, strong hop taste with initially some sharp lemon notes which reduce as a gentle malt becomes more evident. KBR: Sweetish element in the start, turning dry, with later creamy hints.

FINISH: Quite a sharp citric, almost honeyed, hop tang. KBR: Light, fruity bitterness.

OVERALL: A very pleasant drinking golden ale. KBR: Has wonderful balance and a good complexity.

GENERAL: First brewed 1994. Also sold as **La Clermontoise**.

JDW: 7 / 7 KBR: 7 / 7

OTHER BEERS

Papy Jo (3.2% alc/vol.): First brewed in 1996, this beer represents the perfect crossover between Stephane's beer brewery and his family's cider business. Made by blending La Ploquette with fresh apple juice. Papy Jo is the name Stephane called his grandfather when he was a child.

BARS, CAFES & SHOPS RECOMMENDED BY THE BREWERY

None recommended.

Brasserie St. Guibert

✉ Rue de Riquau 1, 1435 Mont-Saint-Guibert, Brabant.
☎ 010 65 42 11 Fax: 010 65 42 26.
480,000hl (in 1994).

This is, like Jupiler, another of Interbrew's Wallonian operations. Also like Jupiler it is massive in scale which makes it rather surprising that it was scheduled for closure by the end of 1996 with its production moving to Leuven. There has been a brewery here since 1837 but you would be hard pushed to imagine what it looked like then.

Being part of a large group like Interbrew the beers produced tended to rotate between their plants but St.Guibert became known for the Leffe range of beers which were the mainstay of the brewery for over twenty years and with good marketing have been well accepted worldwide as archetypal abbey beers.

By early 1996 production of Leffe Triple, Leffe Vieille Cuvée and Vieux Temps had already moved from St. Guibert but the following beers were still being produced.

Leffe Blonde (6.7% alc/vol.) 25cl,33cl,75cl,300cl bottles and draught.
Known Ingredients: Pilsener and aromatic malts. English and Australian hops. A surprisingly light beer for its strength with a dry, spicy hop nose; smooth full flavoured malt and hop palate and a dry finish.

Leffe Brune (6.5% alc/vol.) 25cl,33cl,75cl,300cl bottles and draught.
Known Ingredients: Pilsener, torrefied and aromatic malts. English and Australian hops. A predominantly dark malt beer with a little fruit in the nose, chocolate in the palate and burnt malt in the finish.

Leffe Radieuse (8.3% alc/vol.) 25cl, 33cl, 75cl bottles.
Known Ingredients: Pilsener, torrefied and aromatic malts. English and Australian hops. Spiced with bitter orange peel and coriander. A lightly spiced aromatic hop nose with an alcoholic spicy malt palate and a warming, bitter, very burnt malt finish.

Leffe Rousse (6.7% alc/vol.) Draught.
Known Ingredients: Pilsener, torrefied and aromatic malts. English and Australian hops. All 16,000 hl goes into barrels destined for the Italian market. Believed to be of the pale ale style.

Brasserie Silenrieux

✉ Rue Noupré, 5630 Silenrieux, Namur.

☎ 071 63 32 01 Fax: 071 66 82 04.

Monday-Friday 0830-1700. Weekends on demand.

Pre-arranged only. 15 days notice. In French and English. No charge. Tasting possible.

SHOP Cases, bottles and glasses.

500hl (in 1994).

→ The village of Silenrieux is half way between Beaumont and Philippeville on the N40. From Philippeville, drop down hill into village, turn left at the bottom and turn right at the T-junction. The cafe and brewery are on the right after 50 metres.

A tiny village amid the rolling plains west of Philippeville is perhaps an unlikely setting for a ground-breaking brewery, but Brasserie Silenrieux owes its very existence to local agriculture and, to this day, still promotes the products of its local farmers.

In February 1992 the brewery was started by a co-operative called Agripur which wanted to make greater use of two particular grains, which had recently been reintroduced into Wallonia, by using them in the brewing process. The business was later bought by a syndicate of businessmen, two of whom now work full time at the brewery.

Most ale drinkers will be familiar with grain other than malted barley being used in beer (i.e. wheat, oats, rye and occasionally maize) but few will have sampled the likes of buckwheat and spelt beers.

Buckwheat, sometimes known as black wheat, is an ancient grain with its origins in Asia and its use spread throughout the world only to fall from favour in Europe in the 1950s. Known as "sarrasin" in French, it was re-introduced into the Silenrieux area in 1989.

Spelt (epeautre in French) is a close relative of wheat which has the characteristically smooth but longer and more slender ears. The main reason for it not being more popular in the marketplace is due to the fact that spelt has strong husks around the grain which need to be removed by the additional process of husking prior to milling. The Spelta Mill at Neuville, near Philippeville, has this facility which has given Silenrieux easy access to a rare grain.

We know of no other Wallonian brewery using buckwheat and only Silenrieux, Blaugies and Mibrana using spelt.

The actual use of buckwheat and spelt in brewing also has inherent problems due to the fineness of the milled grain, which tends to clog up the works when filtering the wort from the mash tun (the same problem occurs when using wheat, but this problem can be eased if there is sufficient barley in the mash to act as a natural filter). However, Silenrieux has invested in a quite unique mash tun which filters the wort from the sides rather than the bottom. This piece of equipment – the only one of its type we have seen – represents a good deal of commitment to the use of such odd cereals which, the brewery believes, adds specific properties to its beers. Spelt, for instance, is said to impart a fruity aroma and a multi-layered taste as well as producing a good head.

We could wax lyrical about buckwheat and spelt, but in the finished products they give only hints of their properties. Joseph, one of the spelt beers, is essentially a bière blanche – presumably due to the similar characteristics of its cousin, wheat – but has an odd fruity note absent from normal white beers. Sara possesses a gently herbal, dark fruit character which we believe to be from the buckwheat.

The brewery acknowledges the assistance of the CIREP laboratory in Nevele and the brewing laboratory at Louvain-la-Neuve in the original development of its Joseph and Sara beers. These relationships have been maintained through the subsequent introduction of its Super Noël, Pavé de l'Ours and the "tweaking" of Sara in March 1995 to give it a more marketable palate.

Silenrieux currently brews once weekly in summer and once or twice per month in winter, with Joseph accounting for more than half of its annual output. Watch out for a beer they hope to produce one day – the plan is to use seven different cereals!

The brewery shares the building with a bar, also owned by the syndicate, which offers the full range of Silenrieux products including draught versions of Joseph and Sara and other beers in season. Called Chez l'Père Sarrasin (at the house of Father Buckwheat), the bar also sells bar snacks and local products such as cured meats, cheeses and honey and has internal windows looking onto the brewplant.

JOSEPH

6% alc/vol 25cl crown corked, 75cl corked & crown corked bottles and draught.

Known Ingredients: Pilsener malt, spelt. Lightly hopped. Spiced with bitter oranges.

Appearance: Lemon/gold colour with a slight wheaty tinge. Hazy with sediment.

Nose: Fresh lemon and a distinctive but unusual grainy note with a little yeast.

Palate: Nice clean, fresh, limey taste with some gentle hops and a touch of malt. Gently bitter and dry. Addition of sediment muddies the taste, but makes it more mellow with a better balance. KBR: Has a sharp citricity masking the discrete bitter notes.

Finish: Dry with a light bitterness and a distinctive, interesting malty element. KBR: Quite bland finish leaves you wanting more.

Overall: Interesting beer. A good, refreshing summer beer with a strangely distant but elusive complexity. KBR: Has an unfortunate clinical quality.

General: Pouring two or three glasses from a bottle, the first will be bright and very unlike a bière blanche in appearance. The beer changes enormously with the addition of sediment so we recommend trying it without first. On draught, Joseph is very different (arguably better) and it is always served with a distinct hazy bloom, leading us to believe this is how it should be drunk. **JDW: 8 / 8 KBR: 7 / 7**

PAVÉ DE L'OURS

8.5% alc/vol. 75cl corked & crown corked bottles.

Known Ingredients: Pilsener malt. Hop extract for bitterness and Saaz for aroma. Spiced with honey.

Appearance: Pale gold with a honeyed hue.

Nose: Distinct fresh hop with a sweetish background and some mustiness. KBR: A light trace of bitter honey.

Palate: Strong hop element with a good deal of pale malt. Nice tangy honey in the background which gets gradually stronger. Starts sweet but hop bitterness gives it a good, if slightly harsh, balance.

Finish: KBR: Hoppy bitterness gives way to a growing, eventually cloying, honey. JDW: Tangy honey grows, adding bitterness.

Overall: Well balanced at first, becoming cloying and sweet later. Honey beers tend to cloy by their nature but in this case it is offset well by the hops. KBR: Excellent beer which has acquired more "farmhouse" character. JDW: Aroma gives little clue to what palate holds.

General: Contract beer brewed for Philippe Plouvier from Biercée. Previously brewed by Brasserie Binchoise which now produces Bière des Ours to a similar recipe. Roughly translates as "the way (or path) of the bear". **JDW: 9 / 8 KBR: 8 / 8**

SARA

6% alc/vol. 75cl corked & crown corked bottles and draught.

Known Ingredients: Pilsener, caramel and black malt, buckwheat. Styrian Goldings and Record hops. Spiced with coriander.

Appearance: Lovely red/brown colour.

Nose: Good, dark, fruity malt with spicy characteristics and rich treacle notes in the distance. KBR: Distinct hints of ginger and black pepper. JDW: Herbal notes.

Palate: Intriguing initial impact of taste and texture, seeming both watery yet thick and creamy at the same time. Citric, fruity and malty with suggestions of a sweet dryness and a distinct herbal element. Develops a bittersweet tang with ginger and coriander spiciness. JDW: Both vinous and orchard fruits are present, while the dryness has a gentle ginger character to it.

FINISH: A disappointing way to end – just dry, fruity, bittersweet malt.

OVERALL: A good rich beer with plenty of interest in the nose and palate, let down by its bland finish. Wonderful beer to have on draught.

GENERAL: Sara is short for "sarrasin", French for buckwheat. Poor sales prompted the brewery to change the recipe in 1995. In contrast to the brewery's belief, we find the new beer to be more distinctive. The label used to depict a female version of the Joseph label, now it sports a scantily-clad siren tempting drinkers into her buckwheat field! Does sex sell? Let's wait and see!

JDW: 8 / 8 KBR: 7 / 8

SUPERNOËL

7.5% alc/vol. 75cl corked & crown corked bottles and draught.

KNOWN INGREDIENTS: Pilsener, caramel and black malt, spelt. Saaz and Record hops.

APPEARANCE: Dark chestnut brown with a short-lived beige head.

NOSE: Wonderfully rich and spicy with herbal, fruity notes mingled in with slightly roasted malt. Distinct whiffs of alcohol. KBR: Woody notes. JDW: Touch of chocolate.

PALATE: Rich, full and complex malt with a well-balanced bitterness. Elements of fruit, spice, herbs and a gentle roastiness. Spicy hops still manage to come through the full taste giving it some dryness. JDW: Gentle chocolate notes.

FINISH: Dry with heavily roasted malt yet retaining a good balance. Has slight astringency. JDW: Strongly chocolatey. KBR: Strangely thin with a slightly jarring tartness contrasting the dark roast.

OVERALL: A very good Christmas beer. KBR: Not as warming as I would like. JDW: Very malt based but with enough complex elements to lift it beyond being just a malty beer.

GENERAL: Was a great success in its trial in 1994, prompting the brewery to brew more for 1995.

JDW: 7 / 8 KBR: 7 / 6

OTHER BEERS

La Foire Verte (6% alc/vol): Produced for a local festival in 1994 using buckwheat. Wheaty and citric with a wonderful texture but sadly lacking in the taste department.

BARS & CAFES RECOMMENDED BY THE BREWERY

A LA PORTE DE FRANCE, Rue de France 1, Philippeville.
AUBERGE DE BEAUPONT, Rue de Beaupont 44, Silenrieux.
A LA TAVERNE DU PÈRE SARRASIN, Rue Noupre, Silenrieux.
L'EAU BLANCHE, Rue G. Joaris 27, Lompret.

BEER SHOPS RECOMMENDED BY THE BREWERY

DELHAIZE, Rte de Sergeilles, Cerfontaine.
UNIC, Rue de Bourlers 1, Chimay.
UNIC, Rue de France 39, Philippeville.
BRASSERIE MAGOTTEAUX, Rue de la Station 41, Froidchapelle.

Brasserie de Silly

✉ Rue Ville Basse 141, 7830 Silly, Hainaut.

☎ 068 54 16 95 Fax: 068 56 84 36.

🕓 Mon-Sat 0800-1200, 1400-1730.

Pre-arranged only. 28 days notice. In French. Free admission. Tastings available.

SHOP Cases only and glasses.

15,000hl (in 1994).

➔ Silly is just off the N57 just south of the N7 between Ath and Enghien. The brewery is at the north end of the village square.

You occasionally come upon a word which is perfectly sensible in the native language but means something totally different to those who speak a different tongue. Brasserie de Silly is just one such case. But whereas the "Mad Brewers" (De Dolle Brouwers) of Diksmuide in Flanders intentionally gave themselves an unusual tag, the Silly brewers have a perfectly rational explanation. The name comes from the fact that it is located in the centre of the village of Silly, which in turn takes its name from the River Sylle.

The brewery hasn't always been called Silly, however. When it was founded in 1850 it went under the name Cense de la Tour before later being re-christened Mynsbrughen after the family name of the current owner's mother. The final chapter of the story was in 1974 when the present name was chosen, apparently because it was easier to remember and gave a greater affinity with the area, thereby generating more local loyalty. Another consideration might have been that there were originally three breweries in the village but by 1974 it was the sole survivor thereby picking up the mantle as "the" Silly brewery.

The range of beers at Silly is vast – even after taking into account the label beers – although it should be noted that some appear to be based on other brews. Sixteen is a lot of different beers to justify in terms of production, promotion and marketing but the brewery seems to be doing well in Wallonia and exports are on the increase. Not only is there a huge range, there is also an unusually diverse amount of bottle sizes – for instance Scotch de Silly comes in 25cl, 33cl, 75cl, 150cl and on draught!

Despite the breadth and diversity of the range we find there is a distinctive house character to most of its ales (JDW often describes this as a vegetable taste, KBR identifies it as tannic fruit).

Perhaps best known of its products is Saison de Silly which is sold in most of the local bars on draught and represents a good example of what the brewery is all about. The Saison, along with its Super 64 and Brug Ale, shows that the brewery is still promoting honest, good quality, traditional, local ales many of which have been made for decades. A point of concern, though, is that Silly Pils is growing in popularity and now accounts for about 40% of the brewery's total annual output.

The taking over, in 1975, of the Tennstedt Decroes brewery in the nearby town of Enghien introduced the Spéciale Double Enghien (now called Double Enghien Brune) to the range, the popularity of which prompted the brewery to introduce a Blonde version in 1992.

Silly still make two table beers which, like those of Brasserie Gigi, have a character absent in the nationally-marketed contemporaries from the major brewers. Didier van der Haegen, the present owner of Silly, informed us that Belgian children once had the choice of drinking either table beer or milk at school, and believes the demise of ales (compared to the bottom fermented beers the younger generation now prefer) started when table beer was dropped by the education authorities. When he was elected as representative of small breweries at the CBB he was horrified to find that school parties visiting its museum were not offered a glass of table beer – a situation which has now been resolved.

Hopefully drinkers will remember the Silly brewery for its beers rather than its name. And if an Englishman starts making his beer under the name "Bête Brewery", perhaps the Walloons will then understand what's in a name.

BOCK

2.7% alc/vol. 33cl crown corked bottles.

APPEARANCE: Pale gold with little head.

NOSE: A gentle hoppiness.

PALATE: Dry but with a little sweet malt and a touch of citric hop.

FINISH: Dry and lightly bitter with a lingering fruity grain.

OVERALL: For such a weak beer it has a commendably interesting taste.

GENERAL: A blend of Royal Blonde and Silly Pils. Also sold as **Triple Bock**.

JDW: 6 / 4 KBR: 7 / 4

BRUG ALE

5% alc/vol. 33cl crown corked bottles.

KNOWN INGREDIENTS: Kent and Hallertau hops.

APPEARANCE: Amber with little head.

NOSE: Hoppy with some dry fruit. JDW: Some vegetable notes.

PALATE: A good, full taste with many different elements and plenty of fruit and hops. A little sweet.

FINISH: Full bittersweet taste which evolves into a fruity dryness. Slightly tannic.

OVERALL: Surprisingly interesting taste for a 5% beer. Possesses the typically Silly fruity ale characteristics.

GENERAL: Best drunk within a year of production. First brewed around 1940. **JDW: 7 / 6 KBR: 8 / 6**

DOUBLE ENGHIEN BLONDE

7.5% alc/vol. 25cl crown corked and 75cl & 150cl corked bottles. Also available on draught.

KNOWN INGREDIENTS: Pale malt. Kent and Saaz hops.

APPEARANCE: Dull old gold with a slight, scummy head.

NOSE: Full malty aroma with some wheatiness and spice, hops, lemon and caramel all noticeable.

PALATE: Good full palate, initially a little sweet, becoming more bitter. Very fruity and malty with some wheat and hops, the latter becoming more pronounced the more you drink.

FINISH: Long lasting, interesting finish which begins with a fruity, bitter malt, before developing into a strong, dry bitterness.

OVERALL: Easy drinking yet characterful ale with many typically Walloon traits. Has a very pleasant smooth, creamy texture.

GENERAL: First brewed in 1992. **JDW: 7 / 6 KBR: 7 / 7**

DOUBLE ENGHIEN BRUNE

8% alc/vol. 25cl & 33cl crown corked and 75cl & 150cl corked bottles.

KNOWN INGREDIENTS: Kent and Hallertau hops.

APPEARANCE: Dull, dark amber colour.

NOSE: Mellow aroma of fruity malt over a spicy hop background.

PALATE: Full, very fruity, bitter, roast malt with an unfortunate metallic edge. The hops give it a freshness surprising for a brune.

FINISH: Lingering roasted, bitter malt and a little spiciness

OVERALL: An overtly fruity beer redeemed by good use of hops in the palate and a strong "after dinner" finish.

GENERAL: First brewed in 1860, taken on by Silly in 1975 after purchasing the Tennstedt Decroes brewery. Until recently sold as **Spéciale Double Enghien**. **JDW: 6 / 6 KBR: 7 / 6**

LA DIVINE

9.5% alc/vol. 33cl crown corked bottles. Also available on draught.

KNOWN INGREDIENTS: Kent hops.

APPEARANCE: Copper coloured with a variable head.

NOSE: Very fruity aroma. KBR: Alcohol and herbs on a dark roasted malt base. JDW: Pear drops.

PALATE: Full tasting with vinous fruit, a gentle acidic hop bitterness and a little roasted malt. Quite a sharp alcohol bite. KBR: Tannic with a touch of herbal tartness.

FINISH: Roast malt and a tangy bitterness with a warming alcohol glow. KBR: Some leftover herbs and tannin.

OVERALL: Frighteningly easy to drink at 9.5%. Uncompromisingly strong, dark and fruity (perhaps a little over-fruity) but distinctly Wallonian ale.

GENERAL: First brewed in 1991. The name along with the depiction of a chapel on the label back up the brewery's claim that it is in the abbey style.

JDW: 7 / 6 KBR: 8 / 7

ROYALE BLONDE

1.5% alc/vol. 33cl and 75cl crown corked bottles.

KNOWN INGREDIENTS: Saaz and Hallertau hops.

APPEARANCE: Dull insipid gold.

NOSE: Earthy, light maltiness.

PALATE: Sweet. KBR: A touch malty with tannic hints. JDW: A little hop bitterness.

FINISH: Dry. KBR: Refreshing, lightly fruity malt. JDW: Hop dryness.

OVERALL: Pleasant enough table beer with more character than most of the mass market brands.

JDW: 5 / 3 KBR: 6 / 4

SAISON DE SILLY

5% alc/vol. 25cl crown corked and 75cl corked bottles. Also available on draught.

KNOWN INGREDIENTS: Kent and Hallertau hops.

APPEARANCE: Rich amber.

NOSE: A distinct earthy fruitiness with a mellow maltiness. KBR: A little metallic.

PALATE: Very interesting, quite sweet blend of malt, hop and fruit with citric and tannic notes and a subtle spiciness.

FINISH: A dry, fruity tang.

OVERALL: A good example of an honest, fruity, saison beer – perhaps too fruity for some.

GENERAL: First brewed around 1900. A number of 25cl bottles have been known to be extremely lively when opened, although this seems to reduce as the beer gets older and if chilled. The beer is a blend of a number of different saison brews, some of which can be well over a year old. Cheapest of the Silly ales (excluding table beers) and appears to be a local favourite.

JDW: 8 / 7 KBR: 7 / 6

SCOTCH DE SILLY

8% alc/vol. 25cl & 33cl crown corked and 75cl & 150cl corked bottles. Also available on draught.

KNOWN INGREDIENTS: Caramel malt. Kent and Hallertau hops.

APPEARANCE: Amber with a slight head.

NOSE: Hoppy malt. KBR: Tannic promise.

PALATE: Quite complex and fairly rich, malty, fruity taste with a fair degree of pear drop alcohol. JDW: Butterscotch hints. KBR: Very tannic with treacle/ toffee hints and some sweetness.

FINISH: Strong alcohol notes enhance a lasting, fruity malt bitterness.

OVERALL: Wonderful, easy drinking Scotch ale. Not particularly traditional in style, but thankfully has not followed the trend towards sweet insipidity.

GENERAL: Although first produced in 1850 the name was not changed to Scotch de Silly until World War II. The draught version has some lactic sourness in the palate and finish but still retains its superbly balanced taste. Can be kept for many years (the brewery states it peaks at 10 years old) but we would recommend it to be drunk within one or two years of purchase.

JDW: 8 / 8 KBR: 7 / 7

SILBRAU DORT

6% alc/vol. 25cl crown corked bottles.

APPEARANCE: Light golden amber.

NOSE: Clean with a dry malt and a sharp citric hop.

PALATE: Sweet and grainy with a touch of citric fruit.

FINISH: Dry and grainy. Sweet hop notes.

OVERALL: Certainly has a Dortmunder style character but is a little too one dimensional to be of any real interest. Odd dark grains of sediment at the bottom of the bottle.

GENERAL: This is a spicy version of Silly Pils with added sugar.

JDW: 4 / 3 KBR: 4 / 3

SILLY PILS

4.8% alc/vol. 25cl crown corked bottles. Also available on draught.

KNOWN INGREDIENTS: Pale malt. Saaz hops.

APPEARANCE: Pale gold with little head.

NOSE: Sweet citric hops. JDW: Some pale malt lurking in the background and that distinctive Silly aroma.

PALATE: JDW: A little sweet with a gentle grainy hop taste. KBR: Sweet start turning to a dry hoppiness with very little taste.

FINISH: Tangy citric bitterness which gradually dries the mouth. KBR: A little fruit.

OVERALL: Pleasant interesting tasting pils with a smoother than usual texture and a caressing mouthfeel.

GENERAL: First brewed in 1948 and, until recently, called **Myn's Pils**.

JDW: 6 / 5 KBR: 6 / 4

SUPER 64

5% alc/vol. 25cl crown corked bottles.

KNOWN INGREDIENTS: Kent and Hallertau hops.

APPEARANCE: Orange amber with a scummy head.

NOSE: Malty fruit with a surprising spicy hop element.

PALATE: Slightly sweet, with a little fruit and a harsh, dry tannic tang. Disappointing after the nose.

FINISH: Slightly dry with a tangy hop overpowering the fruity hints.

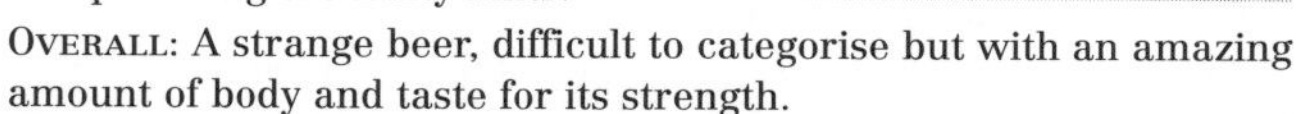

OVERALL: A strange beer, difficult to categorise but with an amazing amount of body and taste for its strength.

GENERAL: First brewed in 1964. With different conditioning this beer becomes **Abbaye de Cambron** as sold at Le Domain at Cambron-Casteau, a ruined abbey north of Mons.

JDW: 6 / 4 KBR: 4 / 5

TITJE

4.8% alc/vol. 25cl & 33cl crown corked bottles. Also available on draught.

KNOWN INGREDIENTS: Pale malt. Wheat. Very few hops. Spiced with coriander and orange peel.

APPEARANCE: Cloudy wheat colour with little or no head.

NOSE: Very unusual. Slightly sour and milky spiced wheat with some yeastiness.

PALATE: Also very unusual. Reasonably complex with elements of malt, wheat, fruit, spice, lemon, yeast and cream. Strangely acidic, even sour.

FINISH: Spicy with lemon, lime and some sourness.

OVERALL: Unique and characterful white beer. Not at all what you would expect.

GENERAL: First brewed in 1990. The draught version is very different with a floral, very wheaty nose, a little spice in the palate and a spicy wheat finish. The word Titje is a slang nickname for inhabitants of the town of Enghien.

JDW: 6 / 5 KBR: 7 / 6

OTHER BEERS

Cervoise de l'Avouerie d'Anthisnes (8% alc/vol.): Very malty character with some fruit and spice.

Cuvée de Hauts Voues (8% alc/vol.): A distinctly malty beer with a bittersweet fruitiness and some spice. Also sold as **La Gueule Noire Koempelbier** when labelled for Corman-Collins.

Villers St. Ghislain Blonde (7.2% alc/vol.): Special brew for Michaux Seconde. A very hoppy beer with an disappointingly tangy finish.

Villers St. Ghislain Brune (8% alc/vol.): Another brew for Michaux Seconde. Pronounced malt character, reminiscent of a British barley wine.

BARS & CAFES RECOMMENDED BY THE BREWERY

CAFE DE LA BRASSERIE, Place, Silly.
TITIEN, Place 17, Bassilly.
LE SALON, Rue Ville Basse 152, Silly.
A L'TONNE, Place 19, Silly.

Brasserie de la Tour

✉ Rue Chera 9, 4180 Comblain-la-Tour, Liège.

☎ 041 69 38 87.

Sat/Sun 1000-1600.

Pre-arranged only. In French, English or Flemish. No charge.

Cases and bottles.

Currently non-productive (see article).

➔ Comblain-la-Tour is just south of Comblain-au-Pont on the N654 south of Liège. The brewery is located at Antoine's house and is difficult to find. Get directions in advance or arrange to meet in the Café des Sports when you phone to arrange a visit.

Antoine Gilissen is a lucky man. He lives in a house idyllically situated on the side of a hill with a commanding view over the rolling countryside around the pretty village of Comblain-la-Tour. He has been successfully self-employed for a number of years and has now fulfilled his dream to build a brewery underneath the house.

He is also an unlucky man. Doing all the construction work himself in his spare time he has built what most visitors would consider a tasteful and quite professional conversion of a garage into a perfectly good, small brewery. The authorities, on the other hand, have taken quite a different view. Recent tightening up of regulations governing the starting up of new breweries has meant that beer needs to be made in a building more akin to a hospital and Antoine has been trying since early 1995 to meet the inspectors' requirements. The most recent set-back was that the walls inside the brewery were deemed not to be smooth enough to facilitate easy washing down – which has meant completely re-rendering them. He finally received the go-ahead from the powers-that-be early in 1996 and produced his first brew in April, intending to be fully up and running by June. After investing a lot of time (and a lot of money) into his venture he remains philosophical about the whole affair and it is good to see that determination will probably win through in the end.

Having been a keen home brewer for a number of years, Antoine has long wanted to brew commercially and perfected the recipe for his sole product, Magonette, with a lot of help from his friends through numerous tasting sessions. Should the business take off he has recipes for some other beers but is content with concentrating on just the one at present.

Magonette is a very adventurous brew with some unusual spices. The beer is named after a highwayman/robber who terrorised the neighbourhood in times past.

Comblain-la-Tour (and hence Brasserie de la Tour) takes its name from the now demolished tower which stood atop the hill close to the brewery.

The area around Comblain-au-Pont is a popular holiday spot for campers and caravanners in the summer and Antoine is hoping that this will become a burgeoning market for his beers. There has been some interest in nearby bars and hotels but in the foreseeable future it appears that Magonette and subsequent products from la Tour will be available only in the very local area.

Antoine is in the enviable position where, if the brewing venture is a success, he can ease in gently by gradually winding down his "real" work. We wish him luck.

MAGONETTE

8.2% alc/vol. 33cl crown corked bottles.

Known Ingredients: Pale malt. Goldings and Hallertau hops. Spiced with cinnamon, hawthorn flowers plus other undisclosed ingredients.

Appearance: Dull orange with little head.

Nose: Peppery, spicy malt and a dry promise. JDW: Earthy and herbal with some hop notes. KBR: Very hoppy nose which only lasts for a few seconds before being replaced with a peppery, fruity malt.

Palate: Very dry, slightly tart malt with interesting herbal elements. JDW: Some astringency and bitterness. Earthy with a touch of fruit. KBR: Vinous bite in the start, with a gorgeous depth of flavour with herbs, fruit, an odd spice plus a good hoppiness.

Finish: Unusually, less dry than the palate. Herbal, fruity malt with a bitter and tart character.

Overall: Very interesting, complex beer where the tartness does not detract from the appeal as you would expect. However, those with a more inhibited palate should approach with caution.

General: First brewed in 1996.

JDW: 7 / 6 KBR: 7 / 6

BARS & CAFES RECOMMENDED BY THE BREWERY

Antoine has been approaching local bars and cafes but hadn't finalised any arrangements at the time of going to press.

BEER SHOPS RECOMMENDED BY THE BREWERY

Magonette is only available from the brewery.

Brasserie de l'Union

✉ Rue Derbecque 7, 6040 Charleroi (Jumet), Hainaut.

☎ 071 35 01 33 Fax: 071 34 02 34.

🕓 Mon-Sat 08.30-17.00.

Pre-arranged only. 28 days notice. In English, French and Flemish. No charge. No tastings available.

SHOP Cases, bottles and glasses.

220,000hl (in 1995).

→ See article.

Union is the only Wallonian outpost of the giant Alken-Maes brewing group (which in turn is part of the French conglomerate Groupe Danone). It is second only in output to the space-age Jupiler beer factory, yet has managed to retain a human scale and is quite personable for an operation of such a size.

It is in an unlikely location surrounded by residential buildings in Jumet, a quiet suburb of the heavily-industrialised ex-mining town of Charleroi. To give accurate directions of how to find it is almost impossible – the best we can advise is to leave at Junction 23 of the A54 and follow the signs in the general direction of the hospital. Once you reach cobbled roads and dense housing, you will have to ask one of the locals.

Judging by the amalgam of different architectural styles, Union has had many different stages of development and redevelopment. The picture above shows the main façade which presumably dates from the art-deco period of the 20s and 30s. The design of this structure does a good job of showcasing the beautiful coppers which can be seen through the huge windows as they curve round a road junction. The rest of the building is of more sombre industrial brickwork, more in keeping with most of its surroundings (as shown on the right).

The brewery has stood on the original site since it was founded in 1864 and is very proud of its long history, which once included a major maltings and the winning of numerous medals from the once-ubiquitous international beer exhibitions.

More recently, however, Union gained notoriety as a pils producer and, even worse, as the continental brewer of Watney's Red Barrel. The latter is still brewed to this day in keg form, albeit solely for export to Italy. The Watney connection came about when Grand Metropolitan owned the parent company in the 70s and Red Barrel and Watney's Scotch are a hangover from that period, proving that a famous British brewing name can still sell beer.

An early Cuvée de l'Ermitage poster.

Today, Union remains a formidable force in Wallonian brewing and produces only top-fermenting beers, some of which are refermented in the bottle. Its large portfolio of beers includes the disappointingly lack-lustre Ciney range, and perhaps its most famous product – Cuvée de l'Ermitage – named after one of the ancient hermitages which abound in the woodlands of southern Wallonia (although there is some dispute as to exactly which one).

We find most of the Union range exudes a slightly artificial quality (despite the use of quality ingredients) and are generally a little on the sweet side. This trait does not seem to have dented the appeal of Union beers, however, with the Grimbergen brews apparently being the best selling Belgian abbey beers in the Netherlands.

We have also noticed a tendency for some of its products to become blander and sweeter in recent years – a shame especially for a beer of Cuvée's pedigree.

CINEY BLONDE

7% alc/vol. 25cl crown corked bottles. Also available on draught.

Known Ingredients: Two row spring malt. German and English hops.

Appearance: Gold with a short-lived head.

Nose: Faint pale malt with a chemical nature. KBR: A distant wheat.

Palate: Sweet. KBR: Metallic with no depth of taste. JDW: Unpleasant detergent-like tang with just hints of malt.

Finish: KBR: Earthy metal notes with a touch of malt. JDW: Dry and a little bitter but the overriding taste is a metallic/chemical tang.

Overall: An unfulfilling beer which neither excites the taste buds nor quenches the thirst.

General: Like the rest of the Ciney range, the label states it is brewed for the Brasserie Demarche in Ciney.

JDW: 1 / 1 KBR: 2 / 2

CINEY BRUNE

7% alc/vol. 25cl crown corked bottles. Also available on draught.

Known Ingredients: Two row spring & winter and special malts. English hops.

Appearance: Deep brown with red highlights.

Nose: Lightly malty with suggestions of a saccharin sweetness. KBR: Metallic with a little caramel.

PALATE: KBR: Watery, with very little taste – just a slightly dry, bitter roasted malt. JDW: Initially a lot of malt which quickly fades but never quite disappears.

FINISH: Some roast malt.

OVERALL: Another disappointing beer. The nose was not particularly impressive but suggested more than the beer could deliver.

GENERAL: The label states it is brewed for the Brasserie Demarche in Ciney. **JDW: 4 / 3 KBR: 2 / 2**

CINEY SPÉCIALE

9% alc/vol. 33cl crown corked bottles.

KNOWN INGREDIENTS: Two row spring & winter and special malts. English hops.

APPEARANCE: Dark brown with cherry red notes and a large, lasting head.

NOSE: KBR: Sweet, fruity malt with some chemical notes. JDW: A slightly sweet, rich fruitiness.

PALATE: KBR: Sweet start, then a dry, roast malt with peppery hints. JDW: Quite sweet with a candy sugar taste marring the full, fruity, chocolatey, bitter, roast malt.

FINISH: KBR: Rich, dry and strong in alcohol with lingering saccharin notes. JDW: Very dry with a tangy chocolate bitterness and lingering saccharin notes.

OVERALL: KBR: Fruity, warming ale, high in roast malt but still has some sacchariness – worth a try though as the best of the Cineys. JDW: Pleasant, fruity malt and bitter chocolate marred by strong candy sugar taste.

GENERAL: Flagship of the Ciney range. **JDW: 5 / 4 KBR: 6 / 5**

CUVÉE DE L'ERMITAGE

8.5% alc/vol. 25cl and 33cl crown corked bottles.

KNOWN INGREDIENTS: Two row spring & winter and special malts. German and English hops.

APPEARANCE: Dark amber brown with a short-lived head.

NOSE: Dark malt. KBR: Smells sweet. JDW: Strong aroma, hints of caramel.

PALATE: KBR: An initial sweetness then a hit of roasted, lightly smokey malt with suggestions of molasses. JDW: Sweet, smooth, rich, malt with a little vinous fruit and a touch of caramel. A little bitter.

FINISH: KBR: Rich and warming, nutty, roast malt with some artificial sweetness. Gives the impression of dryness. JDW: Slighty candied sweetness with a caramel malt tang.

OVERALL: KBR: Full-bodied winter warmer with a long lingering finish spoiled only by a sweetness which seems to have been forced upon it. JDW: A moderately complex beer though the finish disappoints due to the strong, candied sweetness.

GENERAL: Used to be 7.5% and much less sweet.

JDW: 6 / 5 KBR: 7 / 6

CUVÉE DE L'ERMITAGE CHRISTMAS

8% alc/vol. 25cl and 33cl crown corked bottles.

KNOWN INGREDIENTS: Two row spring & winter and special malts. German and English hops.

APPEARANCE: Rich, dark red amber with minimal head.

NOSE: Lashings of warming malt and very fruity.

PALATE: Very rich, warming malt with a distinct but not invasive sweetness. Slight burnt edge to the malt which is tempered by some fruit.

FINISH: Slightly disturbing burnt saccharin which spoils the potentially superb fruity malt finish.

OVERALL: Shame about the burnt edge to the palate and the saccharin in the finish – it could have been an excellent after-dinner beer.

GENERAL: Obviously Cuvée de L'Ermitage with a winter tweak. Can be difficult to obtain.

JDW: 7 / 5 KBR: 7 / 6

GRIMBERGEN BLONDE

7% alc/vol. 25cl & 33cl crown corked bottles. Also on draught.

KNOWN INGREDIENTS: Two row spring malt. German and English hops.

APPEARANCE: Bright golden.

NOSE: A wheaty background. KBR: Spicy and dry. JDW: Hops.

PALATE: KBR: Very full tasting. Principally wheaty character with a dryness, some metal and lactic notes. JDW: Overpoweringly sweet, but behind the saccharin is a gentle blend of hops and wheat with some citric notes.

FINISH: KBR: Wheaty, lactic, creamy. JDW: Dry with gentle bitterness.

OVERALL: KBR: Reasonably interesting blonde ale. JDW: Typifies what the multi-nationals do best.

GENERAL: Grimbergen is just north of Brussels and the label depicts the Phoenix rising from the ashes.

JDW: 4 / 3 KBR: 3 / 4

GRIMBERGEN DOUBLE

6.5% alc/vol. 25cl & 33cl crown corked bottles and 75cl corked bottles. Also available on draught.

KNOWN INGREDIENTS: Two row spring & winter and special malts. English hops. E300 (in 75cl bottles).

APPEARANCE: Deep brown with red notes.

NOSE: KBR: Fruity roasted malt and saccharin. JDW: Gentle, fruity malt.

PALATE: Lots of sweet malt. KBR: Dark and slightly artificially sweet fruity malt which lacks depth. JDW: Fruity, with a little bitter chocolate and some saccharin.

FINISH: KBR: A bland dryness and roasted bitterness with some metal notes. JDW: A mouthdrying bitterness and a slight saccharin malt tang.

OVERALL: Starts promisingly but fades to a disappointing blandness in the end. A 75cl bottle should be shared as it can become very sickly after a glass or two.

GENERAL: 75cl bottles are paper-wrapped while the smaller bottles have standard labels.

JDW: 5 / 4 KBR: 5 / 4

GRIMBERGEN OPTIMO BRUNO

10% alc/vol. 25cl & 33cl crown corked bottles.

KNOWN INGREDIENTS: Two row spring & winter and special malts. German and English hops.

APPEARANCE: Copper/amber in colour. Very little head

NOSE: Big aroma of pear drops. JDW: Sweet and malty. KBR: Fruity malt with a figgy (almost syrup of figs) character.

PALATE: JDW: Quite a harsh taste of caramel malt and pear drops. KBR: Very full taste of a rich figgy sweetness with burnt malt.

FINISH: JDW: Slightly cloying, tangy, caramel malt. KBR: Warming, fruity roasted malt – overpowering, tiresome after just one glass.

OVERALL: Totally uncompromising with a strong pear drop alcohol overlaying a full malty (JDW: caramel; KBR roasted) background. Attacks the tastebuds with a powerful mouthful of taste. KBR: Too strong a taste to drink much of.

JDW: 8 / 7 KBR: 8 / 7

GRIMBERGEN TRIPLE

9% alc/vol. 25cl & 33cl crown corked bottles and 75cl corked bottles.

KNOWN INGREDIENTS: Two row spring malts. German and English hops.

APPEARANCE: Golden colour with a good head.

NOSE: KBR: A dry hoppiness with metallic and wheaty notes. JDW: Citric hop aroma overlying a thick, sweet pale malt.

PALATE: KBR: Quite multi-layered taste with a full and sweetish, slightly wheaty, lactic background. JDW: Loads of smooth pale malt with a harsh bitter hop edge and a slight thickish sweetness in the background. Some lemon notes to the hops.

FINISH: KBR: Some dryness with pronounced alcohol and wheat hints. JDW: Sweet alcohol precedes a bitter hop tang. Slightly astringent.

OVERALL: Certainly leaves you in no doubt as to the alcohol content but comes across as a reasonably full flavoured but quite sweet version of a triple. With less sweetness it has the potential to be a good beer. Better in 75cl form (particularly when aged a little) as the smaller bottles are sweeter, detracting from the taste.

GENERAL: 75cl bottles are paper-wrapped while the smaller bottles have standard labels.

JDW: 6 / 5 KBR: 6 / 5

JUDAS

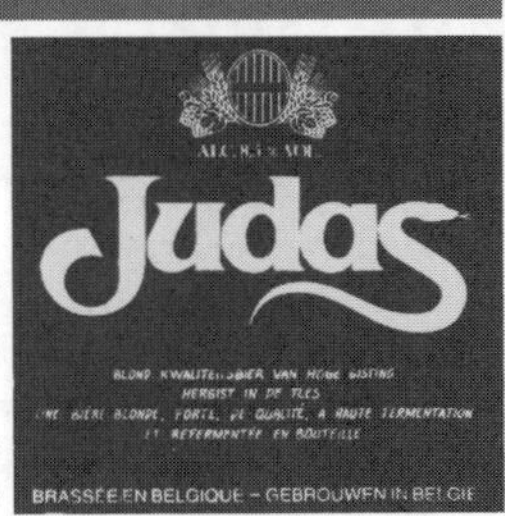

8.5% alc/vol. 33cl crown corked bottles.

KNOWN INGREDIENTS: Two row spring malt. German and English hops.

APPEARANCE: Golden. Good fluffy head.

NOSE: Very hoppy with a full, sweet, pale malt and suggestions of alcohol. KBR: Spicy hints.

PALATE: Starts sweetish though this drops off to a gentle bitterness. A strong pale malt and a distinctive hoppiness which has quite a harsh edge to it. JDW: Occasionally you catch the alcohol notes.

FINISH: Very dry and hoppy with an odd bitterness which has an unfortunate chemical tang in the background.

OVERALL: Quite good example of a Duvel-type golden ale with a strong taste. Not a bad substitute, but lacks the complexity.

GENERAL: The proper Judas glass, although very delicate, makes a wonderful tasting glass.

JDW: 6 / 5 KBR: 6 / 5

WATNEYS SCOTCH ALE

8% alc/vol. 25cl crown corked bottles. Also available on draught.

KNOWN INGREDIENTS: Two row spring & winter and special malts. English hops.

APPEARANCE: Rich, reddish mid-brown with just a scummy head.

NOSE: JDW: Sweet with a well-balanced dark malt and fruit aroma. KBR: Gives you a good idea of the excruciating sweetness to come.

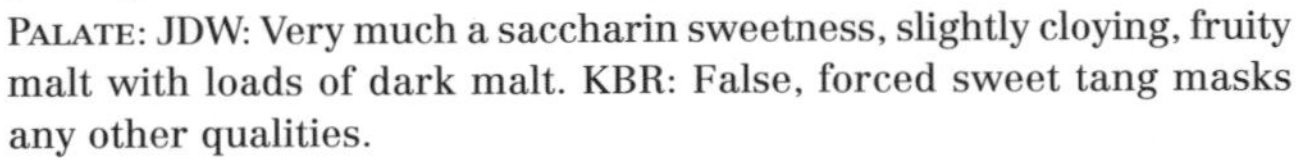

PALATE: JDW: Very much a saccharin sweetness, slightly cloying, fruity malt with loads of dark malt. KBR: False, forced sweet tang masks any other qualities.

FINISH: JDW: Dry and bitter with a fruity, slightly burnt, malt and a little saccharin tang. KBR: Some dryness from the roasted malt comes through but the residues of the sweet palate still marr the taste.

OVERALL: JDW: It certainly doesn't taste 8% and is far too sweet and cloying to be considered a true example of a Scotch Ale – although the trend by the major Continental brewers is towards this excrutiatingly sweet and sticky offering. KBR: Not one of my favourites!

GENERAL: One of the left-over labels from the days when Watney owned the present Alken-Maes group.

JDW: 4 / 2 KBR: 3 / 1

OTHER BEERS

Faro (1.25% alc/vol.).

Rubens Goud (4.3% alc/vol.): Golden/orange coloured beer. KBR: Hoppy, slightly fruity aroma, dry uninspiring malt and hop taste with a short-lived malt and caramel finish. JDW: Yeasty wheat aroma with hints of orange and an odd, grainy, tangy wheat taste and a dry bitter finish.

Watneys Red Barrel (6% alc/vol.): Draught only. 2,000hl per year. All exported.

BARS & CAFES RECOMMENDED BY THE BREWERY

On sale widely through Belgium.

Brasserie À Vapeur

✉ Rue Du Marechal 1, 7904 Leuze-en-Hainaut (Pipaix), Hainaut.

☎ 069 66 20 47 (fax also).

🕓 Mon-Wed & Fri-Sat 10.00-19.00.

Pre-arranged only. 5 days notice. In English and French. 100 Bfr charge. Tastings available. Also last Saturday of the month open days when brewery can be seen working.

SHOP Cases, bottles and glasses.

480hl (in 1995).

➔ Pipaix is just west of Leuze-en-Hainaut and the brewery is on the north side of the school in the centre of the village.

The words Brasserie À Vapeur translate into English as 'The Steam Brewery' which is an apt description for a brewery which uses steam for heat and to power all the equipment for its brewing process. The brewplant – and its operation – is a throwback to the turn of the century and the local tourist information has Vapeur listed as a brewing museum in recognition of its exclusivity as a fine working example of Wallonia's industrial heritage.

It may seem odd to discover an overtly factory-like operation in the heart of a peaceful, rural village but the brewery has been in Pipaix since 1785 and most of the buildings you will see today date back to the end of the last century when even farms were modernised to take advantage of the new, labour-saving technology of the industrial age.

At the rear of the main building is a drive-in yard and a beer shop which stocks all of the Vapeur beers (including many different vintages) and some of the difficult to obtain Walloon beers. On the opposite side of the road from the brewery is the characterful sampling room and a large room with kitchens for entertaining groups.

Since Cosne-Damien Cuvelier and Marie-Alexandrine Moulin started the brewery in 1785, it passed through five generations of the family before Jean-Louis Dits and Anne-Marie Lemaire, two local school teachers, bought it in 1984 by which time much of the operation had fallen into disuse. After years of hard work and dedication (and a tragic accident at the brewery which claimed the life of Anne-Marie), Vapeur has become one of the more impressive beer producers – not in capacity, but certainly in the quality and uniqueness of its brews.

The industrial brickwork of Vapeur's buildings contrasts with the rural setting.

All of Vapeur's beers have an immense depth of complexity – even its light beer – although it must be said that they may not be for the unitiated. Some can have traditional lambic-like qualities, and most will improve for many years if kept well in a good cellar (Jean-Louis released some 10-year-old Saison de Pipaix for its anniversary which had aged superbly despite only being 6.5%). Tastes of different brews can vary a great deal – although the quality seldom drops – which, we believe, adds to the interest of Vapeur's products.

The brewery advises that its beers are best stored on their side if they are to be laid down for some time. Most of them will improve with age, although it should be pointed out that ageing will probably accentuate the sourness.

For beer connoisseurs a visit to the brewery is an absolute must. It is wonderful to see the beer production in its full, steamy flow and an afternoon or evening in the company of the indefatigable and charismatic Jean-Louis and his new wife, Vinciane, is a real experience.

An in-depth feature on a typical Vapeur brewery open day is given at the front of this book.

Opposite the brewery is the characterful sampling room (on the left in the picture) abutting a larger function room with kitchens.

COCHONNE / COCHONETTE

9% alc/vol. 75cl corked & crown corked bottles and 25cl crown corked (under the name **Cochonette**).

Known Ingredients: Pilsener and Munich malts. Kent golding hops. Spiced with coriander, roast chicory, sweet orange peel. Candy sugar.

Appearance: Lovely golden orange colour with a short-lived head.

Nose: Excellent blend of fruit and malt with strong suggestions of sourness. KBR: A little musty with a dry promise and a touch of spice. JDW: Slight orange notes.

Whatever label you choose, it's always the same beer inside the bottle.

PALATE: Hints of sweetness at the start rapidly becoming a pleasant sourness which compliments the bittersweet fruit (orange, lemon, lime, grapefruit and crabapples) and a touch of spice. Sediment takes the bite out of the sourness but makes it pervade the whole palate.

FINISH: Very dry but surprisingly also saliva-inducing from the citric acidity. A lasting pale malt, bittersweet tang.

COMMENTS: Excellent, complex, full-flavoured, refreshing beer which would suit most occasions. Better without too much of the sediment.

GENERAL: First brewed in 1992 but has been getting sweeter as the brewery tries to appeal to the modern taste trend. The cartoon pig on the label was inspired by a Belgian comic and mimics the motions of a Walloon students' drinking song. When the beer went for export to Canada there were comments about its sexual nature, so Jean-Louis mockingly redesigned the labels with the figures wearing scant clothing and the words "censored" across the title. Now, however, the saga has gone full circle and the designs have returned to their "uncensored" versions. Vapeur grudgingly accepts that in some markets it needs to offer the beer in 25cl bottles but decided to give Cochonette a different identity (as they have with Vapeur Blonde) because they believe its beers will not mature in the same way in a 25cl bottle. KBR agrees with the brewery's sentiments and points out that the marks below from him are for the 75cl version, after having found the Cochonette far less complex and lacking the bittersweet fruit to counter the sourness.

Note: The Cochonne available during summer 1996 bore no resemblance to previous vintages (we were told this was due to a change of yeast), so at the time of going to press we have opted to keep the tasting notes of the previous three years' vintages. We can only hope that these notes will apply again soon!

JDW: 9 / 9 KBR: 9 / 9

SAISON DE PIPAIX

6.5% alc/vol. 75cl corked & crown corked bottles.

KNOWN INGREDIENTS: Pilsener and Munich malts. Hallertau hops. Spiced with pepper, ginger, curacao and sweet orange peels.

APPEARANCE: Gorgeous orange / amber colour with a light head.

NOSE: Slightly sour with orange notes in a light malt aroma. KBR: Musty, damp hay – some bottles may even exude an inviting, lambic-like nose.

PALATE: A distinct, though not overpowering, sharp sourness dominates. A good deal of fruit – mostly apple, but some orange and lemon.

FINISH: Dry, lingering acidity prevails over a slight astringency.

OVERALL: A superb blend of tastes and, for a beer of only 6.5%, has a light, unassuming complexity. In some ways, it could almost be described as a fruity, malty version of a superior gueuze. The acidity is reduced a little with the addition of some sediment which may make it more accessible to the uninitiated. KBR: My marks below reflect a young version – well aged it can attain a 10/10.

GENERAL: This is the brew on which the brewery was founded back in 1785, though pepper is now substituted for the original lichen (which sadly is no longer flourishing in today's unclean air).

JDW: 9 / 8 KBR: 8 / 8

VAPEUR EN FOLIE / VAPEUR BLONDE

8% alc/vol. 75cl corked and crown corked bottles. Also available in 25cl crown corked bottles, labelled as **Vapeur Blonde**.

KNOWN INGREDIENTS: Pale malt. Hallertau hops. Spiced with cumin.

APPEARANCE: Bright gold colour with no real head unless forced.

NOSE: Citric with a little fruity grain and a distinct sour promise. When aged it suggests great depth of character and maturity. KBR: Almost a champagne-type character but with an injection of malt and a slight mustiness, especially with sediment.

PALATE: Starts with a citric bite and a powerful sourness which gains a refreshing quality which serves to accentuate the clean but complex, sweet and dry blend of hops, malt, fruit and spice.

FINISH: Gentle acidic crabapple sourness.

OVERALL: Wonderfully complex, full-flavoured and refreshing ale with an amazing balance.

GENERAL: First brewed in 1986. Anyone with a good cellar should consider buying a batch of Folie to lay down as it matures to become even more complex and rewarding than it is in its youth, making it one our favourite beers.

The name derives from the original brew, called **Château de la Follie** which was commissioned by a group of local people and distributed with a label depicting the Château de Follie.

JDW: 9 / 9 KBR: 10 / 10

VAPEUR ROUSSE

8% alc/vol. 75cl corked & crown corked bottles.

KNOWN INGREDIENTS: Pale and amber malts. Hallertau hops. Spiced with coriander, bitter orange peel and roast chicory.

APPEARANCE: Deep orange gold with minimal head.

NOSE: Highly aromatic initially, but short-lived. Mostly a sour malt with a touch of caramel.

PALATE: A large kick of sharp, citric sourness in the start, before developing a bitterness within a fruity, mostly grapefruit, taste. JDW: Hints of fruity spice.

FINISH: Acidic with lingering grapefruit and growing bitterness. KBR: Builds to a crescendo of sour dryness which lasts for ages.

OVERALL: Excellent, characterful, quite complex beer (as long as you can handle the acidity). Its summer refresher qualities are marred only by a slight tendency towards a cloying character.

GENERAL: First brewed in 1987. Acknowledged by the brewery as the sourest of the range which, presumably, has not evolved along the same path of added sweetness as its others. Not the best introduction to Vapeur for beginners.

JDW: 8 / 7 KBR: 8 / 8

OTHER BEERS

Vapeur Legère (4.5% alc/vol.): Unbelievably light, refreshing summer drink with a very delicate taste. Slight gooseberries and grapefruit. Ginger, lime tree leaves, chicory, pepper and bitter orange peel are among the ingredients. KBR: The most quenching beer I've ever had.

BARS & CAFES RECOMMENDED BY THE BREWERY

AU COEUR DE LA GAUME, Rue Dr Hustin 51, Ethe.
BEER CIRCUS, Rue de l'Enseignement 89, Brussels.
L'EXCELSIOR, Grand Place 29, Mons.
LA MERVEILLE DE VYLE, Rue Pont de Vyle 1, Vyle en Taroul.
LE GRAND CHEMIN, Rue Rumez 38, Templeuve.
TAVERNE REMBRANDT, Rue de Bruxelles 1, Enghien.

BEER SHOPS RECOMMENDED BY THE BREWERY

CAVE DE WALLONIE, Rue de la Halle 6, Namur.
CORMAN COLLINS, Rue Xheneumont 1a, Battice.
HEUGHEBAERT, Rue du Faubourg 35, Comines-Warneton.
MUSÉE DE LA BIÈRE, Rue Pont à la Faulx, Peruwelz.
LE MARCHÉ DE NATHALIE, Grand Rue 22, Bouillon.
VIN DU GORLI, Chaussée de Namur 38, Wepion.

Brasserie Vervifontaine

✉ Vervifontaine 100, 4845 Jalhay, Liège.

☎ 087 64 83 03.

🕓 Not known.

Pre-arranged only. In French and English.

Cases, bottles and glasses.

240hl (in 1995).

➔ On main road from Jalhay to Verviers, a few kilometres from Jalhay. You cannot miss the brightly coloured Bière du Lion sign on the far side of a right hand junction.

The large, bright, Bière du Lion sign at the road junction is actually fixed to a private house which belongs to the brewer's parents. The brewery itself is behind this and accessed via the gate off the side road which leads into a spacious yard with the white painted brewery buildings directly in front of you.

The brewery is run by Dominic Thonnard who gave up his job as an industrial chemist in order to run the brewery with occasional help from his father. For the more labour intensive bottling and labelling he enlists the help of a team of workers, but to reduce the labour effort he sends his bottles away to be cleaned commercially after which they return shrink wrapped ready for use.

The brewing operation is spread over two floors with the gas fired mash tun and hop back (converted from old dairy equipment) upstairs and the fermenters downstairs. The three conical fermenters were custom built to Dominic's own design and incorporate an ingenious temperature control system. An electronic box on the wall keeps track of the temperature and allows cold water to run through pipes inside the fermenters to maintain a steady temperature. Also downstairs is a newly converted bottling room and the warm room for refermentation. Sampling of the beers can be done upstairs.

Production is a fairly steady 20hl per month with most of the Bière du Lion being produced in the summer and the Rousse des Fagnes in the winter. Additionally it does three or four 30hl brews of a 8% alc/vol. beer called La Courcellangne for a trade organisation in Courcelles, near Charleroi.

As with most other breweries it is not averse to relabelling its beers for special clients/ occasions – however, it does insist that the label wording always states which beer it is and that it was made by Brasserie Vervifontaine.

It's difficult to miss the sign on the main road.

Rousse des Fagnes is named after the region to the east of the brewery which is famous for its bogs and forests. An attractive new label was in production in mid-1996 depicting a wood nymph in the deep forest.

For such a small, new brewery the Bière du Lion is an impressive way to join the market. We wait in anticipation to sample other brews from Vervifontaine.

BIÈRE DU LION

8% alc/vol. 75cl corked & crown corked bottles.

KNOWN INGREDIENTS: Pilsener malt.

APPEARANCE: Hazy dark wheat with a good creamy head.

NOSE: Mellow yeasty hops. Complex wheatiness making it very like a white beer.

PALATE: Excellently complex, full and rounded. Distinctly creamy and wheaty with some citric hints and a strong hop character. KBR: Some distant herbal notes, distinct lacticity and some orange hints. JDW: Soft and mellow but the citric notes give it a pleasant hint of tartness.

FINISH: A persistent creamy, wheaty, gently bitter tang.

OVERALL: Impressive, easy drinking beer with an excellent texture and a very well balanced palate. Supposed to be in the Duvel style, yet it has a far more pronounced wheaty character.

GENERAL: The beer gets its name from a stone statue of a lion in the vicinity.

JDW: 8 / 8 KBR: 9 / 9

OTHER BEERS

Rousse des Fagnes (6% alc/vol.): Darker beer than the Bière du Lion, usually produced for the winter months and difficult to obtain out of season. Spiced with liquorice and bitter orange peel.

La Courcellangne (8% alc/vol.): An occasional contract brew, made for a trade organisation in Courcelles.

BARS, CAFES & SHOPS RECOMMENDED BY THE BREWERY

None recommended.

BARS/CAFES

The following bars/cafes are suggested as sources of Wallonian beer. Most are recorded in the brewery section against the brewery which proposed them as a source of their beer, while here they are sorted by town within province. We have not visited all of them and cannot therefore vouch for them all personally, but many of the brewery-recommended outlets are small bars primarily dispensing that particular brewery's beers and as such are good places to seek out the full range, or close to it. The source of the recommendation follows the entry, in italics.

BRABANT

Rebecq	**Taverne du Moulin**, Rue Docteur Colson, 1430 Rebecq ***(Lefebvre).***

HAINAUT

Arquennes	**Auberge du Dauphin**, Chaussée de Nivelles 13, 7180 Arquennes ***(Orval).*** Should be able to supply various vintages.
Bassilly	**Titien**, Place 17, 7830 Bassilly ***(Silly).***
Binche	**Chez Boule**, Rue Saint Paul 13 ***(Binchoise).***
	La Chamade, Grand Place 44 ***(Binchoise).***
	Philippe II, Avenue Charles Deliege 18 ***(Binchoise).***
	Taverne Binchoise, Grand Place 41 ***(Binchoise).***
Chimay	**Ferme des Quatres Saisons**, Rue de Scourmont 8b, 6464 Forges-Chimay ***(Chimay).*** Near abbey, good food, all Chimay products.
	L'Eau Blanche, Rue G.Joaris 27, 6463 Lompret ***(Silenrieux).***
	Le Casino, Place des Ormeaux, Chimay ***(Chimay).*** Good food and warm atmosphere.
	All bars in Grand Place, Chimay ***(Chimay).***
Dour	**Ferme des Templiers**, Rue Ropaix 169, 7370 Dour ***(Blaugies).***
	La Saline, Rue Ropaix 39, 7370 Dour ***(Blaugies).***
Enghien	**Taverne Rembrandt**, Rue de Bruxelles 1, 7850 Enghien ***(Vapeur).***
Gilly	**Café de l'Enseignement**, Chaussée de Ladelinsert, 6060 Gilly ***(Abbaye des Rocs).***
Le Rœulx	**Au Commerce**, Place de L'Église, 7070 Le Rœulx ***(Friart).***
	La Grimaudière, Place de L'Église, 7070 Le Rœulx ***(Friart).***
Lens	**La Petite Pise**, Place de la Trimite, 7870 Lens ***(Hameau).***
Mons	**Au Passe-Pierre**, Place de Béguinage 6, 7000 Mons ***(Friart).***
	L'Excelsior, Grand Place 29, 7000 Mons ***(Authors, Abbaye des Rocs, Binchoise, Blaugies, Praile, Vapeur).*** Good atmosphere and decor. Excellent regularly changing list of special beers. Good, knowledgable staff. If you can't see what you want – ask, it is probably in the cellar.
	La Maison des Brasseurs, Grand Place 3/4, 7000 Mons ***(Authors).*** Bar made from brewing kettle. Brewing photos. Interesting painted ceiling. Pleasant bar with moderate Wallonian beer range.
	Podo, Rue de la Coupe 43, Mons ***(Authors).*** Wallonian beers include Vapeur, Lefebvre, Friart, Silly, Achouffe.
	Le Ropieur, Grand Place 14, 7000 Mons ***(Friart).***

Montignies sur Roc	**Taverne du Château**, Place, 7387 Montignies sur Roc ***(Abbaye des Rocs).***
Morlanwelz	**Café le Combattant**, Grand Place, 7140 Morlanwelz ***(Orval).*** Should be able to supply various vintages.
Péruwelz	**Le Ménestrel Muse de la Bière**, Grand Place, 7600 Péruwelz ***(Caulier).***
	Taverne de la Brasserie, Rue de Sondeville 132, 7600 Péruwelz ***(Caulier).*** Caulier's impressive brewery tap (see entry in brewery section). Only open at weekends.
Ronquières	**La Tour Glacée**, Route Baccara 4, 7090 Ronquières ***(Friart).***
Seneffe	**Le Tyberchamps**, Place des Alliés 6, 7180 Seneffe ***(Friart).***
Silly	**Café de la Brasserie**, Place, 7830 Silly ***(Silly).***
	Le Salon, Rue Ville Basse 152, 7830 Silly ***(Silly).***
	A L'Tonne, Place 19, 7830 Silly ***(Silly).***
Soignes	**Les Remparts**, Place de Soignes, 7060 Soignes ***(Hameau).***
Tournai	**La Cave à Bière**, Quai Taille Pierres 3a, 7500 Tournai ***(Authors).*** Reasonable Wallonian range. Beer cuisine.
	Le Moine Austère, Rue Dorez 5, 7500 Tournai ***(Authors).*** Very large beer range. Same owner as beer shop of same name across the road. Some beer cuisine at weekends. We have been served out of date stock on occasion.
	Les Quatre Saisons, Grand Place 68, 7500 Tournai ***(Authors).*** Pleasant bar with good atmosphere and limited but well served range of Wallonian beers.
Tourpes	**Caves Dupont**, Rue Basse, 7904 Tourpes ***(Dupont).*** Friendly village local directly opposite the brewery.
	La Forge, Place, 7904 Tourpes ***(Dupont).***

LIÈGE

Liège	**Le Student**, Rue Saint Gilles 182, 4000 Liège ***(Oleye).***
	La Vaudrée, Rue Val Benoît 109, Liège ***(Authors).*** Truly amazing beer list (around 1,000 with over 20 on draught) including many past and present Wallonian beers. Watch out for the age though. We feel turnover is too slow to do justice to the more obscure beers.
	Le Vieux Guillemins, Rue du Plan Incliné 145, 4000 Liège ***(D'Oleye).***
Rocourt	**Taverne du G.B. de Rocourt**, Chaussée de Tongres 85, 4000 Rocourt ***(Oleye).***
Vyle en Taroul	**La Merveille de Vyle**, Rue Pont de Vyle 1, 4570 Vyle en Taroul ***(Vapeur).***
Waremme	**Café de la Place**, Place Albert 1er 2a, 4300 Waremme ***(Oleye).***
	Le Viking, Avenue Reine Astrid 2, 4300 Waremme ***(Oleye).***

LUXEMBOURG

Achouffe	**Hôtel l'Espine**, Achouffe 19, 6666 Achouffe ***(Achouffe).***
	Petite Fontaine, Rue du Village, 6666 Achouffe ***(Achouffe).***
	Brasserie Taverne, Rue du Village 32, 6666 Achouffe ***(Achouffe).*** The brewery's own bar/restaurant with glass panel giving view into brewhouse.
Bastogne	**Bistro Leo**, Place MacAuliffe, Bastogne ***(Achouffe, Rochefortoise).***
Durbuy	**Relais du Vieux Port**, Place de Durbuy, 6940 Durbuy ***(Fantôme).***

Erezée	**L'Arcade**, Rue Principale, 6997 Erezée ***(Fantôme).*** A restaurant/cafe. Beer cuisine includes dishes with Fantôme and Saison d'Erezée.
Etalle	**Relais d'Estalle**, Place des Chasseurs Ardennais 14, 6740 Etalle ***(Gigi).***
Ethe	**Au Coeur de la Gaume**, Rue Dr Hustin 51, 6760 Ethe ***(Gigi, Vapeur).***
Forrières	**L'Estaminet**, 6953 Forrières ***(Ambly).***
Gérouville	**The Paradise**, Place du Tilleul, 6769 Gérouville ***(Gigi).***
La Roche-en-Ardenne	**Le Bronze**, Place du Bronze, La Roche ***(Fantôme).***
Nassogne	**Le Relais St. Monon**, 6950 Nassogne ***(Ambly).***
Rossignol	**La Civanne**, Rue de la Civanne 285, 6730 Rossignol ***(Gigi).***
Soy	**Comme Chez Soy**, Place Troquet, 6997 Soy ***(Fantôme).*** Restaurant. Beer cuisine.
Villers-devant-Orval	**L'Ange Gardien**, on the crossroads, Villers-devant-Orval ***(Orval).*** Sells Orval beer and cheese as well as excellent Ardennes ham.

NAMUR

Crupet	**La Besace**, Rue du Centre, 5332 Crupet ***(Du Bocq).***
Dinant	**La Couronne**, Rue Sax 1, 5500 Dinant ***(Du Bocq).***
	Sax, Place Reine Astrid 13, Dinant ***(Authors).***
Namur	**L'Ebloussant**, Rue Armée Grouchy, 5000 Namur ***(Caracole).*** Good selection of rare Wallonian beers.
	Le Métropole, Rue Émile Cuvelier, 5000 Namur ***(Du Bocq).***
	Les Artisans Brasseurs, Place de la Station 2, 5000 Namur ***(Authors).*** Excellent bar/restaurant opposite the station. The home of Brasserie Mibrana.
Philippeville	**A la Porte de France**, Rue de France 1, 5600 Phillipeville ***(Silenrieux).*** Good selection on the beer list.
Rochefort	**La Taverne**, Rue de France, Rochefort ***(Rochefortoise).***
	Le Limbourg, Place Albert 1er, Rochefort ***(Rochefortoise).***
	Le Luxembourg, Place Albert 1er, Rochefort ***(Rochefortoise).***
Silenrieux	**A la Taverne du Père Sarrasin**, Rue Noupre, 5630 Silenrieux ***(Silenrieux).*** In the same building as the brewery. Can organise brewery tours. Reasonable selection of regional products. Silenrieux beers on tap.
	Auberge de Beaupont, Rue de Beaupont 44, 5630 Silenrieux ***(Silenrieux).*** Fine food.
Spontin	**Le Cheval Blanc**, Chaussée de Dinant, 5530 Spontin ***(Du Bocq).***
Vresse sur Semois	**La Vieille Pompe**, Membre, 5550 Vresse sur Semois ***(Orval).*** Should be able to supply various vintages.

RECOMMENDATIONS OUTSIDE WALLONIA

The following recommendations, though stocking Wallonian beer, are not actually within the area covered by this book.

BRUSSELS

Brussels	**Bier Circus**, Rue de l'Enseignement 89 ***(Achouffe, Vapeur).*** Only Brussels bar with La Chouffe on tap.
	La Danse des Paysans, Chaussée de Boondael 441, 1050 Brussels ***(Vapeur).***

	Les 2 Grands Gros, Rue du Bourgmestre 1, 1050 Brussels ***(Vapeur).***
	Musée de Schaerbeek, Rue Louis Bertrand, Schaerbeek, Brussels ***(Abbaye des Rocs).***

EAST FLANDERS

Gent	**De Hopduvel**, Robevielstraat 10 ***(Binchoise).***
Huise	**De Gans**, Kloosterstraat 40, 9750 Huise ***(Authors).*** Not very far from Wallonia and they have an excellent range of hard to get Wallonian beers, though some may be older than they should be. Only open Friday to Sunday.
Sint-Lievens-Houtem	**De Pikarden**, Cotthemstraat 6, Sint-Lievens-Houtem ***(Abbaye des Rocs).***

LIMBURG

Teuven	**Oud Teuven**, Rue du Village 9, 3793 Teuven ***(Achouffe).*** La Chouffe on tap.

FRANCE

Paris	**Taverne de Nestle *(Abbaye des Rocs).***
Templeuve	**Le Grand Chemin**, Rue Rumez 38, 7520 Templeuve ***(Vapeur).***

BEER SHOPS

The following beer shops are suggested as sources of Wallonian beer. Most are recorded in the brewery section against the brewery which proposed them as a source of their beer, while here they are sorted by town within province. If the recommendation is from a brewery it is as a source of their beer, if it is from the authors the shop should have a well-stocked, wide selection of Wallonian beers. The source of recommendation follows the entry, in italics.

HAINAUT

Basècles	**Cash Battard,** Grand Rue 234, 7971 Basècles ***(Blaugies).***
Binche	**Binche-Boissons**, Route de Merbes 396, 7133 Buvrinnes ***(Authors, Binchoise).*** On the N55 south of Binche. Good, friendly shop with more than 200 special beers. Wed-Sun 9.00-12.00 Wed-Sat 13.30-18.30
	Cora, Rue de la Franco-Belge, La Louvière ***(Binchoise).***
Chimay	**A.D.Delhaize**, Chimay ***(Chimay).***
	Match, Chausée de Mons 17, 6460 Chimay ***(Chimay).***
	Unic, Rue de Bourlers 1, 6460 Chimay ***(Chimay).***
Comines-Warneton	**Heughebaert**, Rue du Faubourg 35, 7780 Comines Warneton ***(Vapeur).***
Dour	**Durigneux**, Rue de l'Église, Dour ***(Abbaye des Rocs).***
Froidchapelle	**Brasserie Magotteaux SPRL**, Rue de la Station 41, 6440 Froidchapelle ***(Silenrieux).***
Mons	**Cash Battard**, Rue des Viaducs 287, 7020 Mons (Nimy) ***(Blaugies).*** Open on Sunday.
Péruwelz	**Cash Battard**, Rue Neuve Chaussée 139B, 7600 Péruwelz ***(Blaugies).*** Open on Sunday.
	Ets Jacquet, Rue de Sondeville, 7600 Péruwelz ***(Dupont).***
	Le Musée de la Bière, Rue Pont à la Faulx 3, 7600 Péruwelz ***(Authors, Vapeur).*** North end of square. Small shop, large range.
Ploegsteert	**Vanuxeem**, Rue d'Armentières 150, 7782 Ploegsteert ***(Abbaye des Rocs).***

Quiévrain	**A.D. Delhaize**, Grand Rue, 7380 Quiévrain ***(Blaugies).***
Soignies	**Delhaize**, Rue de Mons, 7060 Soignies ***(Hameau).***
Tournai	**Drink Deforest**, Chaussée de Willemeau 207, 7500 Tournai ***(Dupont).***
	Le Moine Austère, Rue Dorez 8, 7500 Tournai ***(Authors).*** Opposite bar of same name. Small shop very large range.
Tourpes	**Superette Linda**, Place, 7904 Tourpes ***(Dupont).***

LIÈGE

Battice	**Corman-Collins**, Rue Xheneumont 1A, 4651 Battice ***(Achouffe, Binchoise, Caracole, Vapeur).***
Verviers	**Born J.P.**, Rue de Stembert 185, 4800 Verviers ***(Gigi).***

LUXEMBOURG

Ansart	**Terre Lux**, Rue du Monument 4, 6730 Ansart ***(Gigi).***
Bouillon	**Le Marché de Nathalie**, Grand Rue 22, 6830 Bouillon ***(Vapeur).***
Gérouville	**La Petite Boutique**, Place de l'Église, 6769 Gérouville ***(Gigi).***
Offagne	**Le Panier du Pays**, Rue du Parc 3, 6850 Offagne ***(Gigi).***

NAMUR

Annevoie	**Drink d'Annevoie**, Chaussée de Namur 60, 5537 Annevoie ***(Caracole).***
Beauraing	**Brasserie Balleux**, Rue de Vignie 84, 5570 Beauraing ***(Caracole).***
Dinant	**Delhaize**, Route de Sergeilles, 5630 Cerfontaine ***(Silenrieux).***
Namur	**La Cave de Wallonie**, Rue de la Halle 6, 5000 Namur ***(Caracole, Authors).***
Philippeville	**Unic**, Rue de France 39, 5600 Phillipeville ***(Silenrieux).***
Rochefort	**Le Central**, Place Albert 1er, Rochefort ***(Rochefortoise).***
Wépion	**Vin du Gorli**, Chaussée de Namur 38, 5170 Wépion ***(Vapeur).***

RECOMMENDATIONS OUTSIDE WALLONIA

The following recommendations, though stocking Wallonian beer, are not actually within the area covered by this book.

BRABANT

Aarschot	**Drink Holemans**, Langdor Sewteenweg 117, 3200 Aarschot ***(Abbaye des Rocs).***
St. Genesius-Rode	**Drankencentrale Wets**, Steenweg op Halle, 1640 St Genesius-Rode ***(Authors).***

BRUSSELS

Brussels	**Bières Artisanales**, Chaussée de Wavre 174, 1050 Brussels ***(Abbaye des Rocs).***
	Drink Delpine, Rue Eugène Cattoir 13, 1050 Brussels ***(Achouffe, Dupont).***

EAST FLANDERS

Gent	**De Hopduvel**, Coupere Links 625, 9000 Gent ***(Authors, La Caracole).***

GRAND DUCHY OF LUXEMBOURG

Oberpallen	**Pal Centre**, Route d'Arlon, 8552 Oberpallen ***(Achouffe).*** Not even in Belgium but it sells Achouffe beers at Luxembourg prices.

THE PRETENDERS

When travelling around Wallonia you may often come across a beer which has a French-sounding title or is perhaps named after a Walloon town, region or abbey and has the main text of the label in French. This does not necessarily mean it is a Wallonian beer.

The reason for the appearance of these beers is usually no more sinister than an abbey has asked a Flemish brewery to make a range of beers under licence, or perhaps a trade and commerce organisation of a particular town has commissioned a brew to be named after their town or village. At its worst, however, a Walloon distributor may have an existing product relabelled to be sold locally – often with an even more misleading "Brasserie de" prefix to their name.

To help you through this confusion we have listed here the Flemish beers with French-sounding names and those made for Walloon abbeys, etc. An entry in this list is not intended to suggest the brewery is trying to mislead anyone, it is simply an aid to the consumer.

It is best to treat any beer that is named after a small locality with caution (especially those starting "Cuvée de") as experience has shown us that the majority are relabelled existing brands and could equally be from a Flemish or Walloon brewery. This is usually in spite of the shop- or bar-keeper's claims that it is a special beer brewed locally.

Beer	***Brewery***	
Abbaye d'Aulne 6	De Smedt	(The Abbaye d'Aulne is south west of Charleroi)
Abbaye d'Aulne 8	De Smedt	
Abbaye d'Aulne 10	De Smedt	
Abbaye d'Aulne Blonde	De Smedt	
Abbaye d'Aulne Spéciale Noël	De Smedt	
Abbaye d'Aulne Triple	De Smedt	
Baptiste	Riva	
Bécasse Framboise Lambic, La	Belle Vue	(Belle Vue relabelled for France).
Bécasse Gueuze Lambic, La	Belle Vue	
Bécasse Kriek, La	Belle Vue	
Belle Vue Framboise	Belle Vue	
Belle Vue Gueuze	Belle Vue	
Belle Vue Kriek	Belle Vue	
Bière de Château de Ramegnies-Chin	Facon	
Bière du Corsaire	Huyghe	
Bière de la Bonde	Van Eecke	
Bière de Mars	Artois	
Bière de Noël	Artois	
Bière des Neiges	Huyghe	
Bière des Nonettes	Huyghe	
Bière du Boucanier	Bios (Piraat labelled for French market)	
Bière du Château	Van Honsebrouck (same as Kasteelbier)	
Bol d'Or	Duysters	
Bourgogne des Flandres	Timmermans	
Cervoise des Ancêtres Grand Cru	Sterkens	
Chapeau Exotic	De Troch	

Beer	*Brewery*	
Chapeau Faro	De Troch	
Chapeau Fraises Lambic	De Troch	
Chapeau Framboise	De Troch	
Chapeau Gueuze	De Troch	
Chapeau Kriek	De Troch	
Chapeau Mirabelle	De Troch	
Chapeau Pêche	De Troch	
Chapeau Tropical	De Troch	
Charles Quint	Haacht	
Coq Hardi Bière Blonde de Luxe	Haacht	
Coq Hardi Bière Bock	Haacht	
Coq Hardi Pils	Haacht	
Coq Hardi Spéciale	Haacht	
Cuvée Château des Flandres	Bios (Produced for the Hopduvel in Gent)	
Cuvée de Briqville	Bios	
Cuvée de Namur Blonde	Huyghe	
Cuvée de Namur Brune	Huyghe	
Cuvée des Flandres Triple	Huyghe	
Cuvée René Grand Cru	Lindemans	
Duchesse de Bourgogne	Verhaeghe	
Filée, La	Bios	
Flanders Triple Grand Cru	Sterkens	
Foudroyante Framboise	Lindemans	
Foudroyante Myrtille	Lindemans	
Foudroyante Pêche	Lindemans	
Fumée d'Anvers	Villers	
Godefroy	Moortgat (Produced for a beer shop, Brasserie du Grand Enclos, north of Bouillon)	
Grand Bière de Blondine	Steedje	
Gueuze Framboise des Ardennes	Timmermans (produced for Corman-Collins	
Guillotine, La	Huyghe	
Hotteuse	Roman (Claimed to be the local beer in Florenville. Possibly because Brasserie Maire used to produce a Hotteuse)	
Hotteuse Grand Cru	Roman	
Leffe Triple	Interbrew	
Leffe Vieille Cuvée	Interbrew	
Lindemans Cassis	Lindemans	
Lindemans Framboise	Lindemans	
Maredsous 6	Moortgat	(Abbaye de Maredsous is north west of Dinant)
Maredsous 8	Moortgat	
Maredsous 9	Moortgat	
Maredsous 10	Moortgat	
Marquise, La	Huyghe	
Mort Subite Cassis	De Keersmaeker	
Mort Subite Framboise	De Keersmaeker	
Mort Subite Gueuze Fond	De Keersmaeker	
Mort Subite Kriek	De Keersmaeker	
Mort Subite Pêche	De Keersmaeker	
Napoléon	De Smedt	

Beer	*Brewery*	
Nounou	Bios	
Obligeoise, L'	Facon	
Pêcheresse	Lindemans	
Petite Pêcheresse	Lindemans	
Poiluchette Blanche de Thy, La	Huyghe	
Poiluchette Blonde, La	Huyghe	
Poiluchette Brune, La	Huyghe	
Queue de Charrue	Verhaeghe	
Queue de Charrue Blonde	Bios	
Rosé de Gambrinus	Cantillon	
Ste.Denise Grand Cru	Sterkens	
St.Laurent Double	Sterkens	
St.Laurent Triple	Sterkens	
St.Louis Cassis Kir Royal	Van Honsebrouck	
St.Louis Framboise	Van Honsebrouck	
St.Louis Gueuze Fond Tradition Lambic	Van Honsebrouck	
St.Louis Gueuze Lambic	Van Honsebrouck	
St.Louis Kriek Lambic	Van Honsebrouck	
St.Louis Pêche Lambic	Van Honsebrouck	
St.Paul Blonde	Sterkens	
St.Paul Double	Sterkens	
St.Paul Spéciale	Sterkens	
St.Paul Triple	Sterkens	
Scaldienne, La	Facon	
Spéciale de Calonne Blonde, La	Facon	
Spéciale de Calonne Brune, La	Facon	
Spéciale Noël	De Smedt	
Timmermans Gueuze Caveau	Timmermans	
Timmermans Pêche Lambic	Timmermans	
Triple de Val-Dieu	Van Honsebrouck (Produced for Corman-Collins)	
Triple Toison d'Or	Anker	
Vieux Bruges Blanche	Van Honsebrouck	
Vieux Bruges Framboise	Van Honsebrouck	(St.Louis relabelled for France).
Vieux Bruges Gueuze Lambic	Van Honsebrouck	
Vieux Bruges Kriek Lambic	Van Honsebrouck	
Vieux Bruxelles Gueuze Lambic	Van Honsebrouck	
Vieux Bruxelles Kriek Lambic	Wieze	
Vieux Temps	Interbrew	

UNDECLARED BEERS

Beers for which we can find no declared brewer

Kelottes – For Brasserie Koo, from Verviers, which appears to be a company which commissions beers from other breweries rather than brews them itself. Du Bocq brew Kelottes White under contract for Koo, but it is not known if they also brew the standard Kelottes.

The Soleilmont range of beers – Cuvée de Noël: Very little information at all on the label. Soleilmont is the name of the Trappist nunnery close to Chimay. Excellent beer, yet strangely familiar! **Soleilmont Blonde**, **Soleilmont Brune**, **Soleilmont Triple**: Like the Noël, these are probably occasional contract brews which appear to change brewery from time to time. Du Bocq, Lefebvre and Silly have all been rumoured to have produced Soleilmont beers on occasion.

BEER INDEX

This is an alphabetical index to the beers of Wallonia which appear in this book. Alternative names for existing brands appear in italics and the page number will refer you to the original beer, where we give alternative names in the general comments section of the beer notes.